essentials

ACCESS 2000
basic

ROBERT FERRETT, EASTERN MICHIGAN UNIVERSITY
JOHN PRESTON, EASTERN MICHIGAN UNIVERSITY
SALLY PRESTON, WASHTENAW COMMUNITY COLLEGE

Prentice Hall

A division of Pearson Education
Upper Saddle River, NJ 07458

Access 2000 Essentials Basic

International Standard Book Number: 1-58076-094-5

Library of Congress Catalog Card Number: 98-88894

Printed in the United States of America

First Printing: *June 1999*

03 02 01 00   4 3 2 1

Interpretation of the printing code: the rightmost double-digit number is the year of the book's printing: the rightmost single-digit number, the number of the book's printing. For example, a printing code of 00-1 shows that the first printing of the book occurred in 2000.

Trademark Acknowledgments

Publisher:
Robert Linsky

Executive Editor:
Sunthar Visuvalingam

Series Editors:
Marianne Fox and
Larry Metzelaar

**Annotated Instructor's Manual
(AIM) Series Editor:**
Linda Bird

Operations Manager:
Christine Moos

Director of Product Marketing:
Susan Kindel

Acquisitions Editor:
Chuck Stewart

Development Editor:
Jan Snyder

Technical Editor:
Asit J. Patel

Software Coordinator:
Angela Denny

Senior Editor:
Karen A. Walsh

Book Designer:
Louisa Klucznik

Design Usability Consultant:
Elizabeth Keyes

Project Editor:
Sherri Fugit

Copy Editor:
Melody Layne

Indexer:
Angie Bess

Layout Technician:
Liz Johnston

Team Coordinator:
Melody Layne

Usability Testers:
Sarah Ann Margulies: B.A. University
of Michigan

Cathy Gillmore   Shell Chemical
Company

Amy Schwalm   Eastern
Michigan
University

About the Authors

Robert L. Ferrett is the Director of the Center for Instructional Computing at Eastern Michigan University. The center provides computer training and support to faculty at the university. He has authored or coauthored more than 30 books on Access, PowerPoint, Excel, and Word, and was the editor of the *1994 ACM SIGUCCS Conference Proceedings*. He has served as a series editor for the *Learn 97* and *Learn 2000* books and has been designing, developing, and delivering computer workshops for nearly two decades. He holds a B.A. in Psychology, an M.S. in Geography, and an M.S. in Interdisciplinary Technology from Eastern Michigan University. He is ABD in the Ph.D. program in Instructional Technology at Wayne State University.

John Preston is an Associate Professor at Eastern Michigan University in the College of Technology, where he teaches microcomputer application courses at the undergraduate and graduate levels. He has been teaching, writing, and designing computer training courses since the advent of the PC, and has authored and coauthored over two dozen books on Microsoft Word, Excel, Access, and PowerPoint. He has served as a series editor for the Learn 97 and Learn 2000 books. He has received grants from the Detroit Edison Institute and the Department of Energy to develop Web sites for energy education and alternative fuels. He has also developed one of the first Internet-based microcomputer applications courses at an accredited university. He holds a B.S. from the University of Michigan in Physics, Mathematics, and Education, and an M.S. from Eastern Michigan University in Physics Education. He is ABD in the Ph.D. degree program in Instructional Technology at Wayne State University.

Sally Preston is President of Preston & Associates, a computer software training firm. She utilizes her extensive business experience as a bank vice president in charge of branch operations. She provides corporate training through Preston & Associates and through the Institute for Workforce Development at Washtenaw Community College, where she also teaches computer courses part-time. She has coauthored nearly 20 books on Access, Excel, PowerPoint, Word, and WordPerfect including the *Learn 97*, *Learn 2000*, *Office 2000 Essentials*, and *Access 2000 Essentials* books. She holds an M.B.A. from Eastern Michigan University.

Acknowledgments

Although the authors are solely responsible for its content, this book and the *Essentials* series as a whole have been shaped by the combined experience, perspectives, and input of the entire authoring, editorial, and design team. We are grateful to the Series Editors, **Larry Metzelaar** and **Marianne Fox**, and to the College of Business Administration at Butler University for hosting the listserv on which the implications and value of every series element was thoroughly discussed and finalized, even as this book was being written. They also hosted a November 1998 seminar for the *AIM* authors and coordinated much of the usability testing on the Butler campus. We acknowledge **Robert Linsky** (Publisher, Que Education and Training) for having provided the initial direction and for having allowed the Essentials 2000 team to shape this edition as we saw fit. You, the reader, are the greatest beneficiary of this ongoing online collaborative effort.

Chuck Stewart adapted the original Que E&T *Essentials* series for corporate training. In early 1998, however, he began revamping the *Office 2000 Essentials* pedagogy to better serve academic needs exclusively. He enlisted the services of Series Editors Metzelaar and Fox because of their extensive background in courseware development, many years of classroom teaching, and innovative pedagogy. Early discussion with the Series Editors revealed the need for the three new types of end-of-chapter exercises you find in the *Office 2000 Essentials*. Chuck continued to provide ideas and feedback on the listserv long after handing over the executive editorship to Sunthar. Together, they completely overhauled the *Essentials* series, paying particular attention to pedagogy, content, and design issues.

Sunthar Visuvalingam took over as Executive Editor for the *Essentials* series in October 1998. He stepped into a process already in full swing and moved quickly to ensure "a level of collaboration rarely seen in academic publishing." He performed admirably the daunting task of coordinating an army of widely dispersed authors, editors, designers, and usability testers. Among the keywords that characterize his crucial role in forging a well-knit learning team are decisive leadership, effective communication, shared vision, continuous pedagogical and procedural innovation, infectious enthusiasm, dogged project and quality management, active solicitation of feedback, collective problem-solving, transparent decision making, developmental mentoring, reliability, flexibility and dedication. Having made his indelible mark on the *Essentials* series, he stayed on to shepherd the transition of the series to Alex von Rosenberg.

Linda Bird (AIM Series Editor and author of both *PowerPoint Essentials* books) and **Robert Ferrett** (co-author of *Office Essentials*, all three *Access Essentials* books, and of the related *Learn* series) made significant contributions to enhancing the concept and details of the new series. A newcomer to the series but not to educational publishing, **Keith Mulbery** seized increasing ownership of *Essentials* and undertook the initiative of presenting the series at the April 1999 National Business Education Association Convention.

Alex von Rosenberg, Executive Editor, manages the Computer Applications publishing program at Prentice Hall (PH). The PH team has been instrumental in ensuring the smooth transition of the *Essentials* series. Alex has been ably assisted in this transition by **Susan Rifkin**, Managing Editor; **Leanne Nieglos**, Assistant Editor; **Jennifer Surich**, Editorial Assistant; **Nancy Evans**, Director of Strategic Marketing; **Kris King**, Senior Marketing Manager; and **Nancy Welcher**, Media Project Manager.

Operations Manager **Christine Moos** and Senior Editor **Karen Walsh** worked hard with Sunthar and Alex to allow authors maximum flexibility to produce a quality product, while trying to maintain a tight editorial and production schedule. They had the unenviable task of keeping the book processes rolling while managing the complex process of transitioning the series to Prentice Hall. Book Designer **Louisa Klucznik** and Consultant **Elizabeth Keyes** spared no efforts in making every detail of the new design attractive, usable, consistent, and appropriate to the *Essentials* pedagogy. **Joyce Nielsen**, **Jan Snyder**, **Asit Patel**, **Nancy Sixsmith**, and **Susan Hobbs**—freelancers who had worked on earlier editions of the *Essentials* and the related *Learn* series in various editorial capacities—helped ensure continuity in procedures and conventions. Project Editors **Tim Tate** and **Sherri Fugit** and Copy Editors **Melody Layne** and **Cindy Fields** also asked sharp questions along the way, thereby helping us refine and crystallize the editorial conventions for the *Essentials* series.

Debra Griggs, who has been teaching out of the *Access 97 Essentials* books at Bellevue Community College, offered many excellent comments and suggestions, and provided great technical expertise throughout the beta-testing stage. **Sarah Ann Margulies**, a retired lawyer and continuing learner, greatly enhanced this book by providing exceptional assistance during the usability testing phase. **Cecil Yarborough**, a Development Editor with PH, also caught several inaccuracies that had been overlooked.

Finally, the authors would like to thank **Asit Patel** for his great technical editing and **Jan Snyder** for seeing this book through development during particularly trying times. **Sherri Fugit** and **Melody Layne** edited the book meticulously. Also, thanks to **Marianne Fox** and **Larry Metzelaar** for taking on the series editorship and doing a great job, even though it must have been far more work than they could ever have imagined. Our particular thanks go to **Sunthar Visuvalingam** for having a vision of what this series should be, and then seeing it through.

Contents at a Glance

Table of Contents

Project 8   Integrating Access with Other Sources of Data and the Internet   191

Introduction

Essentials courseware from Prentice Hall is anchored in the practical and professional needs of all types of students. This edition of the Office 2000 *Essentials* has been completely re-vamped as the result of painstaking usability research by the publisher, authors, editors, and students. Practically every detail—by way of pedagogy, content, presentation, and design—was the object of continuous online (and offline) discussion among the entire team.

The *Essentials* series has been conceived around a "learning-by-doing" approach that encourages you to grasp application-related concepts as you expand your skills through hands-on tutorials. As such, it consists of modular lessons that are built around a series of numbered, step-by-step procedures that are clear, concise, and easy to review. Explicatory material is interwoven before each lesson and between the steps. Additional features, tips, pitfalls, and other related information are provided at exactly the place where you would most expect them. They are easily recognizable elements that stand out from the main flow of the tutorial. We have even designed our icons to match the Microsoft Office theme. The end-of-chapter exercises have likewise been carefully graded from the routine Checking Concepts and Terms to tasks in the Discovery Zone that gently prod you into extending what you've learned into areas beyond the explicit scope of the lessons proper. Following, you'll find out more about the rationale behind each book element and how to use each to your maximum benefit.

How to Use This Book

Typically, each *Essentials* book is divided into seven or eight projects, concerning topics such as creating a database, entering and editing data, customizing fields and tables, and integrating Access with other sources of data. A project covers one area (or a few closely related areas) of application functionality. Each project is then divided into seven to nine lessons that are related to that topic. For example, a project about querying your database is divided into lessons explaining how to create a new query, edit an existing query, select data based on matching criteria, and open multiple queries. Each lesson presents a specific task or closely related set of tasks in a manageable chunk that is easy to assimilate and retain.

Each element in *Access 2000 Essentials Basic* is designed to maximize your learning experience. Following is a list of the *Essentials* project elements and a description of how each element can help you:

- **Project Objectives.** Starting with an objective gives you short-term, attainable goals. Using project objectives that closely match the titles of the step-by-step tutorials breaks down the possibly overwhelming prospect of learning several new features of Access into small, attainable, bite-sized tasks. Look over the objectives on the opening page of the project before you begin, and review them after completing the project to identify the main goals for each project.

- **Key Terms.** This book includes a limited number of useful vocabulary words and definitions, such as ***primary key field***, ***one-to-many relationships***, and ***tab order***. Key terms introduced in each project are listed in alphabetical order immediately after the objectives on the opening page of the project. These key terms are shown in bold italic and are defined during their first use within the text. Definitions of key terms are also included in the Glossary.

- **Why Would I Do This?** You are studying Access 2000, so you can accomplish useful tasks in the real world. This brief section tells you why these tasks or procedures are important. What can you do with the knowledge? How can these application features be applied to everyday tasks?

- **Visual Summary.** This opening section graphically illustrates the concepts and features that you will learn in the project. One or more figures, with ample callouts, show the final result of completing the project. This road map to your destination keeps you motivated as you work through the individual steps of each task.

- **Lessons.** Each lesson contains one or more tasks that correspond to an objective on the opening page of the project. A lesson consists of step-by-step tutorials, their associated data files, screen shots, and the special notes described as follows. Although each lesson often builds on the previous one, the lessons (and the exercises) have been made as modular as possible. For example, you can skip tasks that you have already mastered, and begin a later lesson using a data file provided specifically for its task(s).

- **Step-by-Step Tutorial.** The lessons consist of numbered, bold, step-by-step instructions that show you how to perform the procedures in a clear, concise and direct manner. These hands-on tutorials, which are the "essentials" of each project, let you "learn by doing." Regular paragraphs between the steps clarify the results of each step. Also, screen shots are introduced after key steps for you to check against the results on your monitor. To review the lesson, you can easily scan the bold numbered steps. Quick (or impatient!) learners may likewise ignore the intervening paragraphs.

- **Need to Know.** These sidebars provide essential tips for performing the task and using the application more effectively. You can easily recognize them by their distinctive icon and bold headings. It is well worth the effort to review these crucial notes again after completing the project.

- **Nice to Know.** Nice to Know comments provide extra tips, shortcuts, alternative ways to complete a process, and special hints about using the software. You may safely ignore these for the moment to focus on the main task at hand, or you may pause to learn and appreciate these tidbits. Here, you find neat tricks and special insights to impress your friends and coworkers!

- **If You Have Problems...** These short troubleshooting notes help you anticipate or solve common problems quickly and effectively. Even if you do not encounter the problem at this time, make a mental note of it so that you know where to look when you find yourself (or others) in difficulty.

- **Summary.** This section provides a brief recap of the tasks learned in the project. The summary guides you to places where you can expand your knowledge, which may include references to specific Help topics or the Prentice Hall *Essentials* Web site (http://www.prenhall.com/essentials).

- **Checking Concepts and Terms.** This section offers optional True/False, Multiple Choice, Screen ID, and Discussion Questions that are designed to check your comprehension and assess retention. If you need to refresh your memory, the relevant lesson number is provided after each True/False and Multiple Choice question. For example, [L5] directs you to review Lesson 5 for the answer. Lesson numbers may be provided—where relevant—for other types of exercises as well.

- **Skill Drill Exercises.** This section enables you to check your comprehension, evaluate your progress, and practice what you learn. The exercises in this section build on and reinforce what was learned in each project. Generally, the Skill Drill exercises include step-by-step instructions.

- **Challenge Exercises.** This section provides exercises that expand on or relate to the skills practiced in the project. Each exercise provides a brief narrative introduction followed by instructions. Although the instructions are often written in a step-by-step format, the steps are not as detailed as those in the Skill Drill section. Providing less-specific steps helps you learn to think on your own. These exercises foster the "near transfer" of learning.

- **Discovery Zone Exercises.** These exercises require advanced knowledge of project topics or the application of skills from multiple lessons. Additionally, these exercises may require you to research topics in Help or on the Web to complete them. This self-directed method of learning new skills emulates real-world experience. We provide the cues, and you do the exploring!

- **Learning to Learn.** Throughout this book, you will find lessons, exercises, and other elements highlighted by this icon. For the most part, they involve using or exploring the built-in Help system or Web-based Help, which is also accessible from the application. However, their significance is much greater. Microsoft Office has become so rich in features that cater to so many diverse needs that it is no longer possible to anticipate and teach you everything that you might need to know. It is becoming increasingly important that, as you learn from this book, you also "learn to learn" on your own. These elements help you identify related—perhaps more specialized—tasks or questions, and show you how to discover the right procedures or answers by exploiting the many resources that are already within the application.

- **Task Guide.** The Task Guide that follows the last project lists all the procedures and shortcuts you have learned in this book. It can be used in two complementary ways to enhance your learning experience. You can refer to it, while progressing through the book, to refresh your memory on procedures learned in a previous lesson. Or, you can keep it as a handy real-world reference while using the application for your daily work.

- **Glossary.** Here, you find the definitions—collected in one place—of all the key terms defined throughout the book and listed in the opening page of each project. Use it to refresh your memory.

Typeface Conventions Used in This Book

We have used the following conventions throughout this book to make it easier for you to understand the material:

- Key terms appear in ***italic and bold*** the first time that they are defined in a project.

- Text that you type, as well as text that appears on your computer screen as warning, confirmation, or general information, appears in a special `monospace` typeface.

- Hotkeys, the underlined keys onscreen that activate commands and options, are also underlined in this book. Hotkeys offer a quick way to bring up frequently used commands.

How to Use the CD-ROM

The CD-ROM that accompanies this book contains all the data files for you to use as you work through the step-by-step tutorials, Skill Drill, Challenge, and Discovery Zone exercises provided at the end of each project. The CD contains separate parallel folders for each project. The filenames correspond to the filenames called for in this book. The files are named in the following manner: The first three characters represent the software and the book level (such as AC1 for the *Access 2000 Essentials Basic*). The last four digits indicate the project number and the file number within the project. For example, the first file used in Project 1 is 0101. Therefore, the complete name for the first file in the *Access 2000 Essentials Basic* book is AC1-0101.

Files on a CD-ROM are read-only; they cannot be modified in any way. To use the provided data files while working through this book, you must first transfer the files to a read-write medium, where you can modify them. Because classroom and lab rules governing the use of storage media vary from school to school, this book assumes the standard procedure of working with the file(s) on a 3.5-inch floppy disk.

A word of caution about using floppy disks: As you use a data file, it increases in size or automatically generates temporary work files. Ensure that your disk remains at least one-third empty to provide the needed extra space. Moreover, using a floppy for your work disk is slower than working from a hard drive. You will also need several floppy disks to hold all the files on the CD.

- **Copying to a 3.5-inch floppy disk.** For security or space reasons, many labs do not allow you to transfer files to the hard drive at all. The only way you can transfer Microsoft Access databases to a floppy disk is to copy the files manually. Unlike the other Office applications, Access does not have a Save As command for databases. This means that you cannot open and save each data file individually with a different name, as you may have done while working with Word, Excel, or PowerPoint.

  First, select the files on the CD that you want to copy and ensure that their combined size (shown on the status bar of the Explorer window) will fit on a 1.44MB floppy disk. Right-click on the selection with your mouse, choose Send To on the context menu that appears, and then choose 3 1/2 Floppy on the submenu. After copying, select the copied files on the floppy disk and right-click the selection with the mouse again. This time, choose Properties, choose the General tab on the Properties dialog box that appears, and then uncheck the read-only attribute at the bottom of this page. Because the original files on the CD-ROM were read-only, the files were copied with this attribute turned on. You can rename files copied in this manner only after you have turned off the read-only attribute.

  Although you can use the same method to copy the entire CD contents to a large-capacity drive, it is much simpler to use the installation routine in the CD-ROM for this purpose. This automatically removes the read-only attribute while transferring the files.

- **Installing to a hard drive or Zip drive.** The CD-ROM contains an installation routine that automatically copies all the contents to a local or networked hard drive, or to a removable large-capacity drive (for example, an Iomega Zip drive). If you are working in the classroom, your instructor has probably already installed the files to the hard drive and can tell you where the files are located. You will be asked to save or copy the file(s) you need to your personal work area on the hard drive or to a floppy work disk.

Otherwise, run the installation routine yourself to transfer all the files to the hard drive (for example, if you are working at home) or to your personal Zip drive. You may then work directly and more efficiently from these high-capacity drives.

CD-ROM Installation Routine

If you were instructed to install the files on a lab computer or if you are installing them on your home computer, simply insert the CD-ROM into the CD-ROM drive. When the installation screen appears, follow these steps:

1. From the installation screen, click the Install button.
2. The Welcome dialog box displays. Click the Next button.
3. The Readme.txt appears. The Readme.txt gives you important information regarding the installation. Make sure that you use the scrollbar to view the entire Readme.txt file. When you finish reading the Readme.txt, click the Next button.
4. The Select Destination Directory displays. Unless you are told otherwise by your instructor, the default location is recommended. Click Next.
5. The Ready to Install screen appears. Click Next to begin the installation.

   A directory is created on your hard drive where the student files will be installed.
6. A dialog box appears, confirming that the installation is complete.

The installation of the student data files allows you to access the data files from the Start menu programs. To access the student data files from the Start menu, click Start, click Programs, and then click the *Essentials* title you installed from the list of programs. The student data files are in subfolders, arranged by project.

Uninstalling the Student Data Files

After you complete the course, you may decide that you do not need the student data files any more. If that is the case, you have the capability to uninstall them. The following steps walk you through the process:

1. Click on the Start menu, and then click Programs.
2. Click the *Essentials* title that you installed.
3. Click Uninstall.
4. Click one of the Uninstall methods listed:

   - Automatic—This method deletes all files in the directory and all shortcuts created.
   - Custom—This method enables you to select the files that you want to delete.

5. Click Next.
6. The Perform Uninstall dialog box appears. Click Finish. The Student data files and their folders are deleted.

The *Annotated Instructor's Manual*

The *Annotated Instructor's Manual* (AIM) is a printed copy of the student book—complete with marginal annotations and detailed guidelines, including a curriculum guide—that helps the instructor use this book and teach the software more effectively. The *AIM* also includes a Resource CD-ROM with additional support files for the instructor; suggested solution files that show how the students' files should look at the end of a tutorial; answers to test questions; PowerPoint presentations to augment your instruction; additional test questions and answers; and additional Skill Drill, Challenge, and Discovery Zone exercises. Instructors should contact Prentice Hall for their complimentary *AIM*. Prentice Hall can be reached via phone at 1-800-333-7945, or via the Internet at http://www.prenhall.com.

Project 1

Getting Started with Access

Objectives

In this project, you learn how to

➤ Copy and Rename a Database File

➤ Open and Close a Database

➤ Open and Close a Database Table

➤ Identify Access Window Elements

➤ Exit Access and Windows

Key terms introduced in this project include

- database
- Database window
- field
- import
- launch
- link
- object
- Office Assistant
- properties
- query
- read-only
- record
- ScreenTip
- table
- What's This?

Why Would I Do This?

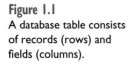icrosoft Access is a **database** program that allows you to store, retrieve, analyze, and print information. Companies use databases for many purposes: for managing customer files, for tracking orders and inventories, and for marketing purposes. An individual might set up a database to track household expenses or manage a list of family, friends, and business addresses. Teachers often set up a database to track student grades and other class information. A database allows the user to access and manage thousands, even millions of pieces of data in an organized, efficient, and accurate manner.

Tables are the foundation of the database, because they store the data and provide the structure by which it is organized. Each table stores a set of related data. Tables are made up of **records** that include related information about one object, person, event, or transaction. Records are displayed in rows. Each category of information in a record is known as a **field**. Fields are displayed in columns; the field name appears in the database table as a column heading. As such, a table organizes data within a predefined structure.

To make the best use of your time, you will use the numerous databases included with this book. In most instances, you will open and modify these sample files rather than create them from scratch. In this project, you learn how to copy and rename a database file. You also open a database and a database table in Access to get a taste of what databases look like. Finally, you learn how to get help and exit Access.

Visual Summary

When you have completed this project, you will have worked with a database that looks like Figure 1.1:

Figure 1.1
A database table consists of records (rows) and fields (columns).

Lesson I: Copying and Renaming a Database File

A large number of database files are included on your student disk. Because you cannot open the databases on your CD-ROM and make changes, you will need to make copies of each file, place the files on another disk drive, and give each file a new name—one that describes the function of the database.

Because many computer labs do not allow you to save files to the hard drive, it is assumed that you will be saving the files to drive A:. If you are using a hard drive to save your files, you can use the Windows Explorer to copy each file from the CD-ROM to your folder on the hard drive. It is important to follow the procedure starting with Step 8 to remove the **read-only** status for each file you copy from the CD-ROM.

To Copy and Rename a Database File

1 **Click the Start button on the Taskbar, and select Programs from the Start menu.**

2 **Find Microsoft Access in the Programs menu, and click it with the left mouse button.**
This **launches** (runs) the Access program.

3 **Select Open an existing file from the Microsoft Access dialog box, and click OK.**
The Open dialog box is displayed.

4 **Place the CD-ROM that came with this book in the proper drive, then click the list arrow at the right end of the Look in text box and select the CD-ROM that contains the project files.**
The files supplied with the book may be on a CD-ROM that would be on drive D: or E: (or some other higher letter), or they may have been placed on a network drive if you are using this book in a classroom setting.

5 **Open the Student folder on the CD-ROM that contains the AC1-0101 database file.**
The project databases included with this book are displayed.

6 **Make sure you have an empty disk in drive A:. Click the right mouse button on the AC1-0101 file.**
The file may appear as AC1-0101.mdb. This is the same file, but your computer has the file extensions turned on.

 Including the .mdb Extension When Renaming
The filenames for your project files may show this database extension: .mdb. This shows you if the Hide MS-DOS file extensions option has not been turned on in the Windows Explorer View, Options menu. If the extensions are showing, then the file extension (.mdb) must be included when renaming the file. In the previous example, the new file-name would be Address Book.mdb. The rest of the procedure remains the same.

continues ▶

To Copy and Rename a Database File (continued)

A shortcut menu is displayed (see Figure 1.2).

Figure 1.2
The shortcut menu is opened by clicking the right mouse button on the filename.

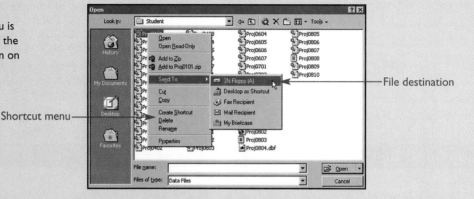

Shortcut menu ——

File destination

7 **Select Send To, and choose 3 1/2 Floppy (A:).**
The AC1-0101 file is copied to drive A:.

> If you are saving your work to a hard drive, the procedure in Steps 6 and 7 won't work. Instead, find the file on the CD-ROM, and right-click it. Select Copy from the shortcut menu. Move to your folder on the hard drive, and right-click in an open area. Select Paste from the shortcut menu.

8 **Select drive A: from the Look in box, then right-click AC1-0101 and select Properties from the shortcut menu.**
Notice that the Attributes at the bottom of the Properties dialog box say that the file is read-only. This happens when you copy a file from a read-only storage medium such as a CD-ROM. You need to change this to Archive before you can make changes to the database.

9 **Click the Archive check box to select it, and then click the Read-only check box to deselect it. Click OK.**

10 **Right-click AC1-0101 and select Rename from the shortcut menu.**
The filename is highlighted.

11 **Change the name of the file to Address Book, then press `Enter`.**
The name of the file is changed (see Figure 1.3). Leave the Open dialog box displayed to continue with the next lesson.

Figure 1.3
The filename has been changed.

New filename

File location ——

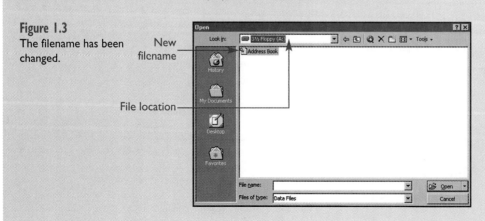

Differences Between Access and Other Office Applications
In other Microsoft applications such as Word, Excel, or PowerPoint, you may
have made copies of files by opening them in the application and then choosing
the File menu's Save As option. The Access program uses files differently than
most other programs. The Save As menu option saves only what is selected, not
the whole database.

Lesson 2: Opening and Closing a Database

Typically, the first thing you do when you launch Access is open an existing database. You
can open any database you have created, any database that is included as part of this
course, or any database that was included in the Access program.

In this lesson, you open a sample database, called Address Book, that contains the same
kind of information you would include in a personal address book. Access can easily manage
a database that lists contact information about family members, friends, and associates.

To Open and Close a Database

1 **If the Access program is not already running from the previous
lesson, launch Access, click OK, click the list arrow next to the
Look in text box, and find the disk drive and folder that contain the
Address Book database.**
If you left the program running at the end of the previous lesson, the Address
Book database will already appear in the Open dialog box.

2 **Click Address Book to select it, then click the Open button to open
the database.**
The sample Address Book database appears onscreen (see Figure 1.4). The
Database window lists all the tables in the database. The various database
objects, such as tables, forms, and reports, are displayed. Object buttons
are displayed down the left side of the database window. Action buttons
(Open, Design, and New) are found in the Database window toolbar. You
can create or open tables from this window. You can also change the design
of existing tables.

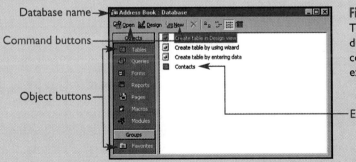

Figure 1.4
The Database window
displays object buttons,
command buttons, and
existing tables.

continues ▶

To Open and Close a Database   (continued)

③ Click the Queries object button.

The Queries object button is displayed on the left side of the window, along with the other object buttons. Clicking the button displays the only *query* in this database, named Indiana (see Figure 1.5). A query is used to sort, search, and limit the data to only those records that you need to examine.

Figure 1.5
Clicking the Queries object button displays all of the queries contained in the database.

Queries object button—

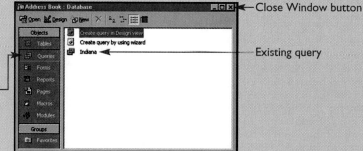

—Close Window button

—Existing query

④ Close the database by clicking the Close Window button (the X icon) on the upper-right corner of the database window, as shown in Figure 1.5.

Do not click the Close button on the right edge of the program title bar. The database window closes, but the Access program is still running.

 If you accidentally close the whole Access program, just launch Access again. You will not lose any work by making this mistake.

 Shortcuts to Opening a Database
You can open a database with the commands used in the preceding steps, but two shortcut methods are also available. You can open a new database by clicking the New button on the Database window toolbar, or by pressing Ctrl+N (holding down Ctrl and pressing the letter N). You can open an existing database by clicking the Open button on the Database window toolbar or by pressing Ctrl+O (holding down Ctrl and pressing the letter O). If you prefer to use the menu, you can select either New or Open from the File menu to create a new database or open an existing one.

Lesson 3: Opening and Closing a Database Table

Tables are the data storage areas of most databases. Access sets up tables as grids in which you can enter, edit, and view all the related information in your database. When you want to work with a table, you first open the database that contains the table, then open the table.

In this lesson, you open a table in the Address Book database that you opened and closed in Lesson 2.

To Open and Close a Database Table

① Click the <u>O</u>pen button on the toolbar.
The Open dialog box is displayed. If necessary, change to the drive or folder containing the database files for this book.

② Click Address Book to select it, then click <u>O</u>pen.
Access opens the Address Book database and displays the Database window. It opens to the object window that was in use when the program was closed; in this case, the Queries window.

③ Click the Tables object button, then select the Contacts table, if necessary (see Figure 1.6).

Open button ⟶

Figure 1.6
Click the <u>O</u>pen button to open a table.

The Contacts table is selected

④ Click the <u>O</u>pen button on the toolbar (see Figure 1.6).
Access displays the Contacts table onscreen. Tables contain a grid of information made up of records and fields. Remember: A record is a row of related data, whereas a field is a column of the same type of data.

Depending on the size of the table window, you may not be able to see all the information in the database table. To display other information, you can scroll the window using the horizontal and vertical scrollbars (see Figure 1.7).

Fields

Records —

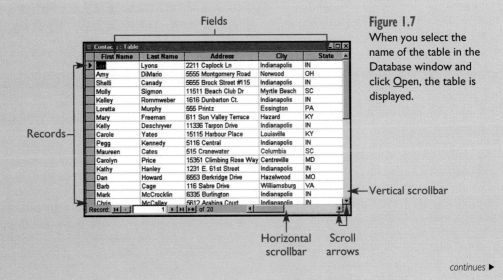

Figure 1.7
When you select the name of the table in the Database window and click <u>O</u>pen, the table is displayed.

Vertical scrollbar

Horizontal scrollbar

Scroll arrows

continues ▶

To Open and Close a Database Table   (continued)

5 **Click the right scroll arrow on the horizontal scrollbar until you scroll to the last field.**
Access displays the information in the ZIP and Phone fields that you may not have been able to see.

6 **Click the left scroll arrow until you scroll back to the first field (First Name).**
You learn more about scrolling through records, entering new records, and sorting records in Project 3.

7 **Click the Close button in the upper-right corner of the Contacts table.**
The database window is still open. Keep the Address Book database open to use in the next lesson.

Lesson 4: Learning About the Access Window

The look of the Access window changes, depending on what you are doing with the program. You may recognize many parts of the Access screen as familiar parts of every Windows program—elements such as the Minimize, Maximize/Restore, and Close buttons, as well as the scrollbars.

Other parts of the Access screen offer features that can help you complete your work quickly and efficiently. For example, the menu bar and toolbar are convenient features that you will use in most of the projects in this book.

When you first launch Access, you see only a few items on the menu bar, and most of the buttons on the toolbar are dim (or grayed), which means that they are unavailable. When you open a database, additional menu items appear on the menu bar, and most of the toolbar buttons become available.

As you open and work with individual objects within the database, you see that menu options and toolbar buttons change in relation to the type of object you selected. This lesson explains what you can expect to see in most Access windows.

To Learn About the Access Window

1 **Look at the elements that appear in the Access window when the Address Book database is open (see Figure 1.8).**
The Address Book database window should be onscreen from the last lesson, and the Tables object button should be selected. Four key elements appear in the Access window: the title bar at the top of the window, the menu bar below the title bar, the toolbar under the menu bar, and the status bar at the bottom of the window.

Where to Find Names

The title bar displays the program name. It also displays the database name and object type when the Database window is maximized. The other three elements display commands and tools that relate to the current database object shown in the Database window.

Title bar
Menu bar
Toolbar

Database window

Status bar

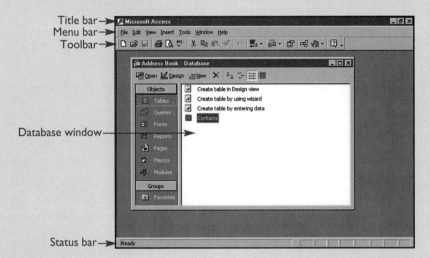

Figure 1.8
Four Access window elements support the Database window.

❷ **Open the File menu.**

Notice that the commands on this menu deal with opening, closing, and working with databases. You can use Access menus the same way you use menus in all other Windows applications. If you choose a menu command followed by an ellipsis (...), Access leads you to a dialog box with additional options. Also notice that shortcut keys are displayed to the right of some menu commands, such as Open.

❸ **Click an unused part of the screen outside the File menu.**

This step closes the menu. You can also close the menu by pressing Esc or clicking the File menu option again.

❹ **Move the mouse pointer over the button at the far left end of the toolbar.**

Access displays a *ScreenTip*, telling you the name of the button—in this case, New (see Figure 1.9).

continues ▶

To Learn About the Access Window   (continued)

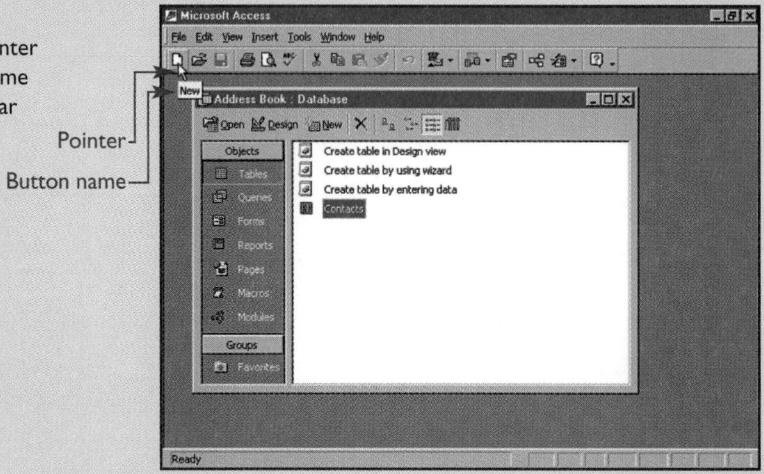

Figure 1.9
You can use the pointer to determine the name of a particular toolbar button.

Pointer
Button name

New

Now take a look at how these elements change when a table is open.

⑤ Select the Contacts table in the database window, if necessary. Click the Open button.

Access opens the table in Datasheet view. You could also double-click the table name to open it. The menu bar, toolbar, and status bar change to reflect the tasks you can perform with tables (see Figure 1.10) .

Figure 1.10
The Access window elements change to reflect table-specific tasks.

Table Datasheet toolbar

View button

⑥ Move the mouse pointer over the View button at the far left of the toolbar.

The View button may be used to display a list of available views for the table and to switch to another view of the table.

⑦ Move the pointer over other buttons in the toolbar.

As you move the pointer over other buttons, read the name that Access provides to get an idea of what each button does. Keep the Contacts table and the Address Book database open for now. At the end of this project, you learn how to close these files and exit Access. In the next lesson, you learn how to use the Access Help system.

Lesson 5: Getting Help

At some point, you may run into problems as you work with your computer and with software such as Access. If you need a quick solution to a problem with Access, you can use the program's Help feature. The Help system makes it easy to search for information on particular topics. In this lesson, you use the **Office Assistant**, an animated guide that helps you search for help, and the **What's This?** feature, which identifies the features of a single screen element.

The Office Assistant is a flexible help feature included with all Microsoft Office applications. It enables you to ask questions, search for terms, or look at context-sensitive tips.

To Get Help Using the Office Assistant

1 **With the Address Book database and Contacts table still open from the preceding lesson, click Help on the menu bar.**
Access displays a drop-down menu of choices. Note that the first item in the Help menu uses the same icon as one of the buttons at the far right of the toolbar. Both of these options launch the Office Assistant. (You can also launch the Office Assistant by pressing F1 at any time.) If the Office Assistant already appears on your screen, all you have to do is click it once to open the Office Assistant window.

2 **Click the Microsoft Access Help command.**
Access opens the Office Assistant, as shown in Figure 1.11.

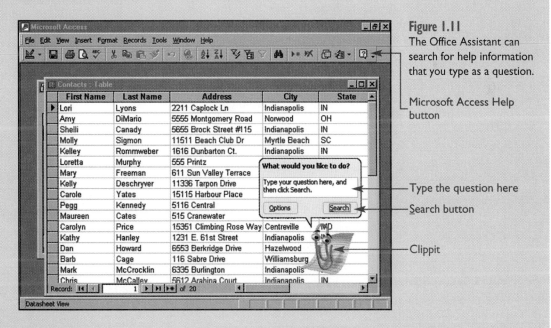

Figure 1.11
The Office Assistant can search for help information that you type as a question.

Microsoft Access Help button

Type the question here

Search button

Clippit

X If you get the Microsoft Access Help window instead of the Office Assistant, close the window and choose Help, Show the Office Assistant from the menu.

The animated Office Assistant shown in the figure is called "Clippit." You may see one of the other images available for the Office Assistant on your screen.

---

continues ▶

To Get Help Using the Office Assistant   (continued)

❸ Type How can I get data from an Excel spreadsheet? **in the text box.**

❹ Click the Search button.

The program searches through your sentence and looks for keywords. Topics related to your question are listed. If there are too many topics to fit in the window, you may need to click the See more button.

❺ Select the topic Import or link data from a spreadsheet.

Access displays the Help window pertaining to this subject (see Figure 1.12). The Help window takes up the right third of the screen, whereas the Access window is reduced to the left two-thirds of the screen.

Figure 1.12
Access displays the Help topic Import or link data from a spreadsheet.

Help topic

Question to the Office Assistant

Show button

Print button

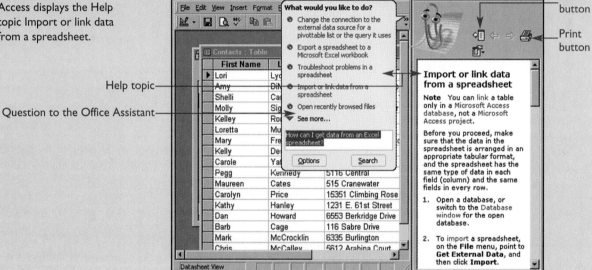

You can scroll down the Help window and read about importing and linking data from spreadsheets. You can click any of the words or phrases in blue to get more information. At the end of the Help window are the words "Additional Resources." You can click this text to see related topics if any are available.

At the top of the Help window are a couple of useful buttons. The first is the Print button, which enables you to print the contents of the Help window. The second is the Show button, which enables you to search for help in a more organized way.

❻ Click the Show button at the top of the Help window.

Another Help panel takes up the middle third of the screen. Three tabs are available—Contents, Answer Wizard, and Index. You may have to drag the Office Assistant out of the way.

❼ Click the Index tab, if necessary. Type spreadsheet **in the Type keywords text box, and click the Search button.**

Two boxes show a list of keywords and a list of topics (see Figure 1.13). Information about the highlighted topic is shown in the Help window.

Contents   Answer   Hide
tab   Wizard tab   button   Index tab   Close button

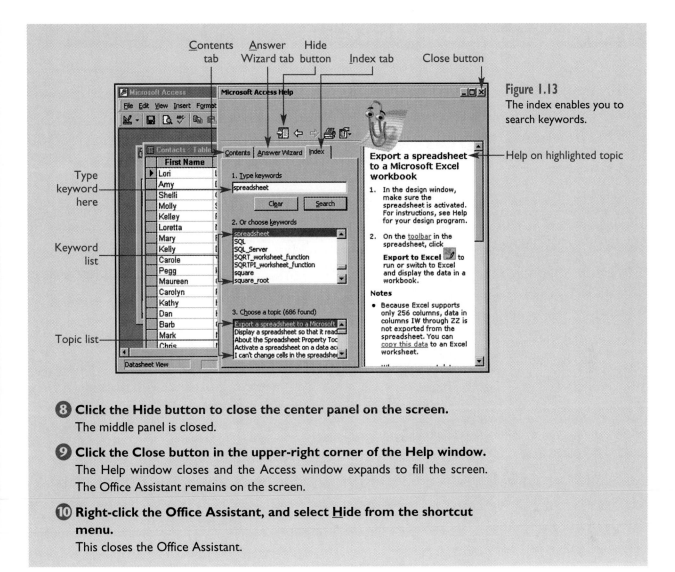

Figure 1.13
The index enables you to
search keywords.

Help on highlighted topic

Type
keyword
here

Keyword
list

Topic list

 8 **Click the Hide button to close the center panel on the screen.**
The middle panel is closed.

9 **Click the Close button in the upper-right corner of the Help window.**
The Help window closes and the Access window expands to fill the screen.
The Office Assistant remains on the screen.

10 **Right-click the Office Assistant, and select Hide from the shortcut
menu.**
This closes the Office Assistant.

ⓘ Learn More About Access from Help
The topic that you found when asking your question says that you can import
or link data from a spreadsheet. Before you even click this option, the Help
menu has already helped you in two important ways. First, you now know
that there is help available on the topic. Second, and much more importantly,
you know that getting data from an outside source is called *importing* or
linking. Using the Help menus frequently will help you develop your Access
vocabulary, which will in turn assist you in finding help!

You can get helpful descriptions of different buttons, menu items, or screen objects by
using the What's This? option. In the following section, you learn how to use this feature.

To Get Help Using the What's This? Feature

1 **Click Help on the menu bar.**

2 **Click the What's This? option.**
The pointer changes to include a large question mark.

3 **Click the Find button on the toolbar.**
A window opens which describes this feature in greater detail (see Figure 1.14).

Figure 1.14
The What's This? feature displays a description of the button or menu selection.

Button description

Find button

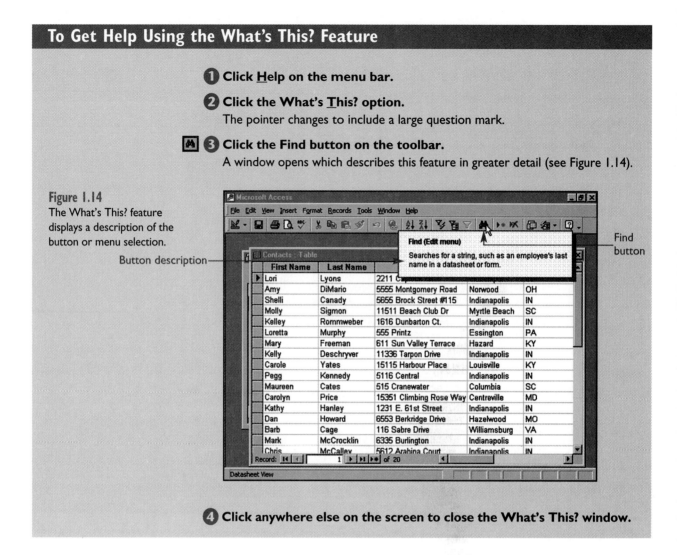

4 **Click anywhere else on the screen to close the What's This? window.**

Several other options that exist for getting help are available from the Help menu. When you clicked the Show button, you used the Index to search through the Help topics alphabetically by keyword. You can also search by topic using the list of topics in the Contents section, or use the Answer Wizard in much the same way as you use the Office Assistant.

Most of your questions about the basic operation of Access can be answered using one of these methods. If you do not find what you need in the Help topics supplied with the program, you can select Office on the Web to connect to Microsoft's support Web page on the Internet.

X To save space, some people delete Help files or don't install them in the first place. If you get a message stating that the Help file can't be found, use your original CD-ROM and add the Help files.

Lesson 6: Exiting Access and Windows

When you have finished working with Access, you should close all open database objects, and exit the program. If you turn off your computer without closing Access or if you lose power, you will probably be able to retrieve most of your data, but some of the recent changes you have made, particularly changes to the structure of a form or report, may be lost. You should get in the habit of saving formatting changes and closing the database before you close Access. You should also exit Windows before you turn off your computer.

In this project, you close the Address Book database, exit Access, and shut down your computer.

To Exit Access and Windows

1 Click the Close button on the Contacts table window.
This closes the Contacts table.

2 Click the Close button for the Address Book Database window.
This closes the Database window and leaves you with the main Access window open.

 Access Prompts You to Save Your Work.
When you close a database object after having made structural changes, the program will automatically ask you if you want to save your work.

3 Click the Close button for the Access program.
Access is closed, and you are returned to the Windows desktop. Here you can launch another program or shut down Windows. If you want to work on the exercises at the end of the chapter at this time, do not close Access or exit Windows until you are done using the computer.

4 To exit Windows and shut down the computer, click the Start button.

5 Click the Shut Down option, then click Yes to confirm that you want to shut down.
Windows checks your programs and files to be sure that they are closed and saved properly, and then shuts down.

6 When the message `It is now safe to turn off your computer` **appears onscreen, turn off the power to the computer and monitor.**
Some computers with power management shut themselves down without this message appearing. If this is the case, you may have to turn off your monitor, but will not have to turn off the power to the computer.

If you are finished with your session at the computer, continue with the "Checking Concepts and Terms" section of this project.

Summary

In this project, you were introduced to some of the fundamental Access procedures and components. You learned how to copy a file from your CD-ROM to a floppy disk and then how to rename the file. You opened and closed a database, and a table in a database. You identified some of the Access window elements and found out how to use various Help features to identify everything from buttons to concepts and procedures. Finally, you exited Access and closed Windows.

You can extend your grasp of Access by looking a little more closely at the Access database window. Move the pointer over buttons and look at the ScreenTips that pop up. See if you can guess what each of the buttons might do. Use What's This? on those that you can't figure out. Don't worry if some of the terms are unfamiliar to you—you'll be adding many of them to your Access repertoire throughout this book!

Checking Concepts and Terms ✓

True/False

For each of the following, check T or F to indicate whether the statement is true or false.

__T __F   **1.** If you click a filename in the Open dialog box using the right mouse button, a shortcut menu will give you the option to rename the file. [L1]

__T __F   **2.** The toolbar and menu bar always remain the same in Access, no matter what window you are working in. [L4]

__T __F   **3.** Once Access is open, you can open a database by using commands found on the menu bar. [L4]

__T __F   **4.** Access includes a feature that can answer questions written in the form of sentences. [L5]

__T __F   **5.** It's OK to turn off the computer when Access is still running. [L6]

__T __F   **6.** You can send an Access database file to drive A: by using shortcut menus in the Open dialog box. [L1]

__T __F   **7.** To close an Access database but leave the Access program running, click the Close button in the title bar of the Access window. [L6]

__T __F   **8.** The Office Assistant is an animated guide that helps you search for help. [L5]F

__T __F   **9.** To exit Windows, you should first click the Start button. [L6]

__T __F   **10.** A record in Access is a category of information that is stored in a column in a table. [L1]

Multiple Choice

Circle the letter of the correct answer for each of the following questions.

1. To put a duplicate of a CD-ROM file on drive A:, you first click the file with the right mouse button and then choose which of the following? [L1]

a. Duplicate from the Tools menu

b. Clone the file from the File menu

c. Send to from the shortcut menu

d. Paste

2. Which of the following is not a type of object that you can display by clicking an object button in the database window? [L2]

a. form

b. table

c. report

d. spreadsheet

3. Which of the following is not a way to open a database? [L2]

  a. Open the <u>F</u>ile menu, and choose the <u>O</u>pen command.

  b. Click the Open button.

  c. Type `Open File`.

  d. Press Ctrl+O.

4. How do you display the name of a toolbar button? [L4]

  a. Place the mouse pointer on the button.

  b. Click the toolbar button.

  c. Point to the toolbar button and click the right mouse button.

  d. Hold down Ctrl and click the toolbar button.

5. Which of the following is not one of the ways you can open the Help program? [L5]

  a. Open the <u>H</u>elp menu on the menu bar.

  b. Press F1.

  c. Click the Office Assistant button on the toolbar.

  d. Press Ctrl+F1.

6. Which of the following is loaded when you select <u>H</u>elp, Microsoft Access <u>H</u>elp from the menu? [L5]

  a. the index of Help topics

  b. a table of contents of Help subjects

  c. the Office Assistant Help utility

  d. a Find window that lets you search through the entire Help file for a single word

7. What does a table consist of? [L3]

  a. rows called records and columns called fields

  b. free-form information about each database item

  c. rows called fields and columns called records

  d. queries, reports, forms, and other database objects

8. When you pause the mouse pointer over a button, what does Access display? [L4]

  a. ScreenTip

  b. ButtonLabel

  c. TaskPointer

  d. ButtonTip

9. What does it mean when the mouse pointer has a question mark attached to it? [L5]

  a. Access has detected an error and is helping you find it.

  b. You have activated the What's This? feature.

  c. The database you've loaded is missing a major component.

  d. You have activated a query or a module.

10. What happens when you close a database object after having made structural changes? [L6]

  a. The program always asks you to save your changes.

  b. You lose your changes if you forgot to save them.

  c. The program automatically asks you if you want to save your work if you have made unsaved structural changes.

  d. Nothing.

Screen ID

Label each element of the Access screen shown in Figure 1.15.

Figure 1.15

A. Table name

B. Open button

C. Table object button

D. New button

E. What's This? pointer

F. ScreenTip

G. Action buttons

H. Close button

I. Title bar

J. Database window

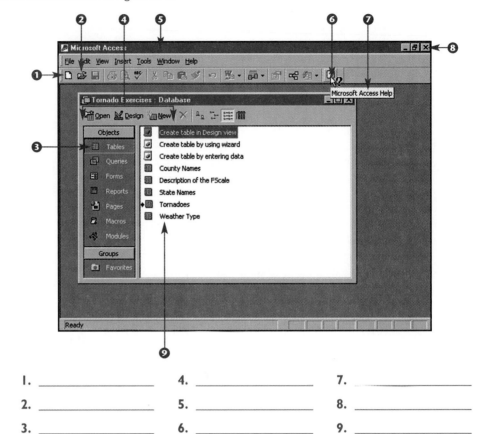

1. _____   4. _____   7. _____

2. _____   5. _____   8. _____

3. _____   6. _____   9. _____

Discussion Questions

1. Some databases have only one table, whereas others have multiple tables that consist of data on the same general topic. For example, a small college might keep all of its student information in one database with several tables. What different but related tables might you find in that database? Can you think of other situations that might require the use of more than one table?

2. Most people who learn Access are already familiar with one or more Office programs, such as Word, Excel, or PowerPoint. From what you've seen so far, what is similar between Access and the other programs? What is different? Do you think the similarities between the programs might help someone learn Access more quickly?

Skill Drill

Skill Drill exercises reinforce project skills. Each skill reinforced is the same, or nearly the same, as a skill presented in the project. Each exercise includes a brief narrative introduction, followed by detailed instructions in a step-by-step format.

1. Opening a Database on the CD-ROM

You have always been interested in a number of places and have wanted to visit them. One place that you've found interesting is Alaska. Over the years, you've gathered pictures and data on geographic sites and area attractions in the state. You have finally decided to organize this data by using a database you were given that contains some geographic information. In this exercise, you open the database on the CD-ROM without copying it to another disk drive.

1. Launch Access.

2. From the Open dialog box, find the AC1-0102 file.

3. Select AC1-0102 and click the Open button. Notice that a dialog box appears, telling you that you can't make changes to this database because it is **read-only**.

4. Click OK to open the database in read-only mode.

5. Click the Close Database button in the Database window title bar to close the database. This will leave Access open for the next exercise.

2. Finding the Help Directions for Creating a Database

The Help features in Access can answer specific questions, or can guide you in database processes and procedures.

1. Click the Microsoft Access Help button at the right end of the toolbar. (If you are not sure which one it is, point to any of the toolbar buttons and wait a moment. A ScreenTip appears that tells you the name of the button.)

2. Type the question How do I copy a database? and click Search. Hint: You don't really need to add that question mark. The program assumes anything you type into the search box is a question!

3. Find one of the options that enable you to make a duplicate copy of your database file and click that option.

4. Look over the instructions.

5. Close the Office Assistant.

3. Opening and Closing a Database Using the Menu

So far, you have opened your database files by using the dialog box that is displayed when you launch Access, and by clicking the Open button on the toolbar. Some people prefer to use menus. Try using the menus occasionally throughout this book. You may find that you actually prefer this method.

1. Choose File, Open from the menu bar at the top of the screen. The Open dialog box is displayed.

2. Find AC1-0102 on the CD-ROM that contains the project files.

3. Make sure you have an empty diskette in drive A:. Click the right mouse button on the AC1-0102 file. Select Send To, and send the file to drive A:.

4. Move to drive A: and select AC1-0102.

5. Right-click the filename, and select Properties from the shortcut menu. Deselect Read-only and select Archive from the Attributes area. Click OK.

6. Right-click the file, and select Rename from the shortcut menu.

7. Change the name of the file to Alaska Information, then click the Open button to open the database.

8. Choose File, Close from the menu.

4. Getting Help Using the Function Key

In Lesson 5, you learned how to click the Microsoft Access Help button and how to use the What's This? option from the Help menu. There is another way to get help, and with this method you don't need to take your hand away from the keyboard to grab the mouse. (Of course, you don't have to move your hand to get to the mouse if you are using a laptop computer, either!)

1. Open the Alaska Information file you created in the previous exercise. Use whichever method you prefer.

2. Press the F1 key on the top row of your keyboard. Notice that the Office Assistant appears, ready for a search.

3. Ask the Office Assistant How do I get online help? and click the Search button in the Office Assistant window.

4. Change online to on line. Do the Help topics change, or is the Office Assistant "smart" enough to figure out what you mean either way?

5. Press the Esc key. Notice that the search box disappears, but the Office Assistant remains on the screen.

6. Leave the Alaska Information database open for the next exercise.

5. Determining What Elements Work with the What's This? Feature

In Lesson 5, you used the What's This? feature to get more details about a button than you would have gotten from a simple ScreenTip, which usually consists of only a word or two. Did you wonder what other screen elements work with the What's This? feature? The buttons mentioned in this exercise can be found in Figure 1.16.

To find out what elements work with the What's This? feature:

Figure 1.16

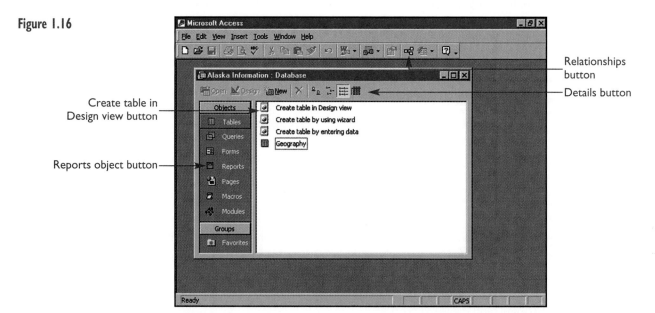

Create table in Design view button

Reports object button

Relationships button

Details button

1. Choose Help, What's This? from the menu. The question-mark pointer is displayed.

2. Move the pointer over the buttons in the toolbar until you find the Relationships button. Notice that the ScreenTips work even when the What's This? pointer is on the screen.

3. Click the Relationships button and read the description. Did it help? (Note: You will use this feature in Project 7.)

4. Hold down ⬆Shift and click F1. Notice that this is a keyboard shortcut for activating the What's This? feature. Click the Reports object button on the left side of the Database window. Did you get a description of what this button does? Click anywhere to turn off the What's This? feature.

5. Hold down (◆Shift) and click (F1) again. Click the Create table in Design view above the Geography table name. Notice that the What's This? feature does not work with some screen elements.

6. Use the same procedure to click the Details button on the right edge of the toolbar in the Database window.

7. Close the Database Window, but leave Access open if you are going to continue to the Challenge section. If not, click the Close button to close Access.

Challenge

Challenge exercises expand on or are related to skills practiced in the project. Each exercise provides a brief narrative introduction followed by instructions in a numbered step format that is not as detailed as those in the Skill Drill section.

1. Finding Out What's New in This Version of Access

If you have used earlier versions of Access, the following exercise will give you an idea of the improvements to this new version. If you have not used Access before, you will get an idea of some of the features of the database.

1. Choose Help from the menu bar.

2. Click Microsoft Access Help.

3. Type How do I design a table? in the Office Assistant text box, and click the Search button in the Office Assistant window.

4. Select What's new about Microsoft Access 2000 from the list of topics. Select Working with Data and Database Design. The results are somewhat limited.

5. Click the Show button at the top of the Help window.

6. Click the Contents tab to view a list of contents.

7. Scroll down to Creating and Designing Tables in the Contents window and click the plus sign to the left of the topic. A list of related topics is displayed.

8. Scroll down to get an idea of the topics that are available. Click one that interests you, and examine it at the Help window.

9. When you are through, click the Close button to close the Help window. Right-click the Office Assistant, and choose Hide from the shortcut menu.

2. Deciding What Fields to Use in a Home Inventory Table

As you review your personal insurance, you realize that you don't have a good idea of what you have bought over the years, or what you should insure and for how much.

Think about what categories would be included in a home inventory database and sketch out a table identifying each of the fields you would use. How detailed do you think you would need to be if you were trying to convince an insurance company that you really owned the items?

To get started, consider whether you'd be better off with a field that contained the age of the items (e.g., 3 for a three-year-old end table), or with a field containing the year the item was purchased. Why would one be superior to the other?

[?] 3. Taking Control of the Office Assistant

Do you like Clippit? He's kind of cute, at least the first few times you see him. Some people, however, get tired of "cute" rather quickly, and would rather use the menu or Microsoft Access Help button to get help when needed than have a paper clip lurking on the edges of the screen. You have complete control over Clippit!

1. Activate the Office Assistant, if necessary. Clippit should appear on the screen, although you might have another figure on your screen.

2. Click the Office Assistant Options button, and go to the Gallery tab in the Office Assistant dialog box. Scroll through the assistants using the Back and Next buttons to see if there is one you like better. If you find one, click OK to activate it. If there are no more assistants available, it means they were not installed.

3. Go back to the Office Assistant dialog box, and select the Options tab. Browse through your options. There is one option that is very appealing if you find the Office Assistant annoying...the Use the Office Assistant check box at the top of the dialog box. If you turn off the check mark and click OK, Clippit will fade away, not to be seen again until you turn it back on using Help, Show the Office Assistant. Close the Office Assistant dialog box.

4. Choose Help, Hide the Office Assistant. This is another way to close the Office Assistant.

[?] 4. Using the Index to Find Help

To get to the Index feature, you will need to open the Help window. If the Office Assistant is active, you will need to type a question, then choose an option to get to this window, even though the question may have nothing to do with what you want to look up. One way to get to the Index (and Contents) tab more quickly is to turn off the Office Assistant.

1. Click the Microsoft Access Help button on the toolbar, if necessary.

2. Click the Options button in the Office Assistant. Click the Use the Office Assistant check box to deselect it, then click OK.

3. Click the Microsoft Access Help button on the toolbar, and then click the Show button, if necessary.

4. Click the Index tab. Type `Table` in the Type keywords text box.

5. Click the Search button. In the Choose a topic area, click Ways to customize a table. Click the graphic to display the Help Screen. Click the numbers on the bottom left corner of the screen, and read the Help information.

6. When you are finished, close the Ways to Customize a Table window.

7. Leave the Help window open for the next exercise.

[?] 5. Using the Help Table of Contents to Read Help Like a Book

The Contents tab works like a table of contents in a book. You can glance down the list of general topics, choose one, then open up help text or sub-chapters.

1. In the first exercise in this section, you clicked the Creating and Designing Tables chapter in the Contents area. Repeat this procedure.

2. Click the plus next to the Adding Fields and Choosing Data Types to see what topics are available.

3. Click the Add a field to a table in Design view topic. This information appears in the window on the right.

4. Click Design view (in blue text) in Step 1. A window pops up showing an illustration of the Design view window and giving some explanation of how to add fields and change data types. Click in the window to close it.

5. Scroll to Step 6 and read the text. Click the How? button at the end of the step. Notice that this takes you to another topic.

6. Close Help, and close the database.

Discovery Zone

Discovery Zone exercises help you gain advanced knowledge of project topics and application of skills. These exercises focus on enhancing your problem-solving skills. Numbered steps are not provided, but you are given hints, reminders, screen shots, and references to help you reach your goal for each exercise.

1. Sending a Database to the Desktop as a Shortcut

In many cases, the same database will be used repeatedly. For example, an inventory database for a small business might be opened many times every day. The same machine, however, might also be used for typing letters, doing budgets and payroll, and other office tasks. It is time-consuming to open Access, then search one or more hard disks or network drives for a database. It would be great if you could place an icon, or shortcut, on your desktop with the name of the database underneath it. That way you could simply double-click it to launch Access and load the database at the same time.

Goal: Figure out how to create a shortcut on your computer desktop.

Use the program's Help features to figure out how to place a shortcut to the Alaska Information database on your desktop. Because this is your first Discovery Zone exercise, you'll get three hints:

> Hint #1: The procedure involves a shortcut menu.
>
> Hint #2: You have seen the procedure on the way to learning something else. If all else fails, review what you have done in this project that involves shortcut menus.
>
> Hint #3: If you are working in a lab with security software, this may not work. It will depend on the level of security set by the lab administrator.

2. Examining Database Properties

As you will see as you go through this book, nearly every element on the Access screen has what are known as **properties**. Properties are the characteristics of a screen element. For example, a number has such properties as its number of decimal places, format, and font size. Databases also have properties. These include the date they were created, whether they are read-only, their size, and several others.

Goal: Find the properties of a database and change one of them.

Use the program's Help features to figure out how to display the properties of a database. Use the Alaska Information database you worked on in this project to test your solution. When you get the Alaska Information Properties dialog box open, change it to a read-only file.

Hint #1: This exercise has no hints. When you solve it, you'll know why.

3. Finding Online Help from Microsoft

Throughout this project, you have used several methods to get help. You have used the Office Assistant, the What's This? button, the Index, and the Contents tab. These are all Help features included with the program. If you have access to the World Wide Web, you can get much more detailed help.

Goal: Explore Microsoft's online help.

Check with your instructor, and if possible, use the Help menu to go to the online help available from Microsoft. Choose to look at Access help, and see what help is available on designing tables. Explore the various categories of help available there.

Creating a Database

Objectives

In this project, you learn how to

➤ **Create a New Database**

➤ **Create a New Table**

➤ **Save a Table Design and Create a Primary Key**

➤ **Add Fields**

➤ **Edit Fields**

➤ **Move Fields**

➤ **Delete Fields**

Key terms introduced in this project include

- data type
- Datasheet view
- Design view
- index
- normalize

- Object Linking and Embedding (OLE)
- primary key
- relational database
- relationship
- row selector

Why Would I Do This?

With Access, you can set up databases to perform a wide variety of tasks. For example, you may want a database (such as the one you create in this project) to keep track of staff training for your company. You can set up various databases to store different sets of related information, and you can create as many databases as you need.

Think of the database as the shell that holds together all related objects. Within the shell, you can create other objects. The fundamental type of object in an Access database is a table. You use tables to store data and organize the information into a usable structure. You can also create other objects, such as forms and queries. You learn about these other database objects later in this book.

In this project, you learn how to create a database and a table from scratch. You also learn how to edit the structure of the table.

 Designing a Database Table

When you design a table, you need to determine what fields will be included. To answer this question, you should consider what kinds of information should be included in a printed report or what information you want to see if you look at a single record on the screen. Consider how you may want to sort or filter the records. For example, if you want to print a list of employee names that is sorted by employee seniority, you need to have a field that contains the date they were hired.

An Access database consists of parts that interact with each other, and it is hard to design one part until you know what the other parts can do. You will have a much better idea of what fields to include in a table once you have learned how to create queries, forms, and reports.

There are six fairly universal rules for designing tables that were originally proposed by Dr. Edgar F. Codd of IBM in the 1960s, and which still hold true today. When you apply these rules to your tables, you are *normalizing* them. The rules are simplified and paraphrased as follows:

- Rule 1: Fields should be atomic; that is, each piece of data should be broken down as much as possible. For example, rather than creating a field called "Name," you would create two fields: one for the first name and the other for the last name.

- Rules 2 and 3: Each record should contain a unique identifier so that you have a way of safely identifying the record. A Social Security Number is ideal, because no two people have the same one. The unique identifier is called a *primary key*. You may select one of the fields in the table as the primary key if that field would never contain duplicate values for different records. If none of the fields is suitable, the program can add a counter field that will automatically assign a unique number to each record as it is entered.

- Rule 4: The primary key should be short, stable, and simple. Addresses and even last names may change several times during a person's life. This is why governments and companies assign permanent, unique identification numbers.

- Rule 5: Every other field in the record should supply additional information about the person or thing that is uniquely identified by the primary key. For example, a table that contains data about employees may include a field that indicates the employee's supervisor. It would be inappropriate to include a field that holds the supervisor's birth date.

- Rule 6: Information in the table should not appear in more than one place. For example, if you tried to create a table of the different committees in an organization and had fields with names such as Chairperson, Member1, Member2, and Member3; the same person could be the chairperson of one committee and Member1 in another. If that person changed his or her name, you would have to change it in more than one place. Avoid numbered field names such as those shown in this example.

In order to conform to these rules, you may need to create more than one table in a database and connect them together. Linking more than one table together is a feature of a *relational database* and is demonstrated throughout this project.

Fortunately, you do not need to understand all of this in order to get started, and the application of these rules will become evident as you use the example tables.

Visual Summary

When you have completed this lesson, you will have created a document that looks like Figure 2.1:

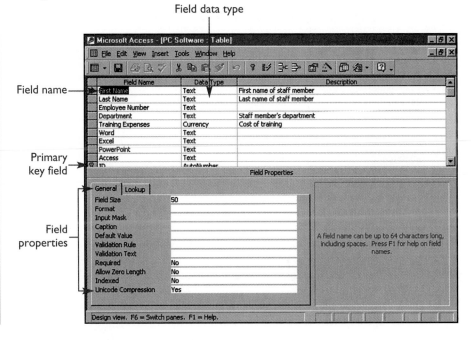

Field data type

Field name

Primary key field

Field properties

Figure 2.1
The table Design view gives you control over the fields in a table.

Lesson 1: Creating a New Database

Remember that the table is the object in which you actually store and define the structure for your data, and the database is the shell that houses all of the related tables and other objects. In this lesson, you create a new database to keep track of the personal computer software training received by your staff.

To Create a New Database

① **Launch Access, then click the <u>B</u>lank Access Database option, and click OK.**

Access displays the File New Database dialog box. Access suggests a default name (such as db1 or db2) for the new database; however, you can assign a more descriptive name here. You can also tell Access where you want to store the database.

② **In the File <u>n</u>ame text box, type Training.**

This is the name you want to use for the new database. After you name the database the first time, you won't have to do it again. As you add or edit records, Access updates the database automatically. As you add new objects, however, you have to save each of them. When you add a table, for example, you must save it. Access then updates the database to incorporate this new database object.

③ **Click the list arrow next to the Save <u>i</u>n text box, and select your drive or folder.**

Access suggests a default drive and folder for saving the new database. Select drive A: unless otherwise instructed (see Figure 2.2).

Figure 2.2
You use the File New Database dialog box to assign a name to your database.

Select a drive and folder

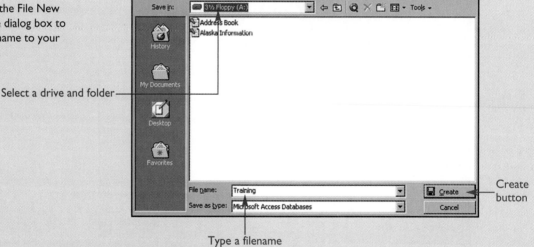

Create button

Type a filename

④ **Click the <u>C</u>reate button.**

Access opens the database window for your new database (see Figure 2.3). The name of the database is displayed in the title bar of the Database window. Notice that there are no tables shown, because you have not created any database objects (yet). Three methods of creating new tables are displayed. Keep the Training database open to use in the next lesson. In that lesson, you learn how to add a new table to the database.

Database name →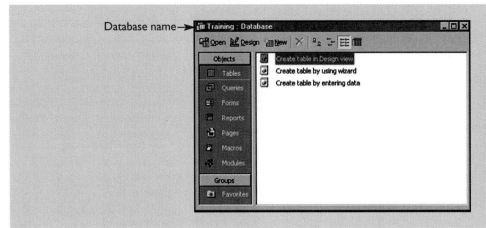

Figure 2.3
The name you assign to your database is displayed in the title bar of the database window.

 Creating Smaller Databases
It's tempting to create one big database that includes multiple tables to meet many different needs, but it's a better idea to create smaller databases, each of which is dedicated to a particular function. Doing so makes managing and using each database much easier. You can relate these smaller databases to one another later, if necessary.

 Other Ways to Create a New Database
There is usually more than one way to perform each function in Access. For example, to create a new database, you can press Ctrl+N, select New from the File menu, or click the New button on the toolbar.

Lesson 2: Creating a New Table

After you create your database, you can add tables to it to store your information. A database is built on one or more tables, each of which holds a distinct set of information. The table defines the structure of the data—what pieces of data you enter and in what order. You should spend some time planning the structure of your database. How many fields do you need? What are their data types? Who will be using the database, and how will they be using the information? If necessary, you can add fields later if you need them, but it is very important to map out the fundamental structure of the table before you get started.

Building a database without a plan is like building a house without a blueprint. The more work you invest in the initial design, the less time you spend in patchwork repairs later. Design your table structures first so that you can immediately put the database to work with confidence.

When you create a new table, you can add any fields you want. Remember that the table consists of records (one set of information—such as the name, address, and phone number for one person) and fields. Fields are the individual pieces of information that together make up a record; for example, an address is a field. To add a field, you type a field name and then select a **data type**, which defines the kind of information you can enter into that field. Table 2.1 explains the various data types you can use. You can also type a description for the field and set field properties. You learn how to set field properties in Project 7.

Table 2.1 Data Types and What They Mean

Data Type	Explanation
Text	The default data type. You can enter up to 255 numbers or letters.
Memo	This type of field is useful when you want to include sentences or paragraphs in the field—for example, a long product description. This type of field is not limited by size.
Number	You can enter only numbers.
Date/Time	You can enter only dates or times.
Currency	You can enter numbers. Access formats the entry as currency. If you type 12.5, for example, Access displays it as $12.50.
AutoNumber	Access enters a value that is incremented automatically with each new record added to a table.
Yes/No	A Yes/No field type limits your data to one of two conditions. You can enter only Yes or No, True or False, or On or Off. For example, you may have a Sent Christmas Card field in your address database that would work best as a Yes/No field.
OLE Object	You can insert **Object Linking and Embedding (OLE)** objects, which are things such as pictures or charts created in another application package.
Hyperlink	A field that enables you to enter active Web addresses.
Lookup Wizard	A field that looks up data from another source.

In this lesson, you create a table containing fields for first names, last names, and department names.

To Create a New Table

❶ In the Tables object button in the Training database window, click the New button.

Access displays the New Table dialog box (see Figure 2.4). You can choose between two views of a blank database, or you can launch one of three wizards to create a new table. The wizards walk you through the process of setting up a table, bringing in a table from another source, or linking the database to another data source without actually moving the information into the database.

Another Way to Create a New Table
You can also create a new table by double-clicking on the Create table in Design view option.

Figure 2.4
The New Table dialog box offers five choices for creating a database.

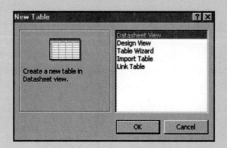

2 Select Design view, and click OK.

You see the table in **Design view** with the default name of Table 1 (see Figure 2.5). The new table, as you can see, contains no fields. To add fields to the table, you must first enter the field names, data types, and descriptions. The insertion point blinks in the first row of the Field Name column. Here, you type the first field name.

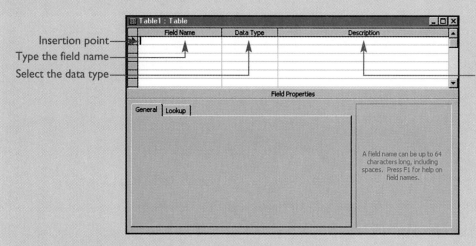

Insertion point —
Type the field name —
Select the data type —

— Type a description of the field

Figure 2.5
The blank table is shown in Design view.

3 Type First Name and press ⏎Enter.

Access enters the field name for the first field. In the lower half of the window, Access displays the field properties you can set (see Figure 2.6). Access moves the insertion point to the Data Type column so that you can choose the type of data you want the field to contain. The most common data type is Text, which is the default. You can click the down arrow (which is displayed when you move to the Data Type column) to display a drop-down list of data types. For First Name, leave the data type as the default, which is Text.

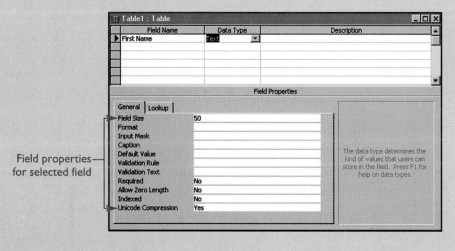

Field properties — for selected field

Figure 2.6
Each field has properties you can set.

4 Press ⏎Enter.

The Text data type is accepted, and Access moves the insertion point to the Description column.

continues ▶

To Create a New Table   (continued)

5 Type `First name of staff member` and press ⏎Enter.
Access enters the field description and moves the insertion point to the next row (see Figure 2.7).

 Where the Description Field is Shown
If you include a description for a field, it is displayed in the status bar whenever you are in ***Datasheet view*** or Form view. Place the insertion point in that field. The information in the status bar provides the user with a more complete description of the purpose of the field.

You are now ready to enter the next field name.

Figure 2.7
The first field of the Table1 table has been created.

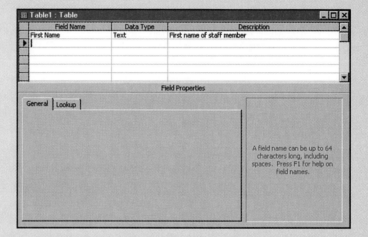

6 Type `Last Name` and press ⏎Enter twice.
This enters the name for the field, accepts the default Text as the data type, and moves the insertion point to the Description column.

7 Type `Last name of staff member` and press ⏎Enter.
As before, Access enters the field description for this second field and moves the insertion point to the next row so that you can add another field. Adding a field description is optional.

8 Type `Department` and press ⏎Enter twice.
Again, this step enters the field name, accepts Text as the data type, and moves the insertion point to the Description column.

9 Type `Staff member's department` and press ⏎Enter.
This is the description for the third field of your table (see Figure 2.8). By adding these fields to the database table, you have taken the first steps toward creating a database to track staff training. Keep both this table and the Training database open. You learn how to save the table in the next lesson.

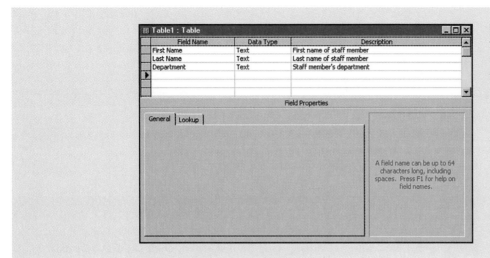

Figure 2.8
The Design view of a database table contains three fields.

 Rules for Field Names and Using Table Design View
You can create a field name using up to 64 characters. Try to use names that are short but meaningful (long names make the system work harder). You can use any combination of letters, numbers, spaces, and characters with a few exceptions: Periods (.), exclamation points (!), single quotation marks ('), and brackets ([ ]) cannot appear anywhere in the name. Spaces are allowed, but not as the first character of the field name.

You can also use the ⌈Tab⇆⌋ key in place of the ⌈↵Enter⌋ key when adding fields, accepting the displayed data type, and entering descriptions in the table Design view.

Lesson 3: Saving a Table Design and Creating a Primary Key

The first time you save the table's design, you are prompted to assign a name. After you save and name the table the first time, it takes only a moment to save changes whenever necessary. If you make changes to the design, such as adding new fields, you must save the changes to the design.

In addition to saving new tables, you should assign or create a primary key field for each table in your database. Each record's primary key field contains a value that uniquely identifies it; no two records can have the same value in their primary key field. Examples of good primary key fields are things such as Social Security Numbers, student ID numbers, or automobile part numbers. You can use this feature to your advantage when you need to establish a **relationship** between one table and another. A relationship connects a field in one table to a field in a second table. Relationships enable you to draw information from more than one table at a time for forms or reports. This topic is discussed in much more detail in Project 7.

Assigning a primary key also ensures that you won't enter the same information for the primary key field more than once in a table, because it won't accept a duplicate entry. Because Access automatically builds an **index** for primary keys, it can easily search for information and sort tables based on the primary key field. An index is a location guide built by Access for all primary key fields that helps speed up searching and sorting for those fields. Indexes can also be created for other fields, as long as they are not OLE or Memo fields.

If you have a unique field, such as an ID number in your table, you can use that as the primary key field. Or you can have Access create a simple counter field.

In this lesson, you have Access create a counter field to use as the primary key field, because you cannot ensure that fields such as First Name, Last Name, and Department will contain unique information.

To Save a Table Design and Create a Primary Key

1 In the Training database, with Table1 open, click the Save button on the toolbar.
You could also open the File menu and choose the Save command. You see the Save As dialog box, which prompts you to type a name for the table (see Figure 2.9). As you can see, the default name that Access provides doesn't tell you much, so you should provide a more descriptive one.

Figure 2.9
You must give the table a name the first time you save it.

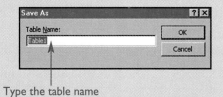

Type the table name

2 Type PC Software and click OK.
This is the name you want to assign to the table for this example. The next time you see the list of tables in the database window, this name will be displayed. The size of a table name isn't limited to eight characters. You can use up to 64 characters, including spaces.

Access displays a reminder that no primary key has been defined (see Figure 2.10). You are not required to use a primary key, but it is a good idea to include one. An easy way to create a primary key field is to have Access create a counter field that automatically assigns a different number to each record in your table.

Figure 2.10
A dialog box warns you that you haven't defined a primary key.

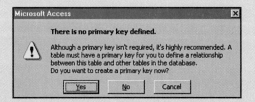

3 Click the Yes button.
Access saves the table and adds a counter field named ID with an AutoNumber data type. This is now the primary key field. Access automatically places sequential numbers in this field as you add new records. Your table in Design view

should look like the one shown in Figure 2.11. Notice the key symbol in the **row selector** for the ID field. The key indicates that the ID field is the primary key field for this table.

Keep the PC Software table of the Training database open. In the next lesson, you learn how to add new fields to the table.

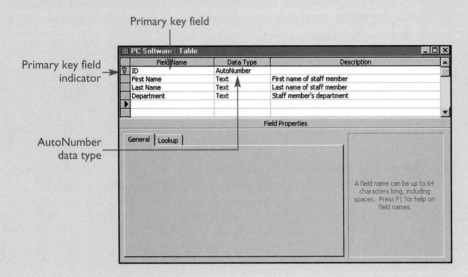

Primary key field

Primary key field indicator

AutoNumber data type

Figure 2.11
The key symbol indicates the field designated as the primary key.

Defining a New Primary Key

To make another field in the database the primary key, click the row selector for the field you want. Then click the Primary Key button on the toolbar. You can also open the Edit menu and choose the Primary Key command. The primary key field is indicated by the key symbol in the row selector.

To save a table quickly, press Ctrl+S.

Lesson 4: Adding Fields

What happens if you decide you want to track more information than you included in your original PC Software table? You can add new fields to store this additional data. Keep in mind, however, that if you have already added records to the table, any new fields in those existing records will be empty until you type information into them. Other database objects such as queries, forms, or reports that are based on the table will not be automatically updated to include the new fields. Because you have not yet created any other database objects that use this table, this is a good time to make changes.

In this lesson, you add seven new fields to your PC Software table—one for training expense, one for employee number, one for employee's supervisor, and one each for four of the Microsoft Office software applications. Try adding these fields now.

To Add Fields

1 With the PC Software table of the Training database still displayed in Design view, position the insertion point in the next blank row of the PC Software table.

This is the row in which you want to enter the first new field name. The row selector arrow should be displayed next to this row (see Figure 2.12).

Figure 2.12
The row selector arrow indicates the current row.

Current row →
Row selector arrow →
Insertion point →

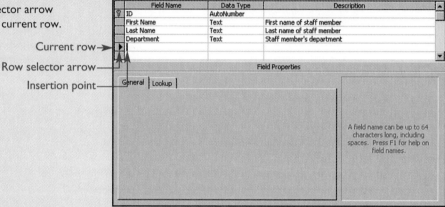

2 Type Cost and press ↵Enter twice.

This enters the name of the field, accepts Text as the data type (it will be changed later), and moves to the Description column.

3 Type Cost of training and press ↵Enter.

This is the description for the new field. When you press ↵Enter, Access moves the insertion point to the next row.

4 Type Employee Number and press ↓.

By pressing ↓, you enter the name for this field, accept Text as the data type, and skip the Description column. Again, the insertion point is in position to add a new field to the table.

5 Type Supervisor and press ↵Enter three times. Click the Maximize button to maximize the Design view window.

Once again, you have added another new field to the table, accepting Text as the data type, skipping the description, and moving to the next row.

6 Type Word and press ↵Enter three times. Use the same procedure to enter fields for Excel, PowerPoint, and Access.

You have now added seven additional fields to the table. Your table should look similar to the one in Figure 2.13, although you may have to scroll up or down to see all of the fields.

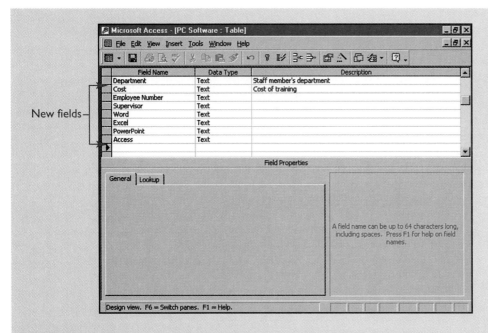

Figure 2.13
You have added seven new fields to the PC Software table.

New fields—

7 **Click the Save button to save your work, and leave both the PC Software table and the Training database open.**
In the next lesson, you learn another way to alter the structure of your PC Software table.

Lesson 5: Editing Fields

As you create your database, you may want to modify the structure. For example, you may want to change field names, choose a different data type, or edit or add descriptions. You make these changes in Design view.

Changing the field type may have an effect on the data in your table. For example, if you type text into a field and then change that field to a Yes/No field, you may encounter problems. Access prompts you to let you know when changes in the field type are made and when they might result in a loss of data. Be sure that you want to make the change before you confirm it.

In this lesson, you edit the name of a field, add a description, and change the field type.

To Edit Fields

1 **In the Design view of the PC Software table, position the pointer on the word Cost (the fourth field name) and double-click.**
This selects the word you want to change (see Figure 2.14). You may have to scroll up to get to this field.

continues ▶

To Edit Fields (continued)

Figure 2.14
To change a field name,
you first select it.

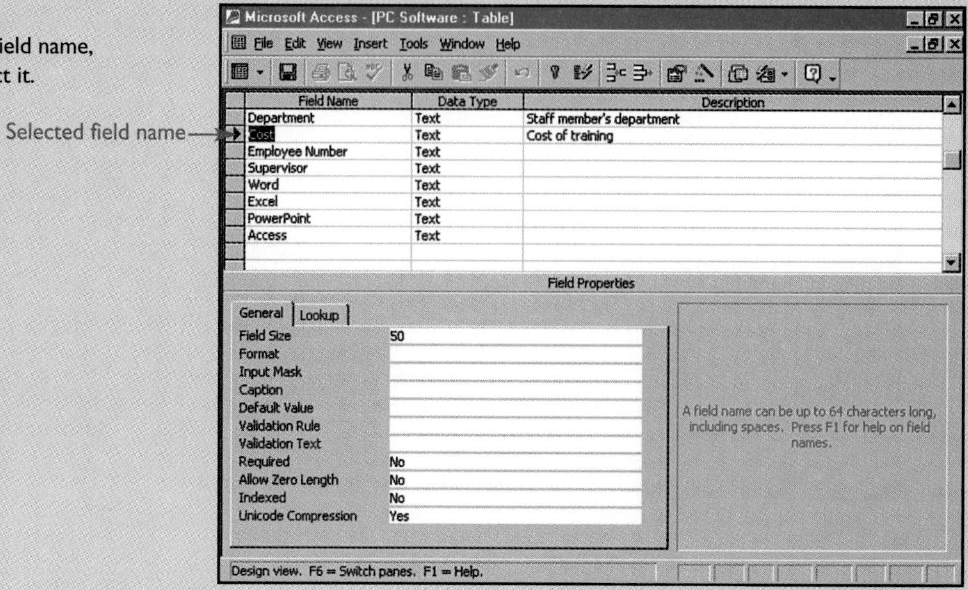

Selected field name ──▶

Field Name	Data Type	Description
Department	Text	Staff member's department
Cost	Text	Cost of training
Employee Number	Text	
Supervisor	Text	
Word	Text	
Excel	Text	
PowerPoint	Text	
Access	Text	

Field Properties

General | Lookup |

Field Size	50
Format	
Input Mask	
Caption	
Default Value	
Validation Rule	
Validation Text	
Required	No
Allow Zero Length	No
Indexed	No
Unicode Compression	Yes

A field name can be up to 64 characters long, including spaces. Press F1 for help on field names.

Design view. F6 = Switch panes. F1 = Help.

2 **Type** Training Expenses.
The existing highlighted text is replaced with the new text.

3 **Click in the Description column for the Supervisor field.**
After moving the insertion point to this field, you can add a description.

4 **Type** Reporting Supervisor.
The description that you enter provides information about what is stored in this field.

5 **Click in the Data Type column for the Training Expenses field.**
Notice that a list arrow is displayed, which indicates a list of data type options is available.

6 **Click the list arrow in the Data Type column.**
A list of choices is displayed (see Figure 2.15) .

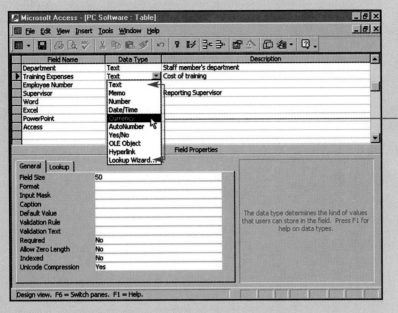

Figure 2.15
When you click the list arrow in the Data Type column, a list of data types is displayed.

List of available data types

 From the list, click Currency.
You have changed the data type to a type that is more appropriate for the information in this field. All data in this field is now displayed with a dollar sign, commas (if needed), and two decimal places.

 Click the Save button on the toolbar to save your work.
Leave both the PC Software table and the Training database open. In the next lesson, you learn how to move fields from one location in the table to another.

Quicker Selection of Data Type
If you know the name of the data type you want to enter in the Data Type column, you don't have to use the mouse to open the drop-down list. Instead, if the data Type is highlighted, you can type the first letter of the data type you want. Access fills in the rest of the characters for you. By typing the letter c, for example, Access fills in Currency.

Changing a Field Name
Changing the field name or description does not have any effect on the data you already have entered in the table. Changing the field name may have an unintended effect, however; if any forms, queries, or reports refer to the field name, you may have to change the references manually to reflect the new name, depending on how your Access program is configured. Otherwise, these database objects will no longer work as they did before.

Lesson 6: Moving Fields

In addition to changing the name and data type of a field, you can change the order in which the fields are displayed in your database. When you enter records, you may want the fields in a different order. In the PC Software table, for example, you may find it easier to enter the employee's number immediately after you enter the employee's name. You may also want to move the ID (counter) field to the end, because you never have to enter anything in this field.

In this lesson, you first look at the table in Datasheet view—the view you use to enter records. You then change back to Design view to rearrange the fields.

To Change Views and Move Fields

 ❶ Click the View button on the toolbar to change from the current Design view to Datasheet view.

If you have not saved your changes to the table, Access will prompt you to save them. Notice that the View button looks different in Datasheet view than it did in Design view. The icon on the View button indicates the view that will be displayed when you click it.

> **X** If the Table Design toolbar is not showing, choose View, Toolbars, Table Design from the menu.

This changes your view of the database to Datasheet view (see Figure 2.16). Datasheet view is the view you use to enter, sort, and edit the records in the database.

The datasheet you see is blank, except for the field names, because you haven't added any records yet. You learn how to work with records in Project 3. In Datasheet view, you cannot make any changes to the structure of the table, although you will be able to change column widths.

Figure 2.16
The PC Software table is displayed in Datasheet view.

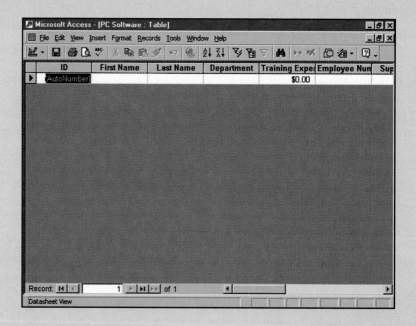

 ❷ Click the View button on the toolbar.
This returns you to Design view so that you can make changes.

3 **Click the row selector for the Employee Number field.**

This step selects the field you want to move. Notice that the entire row is highlighted (see Figure 2.17). You move this field so that it immediately follows the Last Name field.

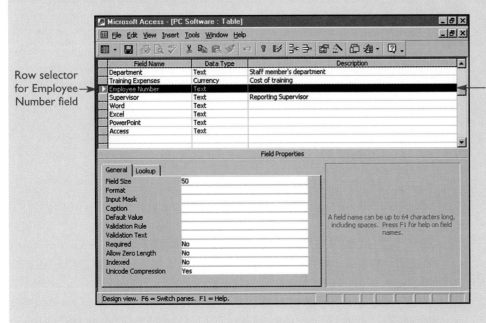

Row selector for Employee→ Number field

Selected row

Figure 2.17
Click the row selector to select the row you want to move.

4 **Click the row selector again with the left mouse button, and hold it down. Drag the row to its new position under Last Name, and release the mouse button.**

As you drag, a small gray box appears under the mouse pointer, along with a horizontal line showing where the row will be placed. When you release the mouse button, Access places the row in its new spot (see Figure 2.18).

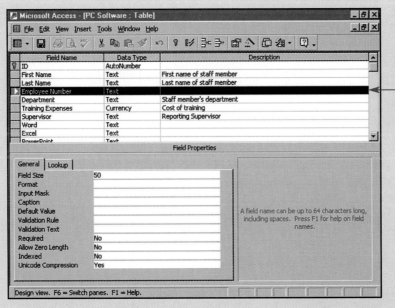

Field has been moved

Figure 2.18
The Employee Number field has been moved to a new location.

continues ▶

To Change Views and Move Fields   (continued)

X If the field you move is displayed in the wrong place after you drag and drop it, don't worry. Just move the field again.

If you see a double-headed arrow as you try to position the mouse, the mouse pointer isn't in the correct spot. If the double-headed arrow is displayed, Access thinks that you want to resize the row height or the Design view window.

 If you accidentally resize rather than move your row, click the **Undo** button (or open the Edit menu and choose the Undo command). The Undo command reverses your most recent action, such as moving a row. Only the most recent change can be undone.

If your window is too small to see all of the rows, maximize the window by clicking on the Maximize button in the upper-right corner of the table window.

5 **Select the ID row, and drag it down to the first empty row of the table.**
This step moves the ID field to the last position in the table. Next, try undoing the move.

6 **Click the Undo button.**
With Access, you can undo some of the changes you make to the database. In this example, however, you decide that you really do want the ID field at the end of the table.

7 **Select the ID row again, and drag it back to the end of the table.**
This moves the ID field back to the end of the table.

8 **Click the Save button to save your work. Keep both the Training database and the PC Software table open in Design view.**
In the next lesson, you learn how to delete fields from your table structure.

Lesson 7: Deleting Fields

Another significant change that you can make to the structure of your PC Software table is to remove fields you no longer need. Suppose that you decide you don't really need a field for the supervisor. Instead of having it take up space in the table design, you can delete the field.

Keep in mind that deleting a field from your table also deletes all the data in that field. Because this may not be what you intended, Access displays a warning that asks you to confirm the change. Read the warning carefully and be sure that you want to delete all the data before you delete the field. If you have already created other database objects such as forms or reports that use this field, they will have to be revised individually.

To Delete a Field

1 **In the PC Software table of the Training database, click the row selector for the Supervisor field.**

Access highlights the entire Supervisor row, showing that the Supervisor field is selected. This is the field you want to delete.

2 **Click the Delete Rows button to delete the row from your table. Click Yes when asked if you are sure.**

Access removes the field from the database table and deletes any data that was in that field (see Figure 2.19). If you had entered any data into this field in the Datasheet view, Access would warn you that the data would be lost.

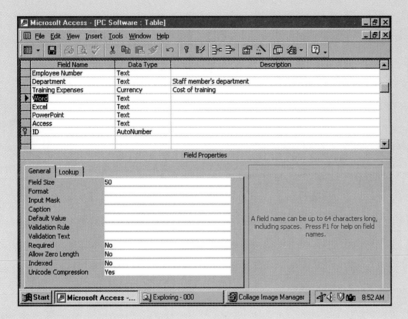

Figure 2.19
The Supervisor field has been deleted.

3 **Click the Save button to save your changes.**

4 **Close the PC Software table by clicking the Close button in the upper-right corner of the table window.**

5 **Close the Training database by clicking the Close button in the upper-right corner of the database window.**

If you are finished with your session at the computer, click the Close button in the upper-right corner of the Access window. Otherwise, continue with the "Checking Concepts and Terms" section.

Summary

In this project, you were introduced to some of the steps required to create a new database. You created your first database, table, and primary key field. You saved the new table, then went back into Design view to modify the structure of the table, adding, editing, moving, and deleting fields.

To expand your knowledge of the table creation process, use the Office Assistant to get more information about the different data types and in what situations each might be used. Type **Data** in the index keyword box, click $\underline{S}$earch, and scroll down to DataType. Select DataType Property from the $\underline{C}$hoose topic box.

Checking Concepts and Terms

True/False

For each of the following, check *T* or *F* to indicate whether the statement is true or false.

__T __F **1.** In Design view, you can move a field by clicking the row selector and dragging the field up or down the field list. [L6]

__T __F **2.** You can include only eight characters in a table name. [L2]

__T __F **3.** The most common data type is Text, the default. [L2]

__T __F **4.** You must have a primary key field. [L3]

__T __F **5.** You can enter only numbers in a Number field. [L2]

__T __F **6.** After you save your table structure, you cannot edit or change it. [L4]

__T __F **7.** A Yes/No field type limits your data to one of two conditions. [L2]

__T __F **8.** When planning a database, you should gather information from the people who will use the database to make sure you understand their needs. [L2]

__T __F **9.** It is best to build one large database with everything in one table. [L2]

__T __F **10.** If you add a new field to a database that already has data in other fields, the new field will be empty until you enter the information. [L4]

Multiple Choice

Circle the letter of the correct answer for each of the following questions.

1. Which of the following is not one of the ways you can create a new database? [L1]

a. Click the $\underline{O}$pen menu, and choose the $\underline{N}$ew Database command.

b. Open the $\underline{F}$ile menu, and choose the $\underline{N}$ew command.

c. Click the New button on the toolbar.

d. Press Ctrl+N.

2. Which of the following is not a valid data type? [L2]

a. Currency

b. Yes/No

c. Text

d. Text & Numbers

3. How do you select a row in Design view of a table? [L6]

a. Drag across the entire row.

b. Click the row selector next to the row.

c. Click the Select Row button on the toolbar.

d. Press Ctrl+R.

4. If you let the program create a primary key for you, what field name does it use? [L3]

a. counter

b. ID

c. MDB

d. primary

5. In table Design view, how do you select a data type? [L2]

    a. Open the Edit menu, and choose the type you want.

    b. Click the Data Type button on the toolbar.

    c. Press Ctrl+D.

    d. Select the data type from the list.

6. In table Design view, a black arrow appears on the row selector of which of the following? [L6]

    a. a row that has an error in the data

    b. the primary key

    c. a duplicate field definition

    d. the row you are editing

7. In Design view, how can you tell that a field is the primary key? [L3]

    a. The status bar displays text when you have the field selected.

    b. There is no way to tell in Design view.

    c. The field name is underlined.

    d. The key symbol appears on the row selector button.

8. Why is the Description entry in table Design view handy? [L2]

    a. It appears in the status bar when you enter data in the field in Datasheet view.

    b. It appears as a pop-up label when you place the mouse pointer on the field in Datasheet view.

    c. Access uses it to test data automatically that you enter into the field.

    d. It serves no purpose at all.

9. To change the order of fields in a table in Design view, you select the field and then do which of the following? [L6]

    a. Press Ctrl+O, entering the destination in the dialog box that appears.

    b. Drag the field to the new location.

    c. Press Alt as you select the new location.

    d. Press Ctrl as you select the new location, and then select Swap from the shortcut menu.

10. Field names are limited to how many characters? [L2]

    a. 255

    b. 50

    c. 64

    d. 8

Screen ID

Label each element of the Access screen shown in Figure 2.20.

Figure 2.20

A. Primary key symbol

B. Primary key field

C. Primary key button

D. Properties area

E. View button

F. Row selector indicator

G. Save button

H. Delete Rows button

I. Undo button

J. Table name

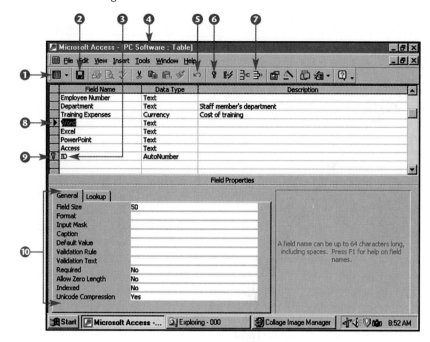

1. _____	4. _____	7. _____
2. _____	5. _____	8. _____
3. _____	6. _____	9. _____
		10. _____

Discussion Questions

1. Access is a powerful database and can be used in the most complex business applications. It can also be used for personal information. If you were to create a database to keep track of your personal information, what tables would it contain?

2. If you wanted to create a table of people to send birthday cards to, what fields would you need to include? Could you get all of the information into one table, or would you need to split it up into two tables? Review the section on normalizing a database at the beginning of this project.

3. Assume you have been hired to set up a database for a small used bookstore. This bookstore prides itself on giving its customers great information. With each book that they sell, they also hand the customer a printout with the following information:

author, name of the book, year of publication, number of pages, publisher, illustrator, author's nationality, and author's date of birth and death. How many tables would you set up for this database? Which fields would go in which table?

4. In the used bookstore database you set up in question 3, what would be a good primary key field for each table?

5. In this project, you created a table that had the first name and last name in separate fields. What is the advantage of separating the first and last names? Why wouldn't it be just as good to have a single field for "Jane Smith"? How about "Smith, Jane"? Should you also create a separate field for the middle name? It might help to think about how you would use the names if you were putting together an address list for a club or other organization.

Skill Drill

Skill Drill exercises reinforce project skills. Each skill reinforced is the same, or nearly the same, as a skill presented in the project. Each exercise includes a brief narrative introduction, followed by detailed instructions in a step-by-step format.

1. Keeping Track of Your Books

You are an avid reader, and have been collecting books for years. You've also borrowed books from the library over the years, and sometimes you can't remember whether you own the book or not. To make matters worse, you read a lot of mysteries, and you sometimes pick up a book and can't remember whether you've read it. You decide it is time to create a database to keep track of your collection.

1. Launch Access, and select the Blank Access Database option.
2. Type `Book Collection` in the File name text box.

3. Use the Save in drop-down list box to select the drive and/or folder in which you want to save your database.
4. Click the Create button.

2. Creating a Table to Store Book Information

Now that you have created a database, it is time to decide what fields you want to include. Give this a little thought.

1. Click the New button to create a new table.
2. Select Design view.
3. Type `Author Last Name` in the Field Name column.
4. Accept Text as the Data Type.
5. Type `Last name of the author` in the Description column.

6. Add the following fields. Make them all Text fields, and add a short description in the Description column.

   ```
   Author First Name
   Book
   Year Published
   Type of Book
   Publisher
   Pages
   ```

3. Saving the Table Design and Adding a Primary Key Field

Now that you have put this much work into your new database, it is probably a good time to save what you've done. You could press the Save button, but you can click the View button and get the same results.

1. Click the View button on the toolbar.
2. Click Yes to save your changes.
3. Name the table `Books`.

4. Click Yes to let Access insert a primary key field.
5. Maximize the table window, and scroll to the right to see your fields.
6. Click the View button to return to the Design view.

4. Adding and Deleting Fields

After some thought, you decide that you would like to make some changes to your database. You find that you are spending far more time typing than you'd like, and the name of the publisher is the culprit. You can't imagine a need for this field in the future, so you decide to eliminate it. You also realize that you should have included a field for whether or not you have read the book.

1. Place the insertion point in the first empty row in the list of fields.
2. Type **Read?** in the Field Name column.
3. Accept Text as the data Type.
4. Type **Enter Y or N only!** in the Description column.
5. Click the row selector in the Publisher field.
6. Click the Delete Rows button to remove the field.
7. Click the Save button to save your changes to the structure of the table.

5. Editing the Data Type of Fields

Two of the fields, Pages and Year Published, are always going to be numbers. You decide that it would be a good idea to change the data type.

1. Click the Data Type column of the Year Published field.
2. Click the list arrow to display the drop-down menu.
3. Select Number from the list.
4. Highlight the data type in the Data Type column of the Pages field.
5. Type the letter **n** to change the data type to Number.
6. Click the Save button to save your changes to the structure of the table.

6. Moving a Field

After some more thought, you decide that you'd like the Pages field to follow the Book field.

1. Click the row selector of the Pages field.
2. Click the row selector of the Pages field again, and drag the field up between the Book field and the Year Published field.
3. Click the View button to change to Datasheet view.
4. Click Yes to save your changes.
5. Check the order of the fields in Datasheet view to make sure the Pages field is in the right place.
6. Close the database, and close Access unless you are going to continue with the Challenge section.

Challenge

Challenge exercises expand on or are somewhat related to skills presented in the lessons. Each exercise provides a brief narrative introduction followed by instructions in a numbered step format that are not as detailed as those in the Skill Drill section.

1. Adding a Table to an Existing Database by Entering Data

You have decided to expand your Alaska database by adding tables that record other information about the Alaskan environment. The first table you want to add is about the wildlife you have seen in your travels.

1. Copy AC1-0201 to drive A: (or other location) and rename it **Alaska Environment**.
2. Open the Alaska Environment database, and double-click Create table by entering data.
3. Enter **Black Bear, Garbage Dump, Seward, 1995** in the first four fields.
4. Click the View button, and name the table **Wildlife I Have Seen**. Do not add a primary key field.
5. In Design view, name the four fields **Animal**, **Surroundings**, **Location**, and **Year**.
6. Close the table, and save your changes.

2. Adding a Table to an Existing Database Using a Wizard

Now that you have added a wildlife table, you decide you ought to have a table for plants you have seen. You know the common names, but decide you ought to leave a place for the scientific names when you get around to looking them up.

1. Double-click Create table by using wizard.
2. Choose the Personal category, and select Plants from the Sample Tables options.
3. For fields, choose `CommonName`, `Genus`, `Species`, `LightPreference`, `TempPreference`, `Photograph`, and `Notes`.
4. Name your table `Plants I Have Seen`. Have the program set a primary key.
5. Do not relate this table to any other table. (You will learn about relating tables in Lesson 7.)
6. Choose to enter information directly into the table.
7. Enter `Dandelion` as the Common Name, and type `Seen all over the place` for the Notes field. Leave all of the other fields blank.
8. Close the table.

3. Adding a Primary Key Field to an Existing Table

Two of your three tables now have primary key fields, and you have decided that maybe the third one should too.

1. Select the Wildlife I Have Seen table, and open it in Design view.
2. Add a new field called `ID`.
3. Make the data type of new field AutoNumber.
4. Click the Primary Key button.
5. Close the table and save your changes.

4. Deleting More Than One Field at a Time

Looking at your Plants I Have Seen table, you realize that you are just doing this for fun, and the odds of you ever looking up the genus and species are very small. Therefore, you decide you want to remove these fields from your table.

1. Select the Plants I Have Seen table, and open it in Design view.
2. Click the row selector for the Genus field, and hold the mouse button down.
3. Drag down, and select the Species field as well.
4. Press Del.
5. Close the table, and save your changes.

5. Add Check Boxes to a Table

You just saw a friend's database that has really neat check boxes for Yes/No fields and decide you'd like to add one to one of your tables. The obvious choice would be a check box in the Geography table for places you have visited.

1. Open the Geography table in Design view.
2. Add a new field called `Visited`.

3. Select Yes/No as the data type.

4. Click the View button, and save your changes.

5. Scroll to the right edge of the table.

6. Click the check boxes for the first two records.

7. Close the table.

[?] 6. Adding a Hyperlink Field

One of the data type options is called Hyperlink. You are not sure exactly what this is or how it can be used in an Access database.

1. Use the Office Assistant to figure out exactly what a Hyperlink field is and how it works. If you are still unsure, go online and check the Microsoft site.

2. Open the Geography table.

3. Go to the Web, and find a site about one of the cities listed in the table.

4. Add a new Hyperlink field called `Local Information`.

5. Enter the URL that you found on the Web for an Alaskan city.

6. Test the URL.

7. Close the table.

Discovery Zone

Discovery Zone exercises help you gain advanced knowledge of project topics and application of skills. These exercises focus on enhancing your problem-solving skills. Numbered steps are not provided, but you are given hints, reminders, screen shots, and references to help you reach your goal for each exercise.

[?] 1. Creating a Lookup Wizard Field

The Lookup Wizard Data type is unlike any of the other data types. It enables you to enter a code, which will fill in the field with information from another source.

Goal: Create a Lookup Wizard field that categorizes the animals listed in the Wildlife I Have Seen table.

Use the program's Help features and online help to figure out how to use a Lookup Wizard field. There are two different ways of using this type of field—you choose which one you want to use. You should create at least three categories for the wildlife types. For instance, one of your categories might be birds.

2. Creating a Primary Key Field Using More Than One Field

Sometimes you want to use information in your database for your primary key field, but no one field is unique. Access offers you a way to use more than one field in combination as a primary key.

Goal: Create a primary key using two fields.

Use the Geography table and create a primary key field out of the Latitude and Longitude fields. (Two places might have the same latitude or the same longitude, but no two places have both the same latitude and longitude.)

Hint: You will need to remove the existing primary key field before you can proceed.

Entering and Editing Data

Objectives

In this project, you learn how to

- ➤ Add Records
- ➤ Move Among Records
- ➤ Edit Records
- ➤ Insert and Delete Records
- ➤ Adjust Column Widths and Hide Columns
- ➤ Find a Record
- ➤ Sort Records

Key terms introduced in this project include

- ■ Clipboard
- ■ current record indicator
- ■ pencil icon
- ■ record selector

Why Would I Do This?

After you create a database and table, you want to be able to put them to work. For your database to be useful, you must enter data into the table (or tables). For example, you can keep track of your business contacts by entering their names, addresses, and phone numbers into the Contacts table of the Address Book database you worked with in Project 1. You can use the Training database you created in Project 2 to keep track of training that your staff receives by entering information about the employees and the training they have received into the PC Software table. As you learned in Project 1, the set of information you enter for each row in a table is called a record.

One reason databases are so useful is that you can work with and modify the records after you enter them. With a paper filing system, you have to cross out, erase, or redo a record when the information changes. With database software, however, you can easily change a record in the table to correct a mistake or to update the information. You can delete records you no longer need, search for a particular record, and sort the records—all quickly and with little effort on your part.

In this project, you learn how to add records to your table, move around in the records within the table, and edit and delete records. You also learn how to search for a particular record and sort your records according to a system that you determine.

Visual Summary

When you have completed this lesson, you will have created a document that looks like Figure 3.1:

Figure 3.1
Records have been added to an empty table.

The table has been sorted on the Last Name field

This field has been edited

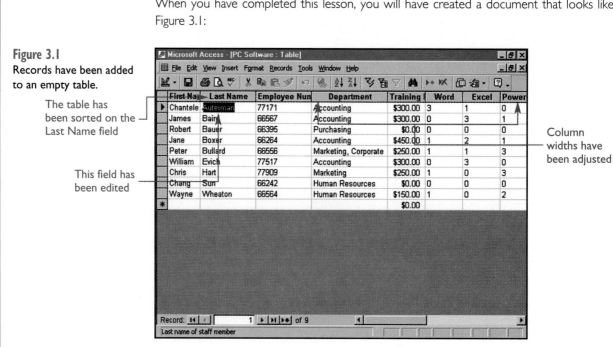

Column widths have been adjusted

Lesson 1: Adding Records

As you recall from Project 2, you worked in Design view when you set up your table structure. In Design view, you can make changes to the fields in the table—change a field name, add a field, change the data type, and so on. Then, when you want to work with the data in the table, you switch to Datasheet view. In this view, you can add records or edit them.

In this lesson, you open a database, Employee Training, which matches your database and your PC Software table from Project 2. You switch to Datasheet view, then add records to the database.

To Add Records

1 Launch Access. Click OK to Open an Existing Database.
Make sure you have a disk in drive A:.

2 Find the AC1-0301 file on your CD-ROM, right-click it, and send it to the floppy drive. Move to drive A:. Rename the file Employee Training, and open the new database.
The database should open to the Tables object button, and a PC Software table should be listed.

3 Click the Open button to open the PC Software table in the Datasheet view.
In this project, you use the Training database you created in Project 2. (Employee Training is a completed version of your work from Project 2.) The PC Software table should be displayed onscreen in Datasheet view. Each of the field names appears along the top of the window. At this point, the table consists of only one row, and it is blank. The insertion point is in the first field, and you see a small, black arrow next to the first field. This arrow indicates the current record (see Figure 3.2).

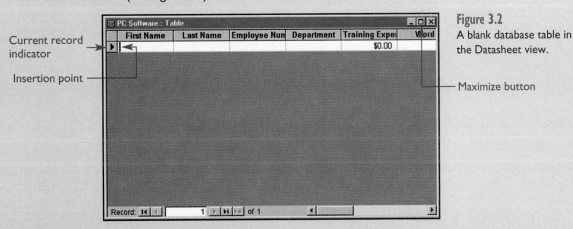

Figure 3.2
A blank database table in the Datasheet view.

4 Maximize the Table window, then type Chantele and press ⏎Enter.
As you type, Access displays a pencil icon in the *record selector*, which is the gray area to the left of the record. You can also use Tab⇄ in place of ⏎Enter when adding data to the table.

continues ▶

To Add Records   (continued)

5 **Type** Auterman **and press** ↵Enter.

The staff member's name is entered, and the insertion point moves to the Employee Number field.

6 **Type** 77171 **and press** ↵Enter.

The employee number is entered, and the insertion point moves to the Department field.

7 **Type** Accounting **and press** ↵Enter.

The department is entered, and the insertion point moves to the Training Expense field.

8 **Type** 300.00 **and press** ↵Enter.

The expense for training this employee is entered, and the insertion point moves to the four fields for specific software training. Notice that Access formats the entry as currency, because in Project 2 you set the data type to Currency after you created this field.

9 **Type** 3 **and press** ↵Enter, 1 **and press** ↵Enter, 0 **and press** ↵Enter, **and finally** 1 **and press** ↵Enter.

The levels of classes taken are recorded in the four application fields. When you press ↵Enter the last time, Access moves to the counter field, which has a value that was automatically entered when you started entering data in the first field.

10 **Press** ↵Enter.

Access saves the record and moves to the next row so that you can add another record (see Figure 3.3). Whenever you move the insertion point off of the record you are editing, Access immediately saves the record or any changes you have made to the record.

Figure 3.3
Access moves to the next row so that you can add another record.

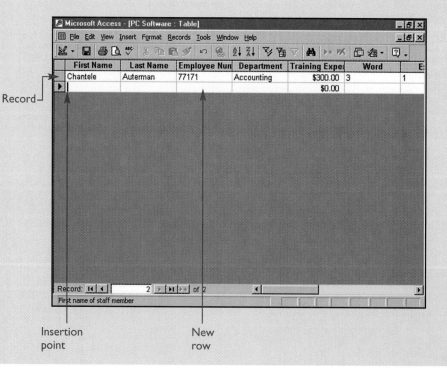

Record

Insertion point

New row

⑪ Use the following list of data to add more records to the database table. (Because of the number of fields in each record, the items are separated by commas. Do not type the commas.)

```
Chang,Sun,66242,Human Resources,0,0,0,0,0
Jane,Boxer,66264,Purchasing,450,1,2,1,3
Robert,Bauer,66395,Purchasing,0,0,0,0,0
Peter,Bullard,66556,Marketing,250,1,1,3,0
James,Baird,66567,Accounting,300,0,3,1,1
Wayne,Wheaton,66564,Human Resources,150,1,0,2,0
Chris,Hart,77909,Marketing,250,1,0,3,1
```

Access adds these records to the database table. Keep the Employee Training database and the PC Software table open. In the next lesson, you learn how to move among the records in your table.

Automatic Dollar Signs
You do not need to enter the dollar sign ($) into a currency field. It will be added automatically by the program. Adding the dollar sign does not hurt anything, but if you learn to leave it off, it will save you a great deal of time if you have to enter large amounts of data. Also, if a dollar amount is a whole number, the program adds the .00 automatically, even if you don't type it.

Lesson 2: Moving Among Records

Earlier, you noticed that Access displays an arrow next to the current row. When you want to edit a field to change or update a record's information, you must first move to the row containing the record that you want to change. You can tell what row you have moved to because a black triangular arrow, called the **current record indicator**, is displayed in the record selector box to the left of the current row.

You can move among the records in several ways. If you can see the record you want on the screen, you can simply click it to select it. If you have numerous records in your table, however, you may have to scroll through the records until you can get to the one you want.

To move to a particular record, you can use the vertical scrollbar, the navigation buttons displayed along the bottom of the window, or the arrow keys on the keyboard. Table 3.1 explains how these navigation buttons and keys work.

Table 3.1 Moving Among Records with the Navigation Buttons and Keys

To Move To	Buttons	Keyboard
First record in table	[◄◄]	Ctrl + Home
Previous record in table	[◄]	↑
Next record in table	[►]	↓
Last record in table	[►►]	Ctrl + End
New record at end of table	[►*]	Ctrl + +

In this lesson, you move among the records in your table using each of these navigational methods.

To Move Among Records

1 **With the PC Software table of the Employee Training database open, move the mouse pointer to the record selector at the left of the Wayne Wheaton record and click.**
The record is selected.

2 **Press** Ctrl + Home. **Access moves you to the first record in the database table. Notice the current record indicator arrow to the left of the active record (see Figure 3.4).**

Figure 3.4
Pressing Ctrl + Home moves you to the first record.

Current record indicator →

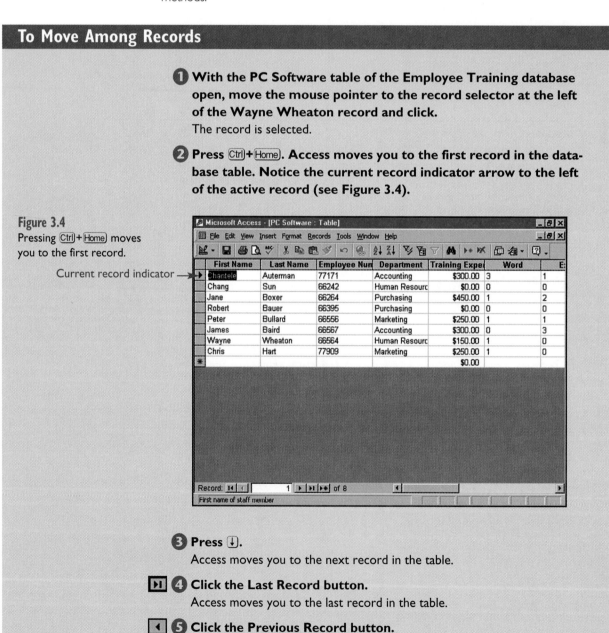

3 **Press** ↓.
Access moves you to the next record in the table.

[►►] **4** **Click the Last Record button.**
Access moves you to the last record in the table.

[◄] **5** **Click the Previous Record button.**
Access moves you to the previous record in the table.

▐◀ **⑥ Click the First Record button.**
Access moves to the first record in the table.

▶✳ **⑦ Click the New Record button.**
The pointer moves to the next empty record.

Now that you know how to move among the records in your table, the next lesson shows you how to make changes to the records. Keep the Employee Training database and the PC Software table open as you continue with Lesson 3.

 If you click a particular field in the table and enter the editing mode, the Ctrl+Home and Ctrl+End commands only move to the beginning and end of the current field. These commands move to the beginning and end of the table if a field or record is selected.

Lesson 3: Editing Records

As you work with the data in the database table, you find that you need to make changes from time to time. In your PC Software table, for example, you might want to correct a typing mistake or change other information. You can update or correct any of the records in your table while you are in Datasheet view.

The first step in editing records is to move to the record that you want to change. Next, you have to move to the field that you want to edit. To move among fields using the mouse, click in the field to which you want to move. When you click, Access places the insertion point in the field and does not select the entire text in that field.

You can also use the keys listed in Table 3.2 to move among fields. When you use these keys, Access moves to the specified field and selects all the text in that field.

Table 3.2   Moving Among Fields with the Keyboard

To Move To	Press
Next field	Tab⇄ or →
Previous field	⬆Shift+Tab⇄ or ←
First field in record	Home
Last field in record	End

When you are in a field, you can add to, edit, or delete the current entry. Try moving among the fields and making changes now.

To Edit Records

① With the PC Software table of the Employee Training database open, click after the word Marketing in the Department column of the record for Peter Bullard.

The insertion point is placed where you are going to add new text in the field.

② Type a comma (,), press ⌷Spacebar⌷, and type Corporate.

As you begin typing, notice that Access displays a ***pencil icon*** in the record selector next to the record. This icon reminds you that you are editing the record and that the change has not yet been saved (see Figure 3.5).

Figure 3.5
The pencil icon indicates that you are editing a field.

Edit indicator →

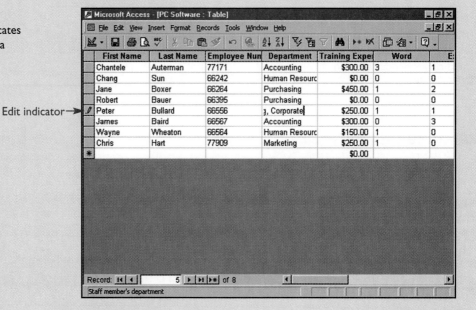

③ Press ⌷↑⌷ twice.

This moves you to the Department field in the record for Jane Boxer. When you move to another record, Access automatically updates the record you just changed.

The text in that field is selected, as shown in Figure 3.6. Anything you type replaces the selected text.

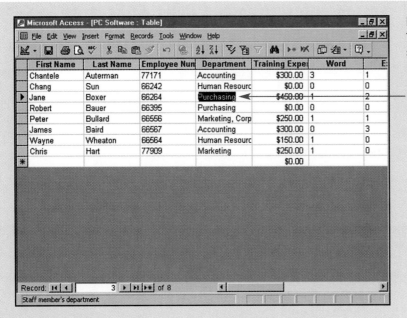

Figure 3.6
Typing replaces the
selected text.

— Selected text

④ **Type Accounting.**
The record has been updated for this employee who has been transferred
to a new department.

⑤ **Press ⬇.**
Access updates the record you just edited and moves to the next record.

Keep the Employee Training database and the PC Software table open. In
Lesson 4, you learn how to insert new records and delete records you no
longer need.

 If you make a change by mistake, you can undo it by immediately clicking the
Undo button, or by opening the Edit menu and choosing the Undo command.
If you are editing a field and decide you don't want to save your edits, press Esc
to ignore your changes.

Saving a Record
You can also save the change you make by pressing ⬆Shift+⬅Enter while still on
the record you are editing. To save a record using the menu, choose the
Records, Save Record command.

Lesson 4: Inserting and Deleting Records

When you first create your database table, you can't always predict exactly what information you'll want to include. As you use your database, you will most likely want to insert new records or delete outdated records.

With Access, you don't have to add all your records at one time. You can add a new record to the end of the table at any time. If you want to enter several records containing similar data, you can enter the data for one record, copy it, paste it into your table, and then edit the data in the new record.

You can delete a record by removing the row from the database table. In this lesson, you insert new records and delete a record you no longer need.

To Insert and Delete Records

1 **With the PC Software table of the Employee Training database open, click in the First Name field of the row marked by an asterisk (see Figure 3.7).**
The insertion point is placed in the First Name field of the empty record where the new information will be added. The current record indicator arrow replaces the asterisk.

Figure 3.7
New records are inserted at the bottom of the table.

Current record indicator →

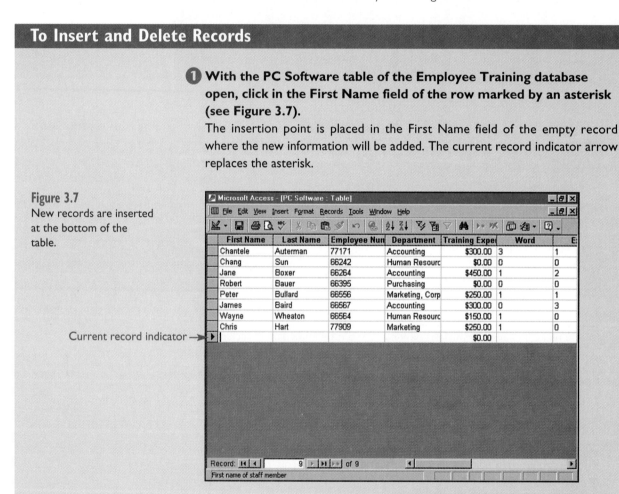

2 **Type the following data for your new record, pressing ↵Enter after each entry. After the last entry, press ↵Enter twice.**
William, Evich, 77517, Accounting, 300, 0, 3, 0, 2

Access adds the new employee record to the end of your table. You can also copy a record and add the copy so that you have two versions of the same record. You may want to do this if you have two or more similar records. This might be appropriate for an inventory database of computer hardware. To practice this skill, you can copy the record you just added.

③ To copy the new record, click in the record selector to select the entire row.
Access highlights the entire row.

 ④ Click the Copy button.
Onscreen, you won't notice anything different after you copy the record. At this point, you have just placed a copy of the selected record into the *Clipboard*, a temporary storage location for whatever you have copied or cut from your document. Next, you paste the copy of the record into your table.

⑤ Click the record selector to highlight the empty record at the end of the table, then click the Paste button.
Access adds the record to the end of the table. Now that you have the basic data in place, you can make any changes necessary for this particular record. Rather than edit this duplicate record just now, you are going to use it to practice deleting a record.

⑥ Click the record selector next to the new record you just inserted.
The record you just pasted is selected. You can also select the record by opening the Edit menu and choosing Select Record when the insertion point is anywhere in the record.

⑦ Click the Delete Record button.
Access wants to be sure that you intended to delete the record, so you are prompted to confirm the deletion (see Figure 3.8). You cannot undo record deletions, so be absolutely sure that you want to delete a record before you confirm the deletion.

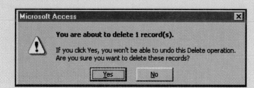

Figure 3.8
Access prompts you to confirm the deletion.

⑧ Click the Yes button.
Access deletes the record and saves the changes to the database table.

Keep the PC Software table open. In Lesson 5, you learn how to change the width of the columns in your table and how to hide and unhide columns.

ⓘ Copying Fields, Deleting and Adding Records
In addition to copying entire records, you can also copy an entry from one field to another. If you want to enter another record for someone from the Marketing Department, for example, you can copy Marketing from the Department field and paste it in the new record.

To copy an entry, move to the appropriate field, and select the text you want to copy by dragging across it. Then click the Copy button. Move to the location where you want to place the copied text, and click the Paste button. Access pastes the selected text.

You can also use shortcut keys: Ctrl+C for Copy and Ctrl+V for Paste.

To delete a record, you can select it and press Del, or place the insertion point anywhere in the record and choose Delete Record from the Edit menu.

 To add a new record, you can click the New Record button on the toolbar.

Lesson 5: Adjusting Column Widths and Hiding Columns

By default, Access displays all the columns in your table with the same width. You can change the column width, making some columns wider so that you can see the entire entry, and making other columns narrower so that they don't take up as much space. The easiest way to adjust the column width is to use the mouse, but it can also be adjusted using Format, Column Width from the menu.

In addition to changing the column width, you can also hide columns you don't want displayed, such as the autonumber field, which is never used for data entry. Adjusting the column width does not change the field size. You learn how to change the field size in Project 7.

To Adjust Column Widths and Hide Columns

1 **With the PC Software table of the Employee Training database open, place the mouse pointer on the line between the First Name and Last Name field selectors.**

The mouse pointer changes to a thick vertical bar with arrows on either side (see Figure 3.9). This pointer indicates that you can now move the column borders.

Figure 3.9
The appearance of the mouse pointer changes when you are preparing to resize a column.

Mouse pointer

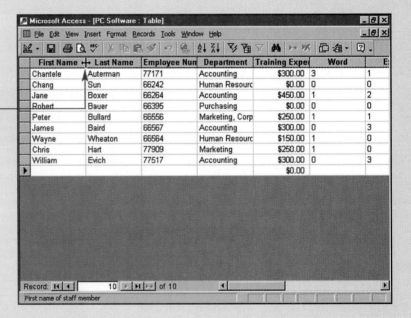

2 **Press and hold down the mouse button and drag to the left until you think the column is narrow enough and you can still see all the entries in the column. Release the mouse button.**

The new width is set. As you drag to the left, you make the column narrower. Notice that you can see the border of the column move as you drag. Don't worry if you cover up part of the field name.

If you don't see the thick bar with the arrows, you don't have the pointer in the correct spot. Be sure that you are within the gray area of the field selectors and that your pointer is sitting directly on the border separating the two columns.

3 Move the mouse pointer to the border between the Department and Training Expense columns, and double-click the mouse button.
Double-clicking is a shortcut method that automatically adjusts the column to fit the longest entry currently displayed onscreen in that column. This often creates a problem when you use long field names, because double-clicking widens the column to show the whole field name if it is the longest entry in the column.

4 Drag across the field selectors for the Training Expense, Word, Excel, PowerPoint, Access, and ID fields. Use the horizontal scrollbar to view the selected columns.
When you drag across the headings, you select all six columns (see Figure 3.10). You can then adjust the widths of all six columns at one time.

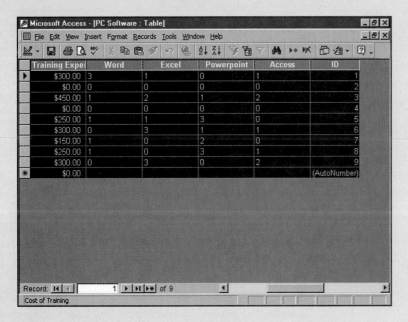

Figure 3.10
You can select several columns and resize them together.

5 Drag the border on the right of the Training Expense column so that it is just big enough to hold the longest entry.
Notice that dragging one of the borders resizes all six columns.

6 Click anywhere in the table to deselect the columns.

7 Scroll to the left. Click in the field selector of the Employee Number field.
Now that you have selected this column, you can practice hiding it.

8 Open the Format menu, and choose the Hide Columns command.
Access hides the column you selected.

continues ▶

To Adjust Column Widths and Hide Columns (continued)

⑨ Open the Format menu, and choose the Unhide Columns command to unhide the column.

Access displays the Unhide Columns dialog box (see Figure 3.11). If the column has a check mark next to its name, the column is displayed. If there is no check mark, the column is hidden.

Figure 3.11
Use the Unhide Columns dialog box to unhide a column.

A check mark indicates that the column is displayed

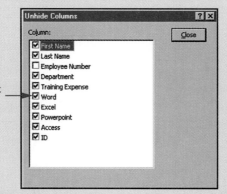

⑩ Click the Employee Number checkbox, and then click the Close button.

Access closes the Unhide Columns dialog box. The Employee Number column reappears on the screen.

Save your work, and keep the PC Software table open. In Lesson 6, you search for specific records in your database.

 Other Ways to Adjust and Hide Columns

You can also use the menus to adjust the column width. Move the insertion point to the column you want to adjust. Then open the Format menu and choose the Column Width command. Type a new value (the width of the column in points). Click the OK button.

You can also hide multiple columns by first selecting them and then selecting the Hide Columns command from the Format menu. In addition, you can use the Unhide Columns dialog box to hide columns. In the list displayed in the dialog box, click the checkbox next to a column to deselect it. This hides the column.

Lesson 6: Finding Records

In a table with many records and many fields, it may be time-consuming to scroll through the records and fields to find a specific record. Instead, you can search for a specific field entry in order to find and move quickly to a record.

For example, if you want to find the Wayne Wheaton record, you can search for Wheaton. It is always faster to select the field you want to use for your search and then search just that field, but you can also search for text in any field in the table. In this lesson, you find a record by first searching a single field and then by searching all fields.

To Find a Record

1 **With the PC Software table of the Employee Training database open, click in the Last Name field.**

It doesn't matter what row in which you click. Clicking anywhere in the field tells Access that you want to search for a particular record using the Last Name field only. The field with the insertion point is searched by default.

2 **Click the Find button.**

Access displays the Find and Replace dialog box (see Figure 3.12). Here you tell Access what you want to find and where you want to look.

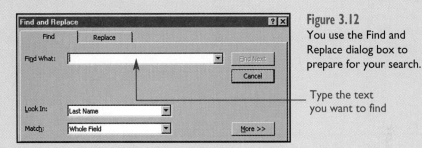

Figure 3.12
You use the Find and Replace dialog box to prepare for your search.

Type the text you want to find

3 **Type Wheaton, then click the Find Next button.**

Access moves to the first match, and the dialog box remains open. You can continue to search by clicking the Find Next button until you find the record you want.

If you can't see the match because the dialog box is in the way, move the dialog box by dragging its title bar.

4 **Drag across the text in the Find What text box to select it, then type Resources.**

This is the next entry you want to find.

5 **Click the list arrow in the Look In drop-down list box, and select PC Software : Table.**

Instead of restricting the search to just the current field, you are now telling Access to look in all fields.

6 **Click the list arrow in the Match drop-down list box, and select Any Part of Field.**

The text you want to find (Resources) won't be the entire entry; it is only part of the field. For this reason, you have to tell Access to match any part of the field. Figure 3.13 shows the options you have requested for this search.

What to find ⟶

What to match ⟶

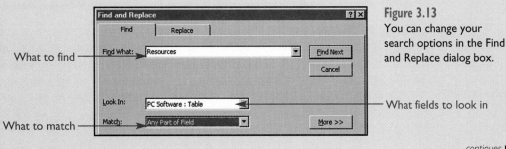

Figure 3.13
You can change your search options in the Find and Replace dialog box.

⟵ What fields to look in

continues ▶

To Find a Record (continued)

7 Click the Find Next button.
Access moves to the first occurrence and highlights Resources in the Department field in the record for Wayne Wheaton. Notice that the search starts from the currently selected record.

8 Click the Find Next button.
Access moves to the next occurrence and highlights Resources in the Department field in the record for Chang Sun (see Figure 3.14).

Figure 3.14
The Find feature can find information in any part of a field.

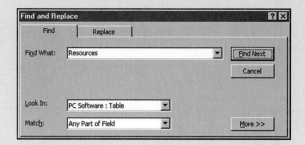

9 Click the Cancel button.
This step closes the Find and Replace dialog box. The last record found remains selected.

Save your work, and keep the PC Software table open. In Lesson 7, you learn how to sort the records in your table.

 Searching Before the Current Record
If you see a message telling you that Access has reached the end of the records and asking whether you want to start searching from the beginning, click the Yes button. By default, Access searches from the current record down through the database. The record you want may be located before the current one.

If you see another message telling you that Access reached the end of the records, Access did not find a match. Try the search again. Be sure that you typed the entry correctly. You may need to change some of the options.

Lesson 7: Sorting Records

Access displays the records in your table in an order determined by the primary key. You learned how to create a primary key in Project 2. If your table has no primary key, Access displays the records in the order in which they were entered.

If you use a primary key, Access sorts the entries alphabetically or numerically, based on the entries in that field. (If a counter field is your primary key, your records will be displayed in the order in which they were entered.) Fortunately, however, you aren't restricted to displaying your data only in the order determined by your primary key. With Access, you can sort the display by using any of the fields in the database table. You can also sort the display using multiple, adjacent fields.

In this lesson, you first sort your data on the Last Name field. You then use the toolbar to sort on the Employee Number field.

To Sort Records

1 With the PC Software table of the Employee Training database open, click in the Last Name field.
Clicking in this field tells Access that you want to base your sort on the Last Name field.

2 Click the Sort Ascending button.
Access sorts the records in ascending alphabetical order (A-to-Z) based on the entries in the Last Name field (see Figure 3.15).

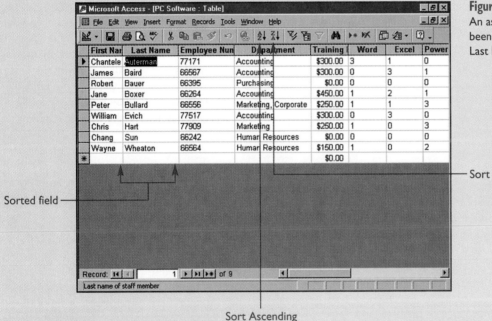

Figure 3.15
An ascending sort has been performed on the Last Name field.

Sort Descending

Sorted field

Sort Ascending

3 Click in the Employee Number field.
Clicking in this field tells Access that you now want to base your sort on the Employee Number field.

4 Click the Sort Ascending button on the toolbar.
Access sorts the table by using the entries in the Employee Number field. Keep in mind that the sort order displayed onscreen does not affect the order in which the records are actually stored.

5 Close the PC Software table.
A dialog box asks if you want to save your changes, which in this case were the changes in sort order.

6 Click the Yes button.
If you have completed your session on the computer, exit Access and Windows before turning it off. Otherwise, continue with the "Checking Concepts and Terms" section.

Another Way to Sort Records

You can also use the Records, Sort command from the menu and select the Sort Ascending or Sort Descending option. As with the buttons, you must first have the insertion point in the field you want to sort.

Sorting by Multiple Fields

To sort by multiple, adjacent fields (for example, last name then first name) select the field name for the first sort, hold down the ◆Shift key, and select the second field to sort (the second field must be adjacent and to the right of the first field). You can also click in the first field selector and drag to the right to select the second field. Click the Sort Ascending or Sort Descending button to perform the sort.

When you have completed a sort, if you wish to return records to their original order, choose Records from the menu, and click Remove Filter/Sort.

If the fields you wish to sort on are not in the proper order (for example, your database Employee Training displays the first name field followed by the last name field) you can move the fields in Design view prior to the sort. By moving the field so that the last name column appears first in your table with the first name field as the next field immediately to the right, you can sort the table by last name, then by first name. You can also move a field by selecting the field, then clicking on the field name and dragging the field to the desired location.

Summary

In this project, you worked with records in a table. You added, edited, inserted, and deleted records, and learned how to move around quickly in a table. You also used two of the more important features of a database—finding and sorting records. You also adjusted the widths of the columns to make the table more readable and learned to hide columns without deleting the field.

You can expand your knowledge of tables by asking the Office Assistant how to design a table. Several topics about table design are available, and some of the basic design concepts are discussed in the topics on creating a table.

Checking Concepts and Terms

True/False

For each of the following, check *T* or *F* to indicate whether the statement is true or false.

__T __F   **1.** You can edit records in Design view. [L1]

__T __F   **2.** When the pencil icon appears in the record selector, it reminds you that the record is being edited and the change has not been saved. [L3]

__T __F   **3.** When you change the column width, you also change the field size. [L5]

__T __F   **4.** When you add a new record, it is added to the end of a table. [L1]

__T __F   **5.** You can undo record deletions. [L4]

__T __F   **6.** The only way to delete a record is to use the Delete Record button. [L4]

__T __F   **7.** You can hide a column so that it does not appear on the screen. [L5]

__T __F **8.** When using the Find and Replace dialog box, the default choice is to search in the field where the insertion point is located. [L6]

__T __F **9.** You can hide only one column at a time. [L5]

__T __F **10.** You create Multiple sorts by choosing non-adjacent fields. [L7]

Multiple Choice

Circle the letter of the correct answer for each of the following questions.

1. Which of the following takes you quickly to the first record in a table? [L2]

a. Ctrl + End

b. Home

c. Alt + Home

d. the First Record navigation button

2. Which command do you use to paste an entire record? [L4]

a. Paste Record

b. Paste All

c. Paste

d. Paste Special

3. Which of the following is not a way to adjust the column width? [L5]

a. Double-click the column border.

b. Drag the column border.

c. Open the View menu, and choose the Column Size command.

d. Open the Format menu, and choose the Column Width command.

4. If you want Access to search all fields in the table, which option do you select in the Find and Replace dialog box? [L6]

a. Current Field

b. Match Case

c. Search Fields As Formatted

d. none of the above

5. Which of the following is not a way to sort the records in a table? [L7]

a. Click the Sort Descending button.

b. Click the Sort Ascending button.

c. Open the Records menu, and choose the Sort command.

d. Open the Tools menu, and choose the Quick Sort command.

6. Which of the following is not a way to delete a record? [L4]

a. Highlight the record, and press Del.

b. Place the insertion point anywhere in the record, and press Ctrl + D.

c. Place the insertion point anywhere in the record, and click the Delete Record button.

d. Place the insertion point anywhere in the record, and choose Delete Record from the Edit menu.

7. Access automatically saves the data you enter to disk when you do which of the following? [L3]

a. Press ◆Shift + ↵Enter.

b. Leave the field in which you entered the data.

c. Choose Save Record from the Record menu.

d. all of the above

8. To hide a column, you should do which of the following? [L5]

a. Select the column, and press Alt + H.

b. Select the column, and double-click the right column separator on the border.

c. Place the insertion point in the column, and select Hide Columns from the Format menu.

d. Place the insertion point in the column, and select AutoHide from the Format menu.

9. Access identifies the record you are editing by which of the following? [L3]

a. the arrow on the record selector

b. the asterisk on the record selector

c. the key symbol on the record selector

d. the pencil icon on the record selector

10. What does the New Record button look like? [L2]

a. an arrow pointing to an asterisk

b. a folder with an arrow on it

c. a folder with a star on it

d. an arrow pointing to a line

Screen ID

Label each element of the Access screen shown in Figure 3.16.

Figure 3.16

A. First record button

B. Paste button

C. Next Record button

D. Sort Ascending button

E. Editing Record indicator

F. New Record button

G. Sort Descending button

H. Previous Record button

I. Empty Record indicator

J. Last Record button

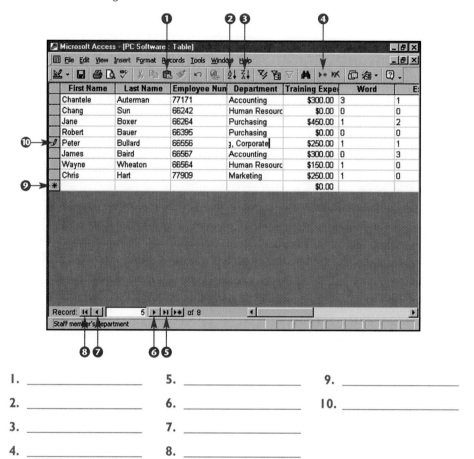

1. _____   5. _____   9. _____

2. _____   6. _____   10. _____

3. _____   7. _____

4. _____   8. _____

Discussion Questions

1. Access does not allow you to insert records into the middle of a table—just at the end. Does the order in which you enter records really matter? Why or why not?

2. Assume that you are designing a database table for automobile parts to use in a store. This table will be used by both the sales personnel at the counter and by the customers at a self-help computer. The table will contain the make of the car, part name, description, number sold year-to-date, quantity in stock, retail price, sale price, and cost. Which, if any, of the fields would you hide? Why?

3. Forms are also used to enter data. With forms, you can lay out the fields so that many fields are on the screen at once, but for only one record at a time. When would you want to use a form rather than a table? When would a table be preferable?

4. In this project, you learned about several different methods of moving around in a table. When might it be preferable to use buttons? Keyboard shortcuts? The mouse?

5. Sorting records is often done in a database. Sorting by last name and first name is an example of sorting on more than one field at a time. Can you think of any other instances when you might need to sort on two fields at once? Would there ever be a reason to sort on three fields?

Skill Drill

Skill Drill exercises reinforce project skills. Each skill reinforced is the same, or nearly the same, as a skill presented in the project. Each exercise includes a brief narrative introduction, followed by detailed instructions in a step-by-step format.

You are working for a company that does research for other companies. Your current project is to conduct a survey for a cable TV company to find out how subscribers feel about five of the channels offered in their basic cable package. You are just starting out and testing your survey with a small number of families. You have set up a preliminary survey and are recording the results in an Access database.

1. Adding Records

You have decided you need ten families for your trial run, so you will need to add two more families to your survey.

1. Find the AC1-0302 database file on your CD-ROM, send it to drive A:, remove the read-only status, and name it **Television Survey**. Open the Questionnaire table.

2. Click the View button to switch to Design view and read the Description column to see what each of the categories means. Click the View button again to return to Datasheet view.

3. In Datasheet view, click the New Record button. Use either the one on the toolbar or the one included with the navigation buttons.

4. Enter the following information into the Questionnaire table. (Note: You can enter checks in the check boxes by clicking on them with the mouse button or pressing ⎚Spacebar⎚.)

5. Close the table, but leave the database open.

Adults	Children	Use	Hours	#1	#2	#3	Doing	Comments
4	0	N	8	DISCOVERY	CNN	SCIFI	Great	More nature shows
1	2	Y		DISNEY	SCIFI		Good	More cartoons!!!

2. Editing Records

While looking over the paper survey forms you have received, you find that you made a couple of mistakes while entering the data.

1. Open the Questionnaire table in the Television Survey database. Make sure you are in Datasheet view.

2. Move down to the 8th record (the one that has only CNN in the favorite channel fields).

3. Highlight CNN, and type **TNT**.

4. Move to the Improve field, and type **No opinion**.

5. Leave the table open for the next exercise.

3. Inserting and Deleting Records

After discussing your sample data with a representative from the cable company, you find that they feel that every household must have at least one of the five channels being tested in their list of favorites. This means that you have one record that needs to be deleted, and you need to find another one to take its place.

1. Click the record selector next to the record with no favorite channels listed. This should be the fourth record.

2. Press Del to remove the record.

3. Click the New Record button.

4. Add the following information:

Adults	Children	Use	Hours	#1	#2	#3	Doing	Comments
2	2	Y	2	TNT	CNN	DISCOVERY	Good	Would like more news & nature shows

4. Adjusting Column Widths and Hiding Columns

You would like to be able to see more of your survey information on the screen at one time. The best way to do that is to reduce the width of several columns, and to hide the ID column.

1. Click the field selector of the ID field, and drag across until you have selected the ID, Adults, Children, Use, and Hours fields.

2. Grab the column separator between any two of the fields, and reduce the column width to the smallest size needed to show all of the data. You will cut off part of the field names.

3. Place the insertion point in the ID field.

4. Choose Format, Hide Columns from the menu.

5. Leave the table open for the next exercise.

5. Finding a Record

Although this is a small sample, you want to be prepared to find data when the full survey is completed.

1. Place the insertion point in the Improve field of the ninth record (the Disney Channel record you added in Exercise 1).

2. Click the Find button on the toolbar, then type **Nature** in the Find What box.

3. Select Any Part of Field from the Match drop-down list.

4. Click the Find Next button. If the first instance is hidden, move the Find and Replace dialog box out of the way. Notice that the first record found is the last record in the table.

5. Click the Find Next button again. A second match is found.

6. Click the Find Next button. When no more matches are found, click OK, and close the Find and Replace dialog box.

7. Leave the table open for the next exercise.

6. Sorting and Printing Records

Your client wants to see the sample survey data in two different orders.

1. Place the insertion point in the Children field, and click the Sort Descending button.

2. Select File, Page Setup, and move to the Page tab.

3. Select Landscape orientation, and click OK.

4. Click the Print button to print the table.

5. Click the Use field selector, and then click the Sort Ascending button. You could print this table if necessary, although it is not necessary to do so at this time.

6. Close the table and save your changes. Close the database, and close Access unless you will be moving on to the Challenge section.

Challenge

Challenge exercises expand on or are somewhat related to skills presented in the lessons. Each exercise provides a brief narrative introduction followed by instructions in a numbered step format that are not as detailed as those in the Skill Drill section.

The table you will be working with in the Challenge section is a list of your CDs in a database called CD Collection. This table has fields for the artist, title, year, label, serial number, and category.

1. Freezing Columns

You may have to use the horizontal scrollbar to scroll back and forth to look at all of the fields for a record. When you scroll to the right, the name of the artist disappears from view. You would like to keep the name of the artist and title on the screen at all times.

1. Copy the AC1-0303 database file to drive A:, remove the read-only status, and rename it **CD Collection**.

2. Open the CD Collection table in Datasheet view.

3. Select both the Artist/Group and the CD Title fields.

4. Choose Format, Freeze Columns from the menu.

5. Scroll to the right to make sure the first two columns don't move off the screen.

6. Close the table, and save your changes.

2. Finding and Replacing Data

When you show a friend a printout of your CD collection, she points out that you misspelled the name of classical composer Gustav Holst, which you spelled "Holzt." You can scan the entire 371 records and try to make sure you find all of the misspelled words, or you can use the Find and Replace feature to do the hard work for you. You decide to try the latter.

1. Open the CD Collection table in Datasheet view.

2. Highlight the CD Title column.

3. Choose Edit, Replace from the menu.

4. Type `Holzt` in the Find What box and `Holst` in the Replace With box. Make sure that you match any part of the field and look in only the CD Title field.

5. Click Find Next to find the first instance of the misspelled word. Replace it with the correct spelling. You will not be able to undo this action.

6. Click Replace All to find the rest of the misspelled words.

7. Close the table and save your changes, if necessary.

3. Copying and Pasting Records

Sometimes you have a CD to enter into the table that is very similar to another one you have already entered. Try copying and pasting a record to save work.

1. Open the CD Collection table in Datasheet view. Use the Find button to find the CD Title called "Too Long in Exile" by Van Morrison. (Hint: you can just type the first couple of words in the Find What box.)

2. Click the record selector to select the whole record.

3. Use the Copy button to copy the record.

4. Click the New Record button, and click the record selector to select the whole record.

5. Click the Paste button to paste the whole record you copied.

6. Change the CD Title field to `Days Like This`. Change the Year field to `1995`. Change the Serial number field to `31452 7307 2`.

7. Close the table.

4. Removing Sorts

You just noticed that there is a command to remove a sort, and you wonder how it works. Does it remove only the previous sort, sort of like the Undo option, or will it go back to the original order even after two sorts? Will it work after you have saved your changes and left the table? Look at the first three records so you can remember which records came first.

1. Open the CD Collection table in Datasheet view. Place the insertion point any-where in the Artist/Group column, and sort in ascending order.

2. Now sort on the Label field in descending order.

3. Choose Records, Remove Filter/Sort from the menu. Notice that the records are back in their original order.

4. Sort by Artist/Group, again in ascending order, then close the table and save your changes.

5. Open the CD Collection table again, and notice that the sort on Artist/Group is still in effect.

6. Choose Records, Remove Filter/Sort from the menu. Did the records go back to their original order?

7. Close the table, and save your changes.

[?] 5. Changing Column Widths Using the Menu

The column widths are not quite right in the CD Collection table. Try the menu option to change the column widths.

1. Open the CD Collection table in Datasheet view. Select the Year column.

2. Choose Format, Column Width from the menu.

3. Click the Best Fit button to narrow the column.

4. Select the Serial number field, then choose Format, Column Width from the menu.

5. Select the Standard Width check box, and click OK.

6. Select the Artist/Group field, then choose Format, Column Width from the menu. Notice that the Column Width is shown as 22.5. Change the number to 30, and click OK.

7. Use the Access Help option to find out exactly what the numbers in the Column Width box are. Could they be points? Eighths of inches? Some other measurement?

8. Use what you found out from the Help source to make the CD Title column exactly 3" wide.

9. Close the table, and save your changes.

[?] 6. Formatting Text in a Table

You have seen text formatting on text in word processing programs and spreadsheets, and you wonder if the same thing can be done with text in Access.

1. Open the CD Collection table in Datasheet view.

2. Use Access help to find out how to turn on the formatting toolbar in Datasheet view.

3. Change the background color to a pale blue (or other light background color of your choice).

4. Change the text to a very dark blue (or other dark font color of your choice).

5. Highlight any CD Title, and click the Italic button. Notice that all of the text in the datasheet is italicized. When you format anything in a datasheet, everything else in the datasheet is formatted the same way.

6. Close the table, and save your changes.

Discovery Zone

Discovery Zone exercises help you gain advanced knowledge of project topics and application of skills. These exercises focus on enhancing your problem-solving skills. Numbered steps are not provided, but you are given hints, reminders, screen shots, and references to help you reach your goal for each exercise.

In these exercises, you will be using the CD Collection database you used in the Challenge exercises. If you didn't do the Challenge exercises, copy AC1-0303 to a disk as CD Collection.

1. Sending a Database to the Desktop as a Shortcut

You buy CDs all the time, and you find that you are opening this database several times a week. It would be a good idea to place an icon representing the database right on your desktop. That way, you will be able to boot your computer and double-click the CD Collection icon to move directly to the database, saving several steps!

Goal: Create, test, and delete a desktop shortcut to a specific database.

Create a desktop shortcut for your CD Collection database, test it, and then delete it from your desktop.

Hint: There are two ways to do this, one within Access and one using Windows. Try to figure out both of them.

2. Using Access Tools

Access has all sorts of tools available to help you enter data more quickly and proofread information when you are finished. The most commonly used tool is the spelling checker, which can be very important to people who are weak in this area. A second, lesser-known tool can be of at least as much help. This is the AutoCorrect feature.

Goal: Use the spelling checker to check spelling and add words to the dictionary, and the AutoCorrect tool to simplify the entry of long text entries.

The spelling checker

- Find two ways to activate the spelling checker.
- Check the spelling of several words in the CD Title column.
- Add one of the words to your dictionary.

The AutoCorrect tool

- Have the program automatically capitalize the first letter of a sentence if it is not turned on.
- Turn on the feature that changes the second letter of two capital letters to lower case, then make an exception for **CD**.
- Create a shortcut that enables you to type **ASMF** and have it replace those letters with **Academy of St. Martin-in-the-Fields (Sir Neville Marriner)**.
- Test the three features you just worked with.

Also: Look at some of the other tools available to use with your table.

[?] 3. Analyzing Your Table

When you look at your fields in the CD Collection table, you notice that the names of the artists are repeated frequently. Knowing that this probably isn't good database design, you'd like to have the table analyzed. You've heard that Access has a procedure to analyze tables.

Goal: Discover how to have Access analyze your table, then run the analysis option.

Use help to find out where the table analysis tool is located. Run the analyzer to see whether the program feels your table should be split into two tables. If Access suggests splitting the table, read why, but do not actually go through with it.

Project 4

Querying Your Database

Objectives

In this project, you learn how to

➤ **Create a New Query**

➤ **Choose Fields for a Query**

➤ **Save a Query**

➤ **Edit a Query**

➤ **Change Field Order and Sort a Query**

➤ **Match Criteria**

➤ **Save a Query with a New Name and Open Multiple Queries**

Key terms introduced in this project include

- column selector
- criteria
- crosstab query
- design grid

- dynaset
- query
- Select query

Why Would I Do This?

The primary reason you spend time entering data into a database is so that you can easily find and work with the information. In your address book database, for example, you may want to display all of your contacts in Indiana. To do so, you would create a **query**. A query asks a question of the database, such as, "Which records have IN as the state?" and then it pulls those records from the database into a subset of records. The subset is called a **dynaset**. You can then work with or print just those records selected by your query.

You can also create queries that display all of the records but only show selected fields. For example, you can display only the Last Name and Employee Number fields in the Employee Training database. You can create a query that searches for values in one field, such as the Indiana example just given, but displays only selected fields in the result. You can also create more complex queries. For example, you can query your Employee Training database to display all staff members who have received training in either Microsoft Excel or PowerPoint. Queries are created and saved so that they can be used repeatedly.

In this project, you create, save, edit, and use a query.

Visual Summary

When you have completed this project, you will have created a document that looks like Figure 4.1:

Figure 4.1
Queries enable you to display selected fields and records that meet criteria you specify.

Records that meet specified criteria are displayed

The query displays only selected fields

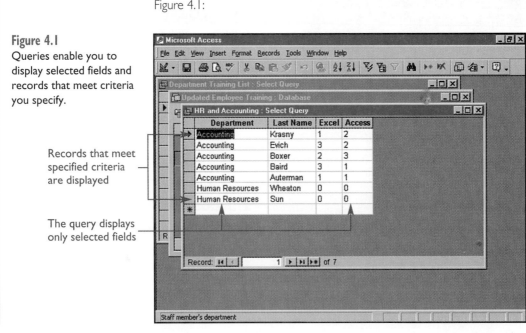

Lesson 1: Creating a New Query

A table is the most common type of object you can include in a database, but as mentioned in Project 1, "Getting Started with Access," there are several other types of objects. A query is another object you can create in a database.

You may remember that when you open the database, you see a database window that lists the tables contained in the database and also includes object buttons for queries, forms, reports, and so on. If you want to add a query to the table, you can start from this window.

In this lesson, you work with the data in the PC Software table of your Employee Training database. The PC Software table on your student disc that you copy and use in this project includes the records you entered in Project 3, "Entering and Editing Data," as well as some additional records. The headings in the revised table have been modified slightly to adjust the size of each column, allowing more information to appear onscreen. You start the procedure by creating a query and adding the table(s) with which you want to work.

To Create a New Query

1 **Launch Access. Click OK to open an existing file.**
Make sure you have a disk in drive A:.

2 **Find the AC1-0401 file on your CD-ROM, right-click on it, and send it to the floppy drive. Move to drive A:, remove the read-only status, and rename the file Updated Employee Training. Open the new database.**
The database should open to the Tables object button, and a PC Software table should be listed.

3 **Click the Queries object button.**
The Queries list displays no queries, because you haven't created and saved any queries yet (see Figure 4.2).

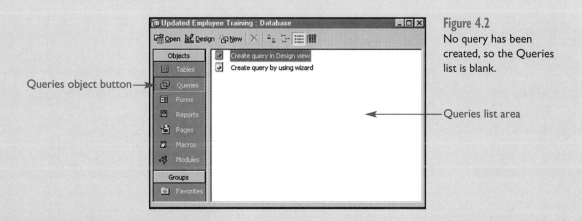

Queries object button

Queries list area

Figure 4.2
No query has been created, so the Queries list is blank.

4 **Click the New button.**
The New Query dialog box is displayed (see Figure 4.3). You can use one of the Query Wizards to create a query. This method works best for specific kinds of queries, such as finding duplicate records. None of the wizards is appropriate for the query you want to create for this example, so use the more general Design View method.

continues ▶

To Create a New Query   (continued)

Figure 4.3
Choose the method you
want to use to create a
new query.

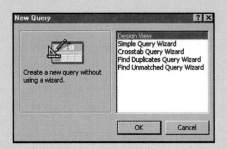

⑤ **Click Design View, and then click OK.**
The Show Table dialog box is displayed (see Figure 4.4). Here you select the
tables you want to use in your query. For complex queries, you can pull information from more than one table. (You learn how to work with multiple
tables in Project 7, "Customizing Fields and Tables.") For this example, you
use just one—the PC Software table.

Figure 4.4
Select the table you
want to use from the
dialog box.

Table available in database

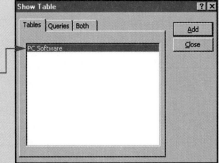

⑥ **The PC Software table is already selected, so click the Add button.**
This step selects the table you want to use. The dialog box remains open so
you can add other tables if necessary.

⑦ **Click the Close button.**
Access closes the Show Table dialog box and displays the Select Query window
(see Figure 4.5). Leave the Select Query window open, and continue with
Lesson 2.

Figure 4.5
Use the query window to
create a new query.

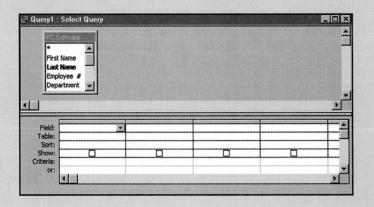

Lesson 2: Choosing Fields for a Query

After you open a new query and select a table, you see a window divided into two parts. The top half of the query window displays a scroll box containing a list of the fields from the table you selected. Notice that the primary key field appears in bold type. In this version of the database, the Last Name field has been designated as the primary key. You can use this field list to choose the fields you want to include in your query.

In the lower half of the query window, you see the **design grid** with rows for Field, Table, Sort, Show, Criteria, and or. All the columns are blank. The design grid controls which fields are included in your query. The simplest type of query, and the one you will probably use most often, is the **Select query**, which displays data that meet conditions you set.

You can create a query that displays just a few fields from a table. You add the fields you want to include in the query to the Field row in the design grid. You can include as many fields as you want in the query, but you must include at least one.

In this lesson, you create a query that contains only the Last Name and Department from your PC Software table. This list might be handy if you need to know who has received training in each department. You can use one of several methods to add fields to your query.

To Choose Fields for a Query

1 In the field list in the top half of the Select Query window, click the Last Name field.

The query window should still be open from the preceding lesson. This step selects the field you want to add to the design grid.

2 Drag the selected field from the field list to the first column in the Field row of the design grid.

As you drag, a little field box is displayed. When you release the mouse button, Access displays the field name in the Field row, and the table name in the Table row (see Figure 4.6). The Show row in this column then displays a check mark in the check box, indicating that this field will be displayed in the query.

 Use a Field but Don't Display It

There are occasions when you may want to use a field but not display its contents. In that case, you would click on the Show box to deselect it.

continues ▶

To Choose Fields for a Query   (continued)

Figure 4.6
Choose the first field for
the query by dragging it
into place.   Field list

Field name

Design grid

Show box   Source of the field

3 **Click in the second column of the Field row in the design grid.**
A list arrow is displayed. Clicking this arrow activates a drop-down list of available
fields.

4 **Click the list arrow.**
Access displays the drop-down list of fields (see Figure 4.7).

Figure 4.7
Use the drop-down list to
select a field to add to the
query.

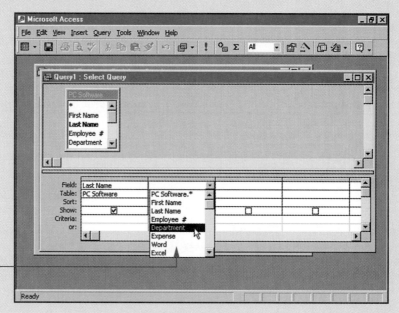

Drop-down list of available fields

 Adding Several Fields at Once
You can select several fields from the field list and add them all at once.
If the fields are listed next to each other, click the first field in the field
list. Then hold down ⬆Shift and click the last field in the field list.
Access selects the first and last fields and all fields in between. You can
also select fields that aren't listed next to each other. Click the first
field you want to select. Then hold down Ctrl and click the next field
you want to select. Continue pressing Ctrl while you click each subsequent field. After you have selected all the fields you want, drag them
to the design grid, and place them in the first empty space in the Field
row. This will add all of the selected fields to the query.

5 Click Department in the list.

The Department field is added to the query. This action has the same effect as dragging the field from the field list.

ℹ **Other Ways to Add Fields to a Query**
You can add fields to the query by double-clicking the field name or by typing the field name in the Field row of the design grid.

---

6 Click the View button on the toolbar.

This displays the records in Datasheet view, using the fields you selected in the query (see Figure 4.8). Notice that the title bar displays Select Query to remind you that you are viewing a dynaset, not the actual table. The difference between a table and a dynaset is that the table consists of all the records with all of the fields; the dynaset consists of a subset of the records.

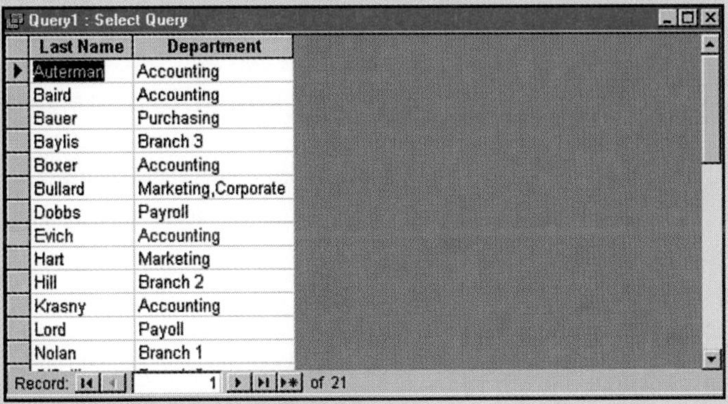

Query1 : Select Query	
Last Name	**Department**
Auterman	Accounting
Baird	Accounting
Bauer	Purchasing
Baylis	Branch 3
Boxer	Accounting
Bullard	Marketing,Corporate
Dobbs	Payroll
Evich	Accounting
Hart	Marketing
Hill	Branch 2
Krasny	Accounting
Lord	Payoll
Nolan	Branch 1

Record: 1 of 21

Figure 4.8
In Datasheet view, you can see that the query now includes two fields.

7 Click the View button on the toolbar.

Clicking the View button now has a different result. This step returns you to the Design view for the query. Keep the query window open in this view. You learn how to name and save the query in the next lesson.

ℹ **Using the Menus to Change Views**
If you would rather use the menus, you can open the <u>V</u>iew menu and select the Data<u>s</u>heet View or the <u>D</u>esign View command, instead of clicking the Toolbar View button.

⚠ **Running a Query**
When you switch from Design view to Datasheet view, you are actually running your query. Instead of switching views, you can open the <u>Q</u>uery menu and select the <u>R</u>un command, or click the Run button on the toolbar.

Lesson 3: Saving the Query

As with any object you add to a database, you must save and name the object if you want to keep it. When you save a query, you save the structure of the query, not the dynaset. The dynaset is the result of running the query, which can be different each time it is run, because it is based on the data in your table. If the records in the table have changed, the resulting dynaset will reflect those changes.

The first time you save a query, you are prompted to give it a name. After that, you can save changes to the query without retyping the name. You can open the File menu and choose the Save command, or you can click the Save button on the toolbar. You can also close the query window, at which point the program will ask if you want to save the query.

In this lesson, you save the query and name it.

To Save the Query

1 The query window, based on the PC Software table, should still be open from the preceding lesson. Click the Save button on the toolbar.

The Save As dialog box is displayed with the name Query1 (see Figure 4.9). Access suggests Query1 as a default name, but as you can see, it isn't very descriptive.

Figure 4.9
Replace the default name with a more descriptive name for the query.

2 Type Department Training List.

This is the name you want to assign the query. You can type up to 64 characters, including numbers, letters, spaces, and special characters.

If Access will not accept your filename, it means that you have used one of the forbidden characters—a period (.), an exclamation point (!), an accent (`), or square bracket ([ ]). Also, you cannot include leading spaces in the query name. If you use a restricted character in a filename, a message box appears telling you that the name you have entered is unacceptable. You can click OK and rename the file, or click the Help button for further information.

Changing a Query Name

If you don't like the name you used—for example, suppose that you accepted the default Query1 name—you can change the name. In Project 8, "Integrating Access with Other Sources of Data and the Internet," you learn how to rename objects such as tables and queries.

3 **Click the OK button.**

Access saves the query and the database. The name of the query is displayed in the title bar of the query window and also in the list of Queries in the database window.

Accepting the Default Choice in a Dialog Box

When you are given choices in a dialog box, one of the buttons will have a dark border. This is the default choice and may be activated by pressing ⏎Enter). If your fingers are already on the keyboard after typing data, it is faster to press ⏎Enter) than to reach for the mouse. Be sure to check the default choice before pressing ⏎Enter) to make certain it is the action you want to take.

---

4 **Click the Close Window button in the upper-right corner of the query window.**

Access closes the query window. The Department Training List query is displayed in the Database window (see Figure 4.10).

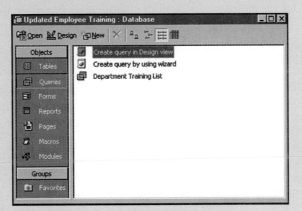

Figure 4.10
The new query is displayed in the Database window.

5 **Click Department Training List on the Queries tab, and click the Open button.**

This reopens the query. The query is now displayed in Datasheet view, instead of Design view. Keep the Department Training List query open; you will use it in the next lesson.

Closing or Saving a Query

You don't have to save the query if you're sure you won't use it again. Just close the query window without saving. When Access prompts you to save, click the No button.

If you decide to save the query, you can do so by choosing File, Save from the menu or by pressing Ctrl)+S).

Lesson 4: Editing the Query

Creating a query takes some practice and a little trial and error. You choose some fields, view the query, make some changes, view the query again, and so on, until you get the results you want.

You can edit the query to add or delete fields. In this project, you add three fields and then delete a field.

To Edit the Query

1 **With the Department Training List query window displayed, click the View button on the toolbar.**

When you opened the query in the preceding lesson, it was displayed in Datasheet view. To make changes, you first have to change to Design view. Now you should see the query window with the field list box at the top and the design grid at the bottom.

2 **Click the Excel field in the field list (you may have to scroll down to find it) and drag this field to the third column of the design grid.**

Access adds this field to the design grid.

3 **Click the PP field in the field list, and drag this field to the third column of the design grid, the same column that currently contains the Excel field.**

Access adds this field as the third column and moves the Excel field over one column to the right. You now have four fields in the query.

> **X** If the PP field appears in the wrong location, drag across the PP name in the column where it appears, and press Del. Repeat step 3. If it is necessary to fill an empty column, click in the Field row of the empty column, click on the drop-down arrow and select the appropriate field for that column from the drop-down field list.

4 **Double-click Access in the field list.**

Access is added in the next empty field. You now have five fields in the query. In your window, you may not be able to see part, or even any, of the fifth column, depending on the size and settings of your computer monitor. Use the horizontal scrollbar to view the field you just added, if necessary.

5 **In the design grid, click the column selector over the PP column.**

When you are in the *column selector* (the thin gray bar just above the field names), you see a black downward arrow for the mouse pointer. When you click the mouse button, the entire column is selected (see Figure 4.11). After you select a column, you can move it or delete it. Try deleting this column.

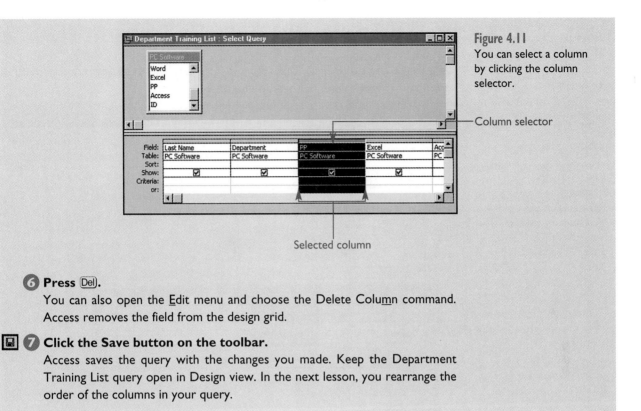

Figure 4.11
You can select a column by clicking the column selector.

Column selector

Selected column

⑥ Press Del.

You can also open the Edit menu and choose the Delete Column command. Access removes the field from the design grid.

 ⑦ Click the Save button on the toolbar.

Access saves the query with the changes you made. Keep the Department Training List query open in Design view. In the next lesson, you rearrange the order of the columns in your query.

Replacing a Deleted Column

You cannot use the Undo command to undo the deletion of a column. If you delete a column by mistake, simply add it again by dragging the name from the field list, double-clicking the field name in the field list, or using the drop-down list in the design grid.

Lesson 5: Changing Field Order and Sorting the Query

The way your query results are arranged depends on two factors. First, the order in which the fields are displayed is determined by the order in which you add them to the Field row in the design grid. If you don't like the order, you can rearrange the fields.

Second, the primary key determines the default order in which the records are displayed. You can change the query's sort order by using the Sort row in the design grid.

To Change the Field Order and Sort the Query

❶ In the Department Training List query Design view, click the column selector above the Department field.

The entire column is selected. After you select a column, you can move it or delete it.

continues ▶

To Change the Field Order and Sort the Query (continued)

2 **Place the pointer on the column selector, and drag Department until it is the first column in the design grid.**

A dotted box is displayed as part of the pointer to signify that you are dragging the column (see Figure 4.12). A dark vertical line also is displayed to indicate the insertion point for the selected column. When you release the mouse button, Access rearranges the columns in the new order.

Figure 4.12
The pointer changes when you move a column in the design grid.

Dark line indicates
new column location

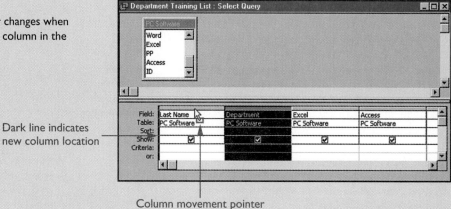

Column movement pointer

3 **Click in the Sort row of the Department field.**

In this example, you want to sort the query by Department. When you click in the Sort box, Access displays a list arrow.

4 **Click the list arrow.**

Access displays a drop-down list of sort choices (see Figure 4.13).

Sort box

Figure 4.13
Choose a sort order for your query from the drop-down list.

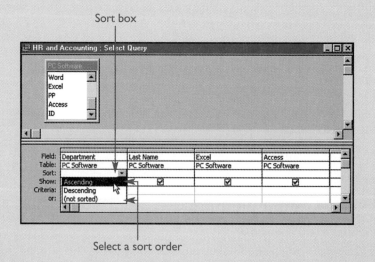

Select a sort order

5 **Click Ascending.**

This selects the sort order (a-to-z) you want to use. You can check the query by changing to Datasheet view.

6 Click the View button on the toolbar.
You can see the results of your query in the Datasheet view, as shown in Figure 4.14.

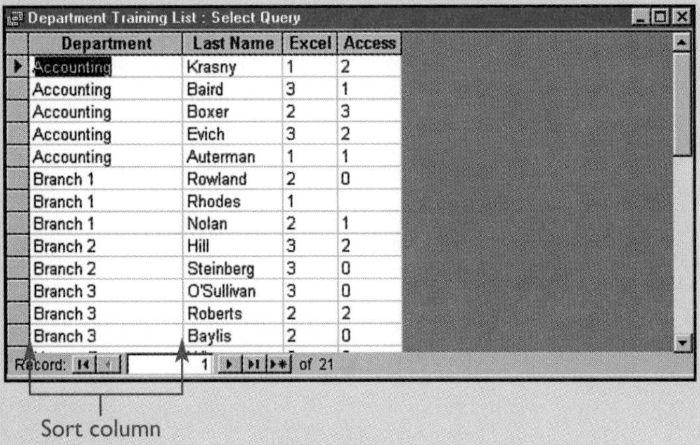

Sort column

Figure 4.14
In Datasheet view, you can see that the query is now sorted by Department.

7 Click the View button on the toolbar again.
The query is once again displayed in Design view.

8 Click the Save button on the toolbar.
This saves the changes you made to the query. Keep the Department Training List query open in Design view as you continue with the next lesson.

Lesson 6: Matching Criteria

So far, the query you have created displays all of the records contained in the Updated Employee Training database, but only shows the fields you selected. You can also use a query to display only certain records—records that match certain **criteria**. Criteria are a set of conditions that limit the records included in a query. A single condition is called a criterion.

You can match a single criterion, such as the last names of staff members who have received training in Excel, or you can match multiple criteria, such as staff members in the Marketing or Human Resources departments who have received training in Access or Excel. In this lesson, you practice using the various types of criteria.

To Match Criteria

1 In the Design view of the Department Training List query, click the Criteria box in the Department column.
The insertion point is moved to this location on the design grid. Here you can type the value that you want to match.

2 Type Human Resources and press ⏎Enter.
Access automatically adds quotation marks around the criteria that has been entered (see Figure 4.15). However, in some cases, such as when entering values that contain any punctuation marks, you must type the quotation marks.

continues ▶

To Match Criteria   (continued)

Figure 4.15
Enter the criterion you
want to match.

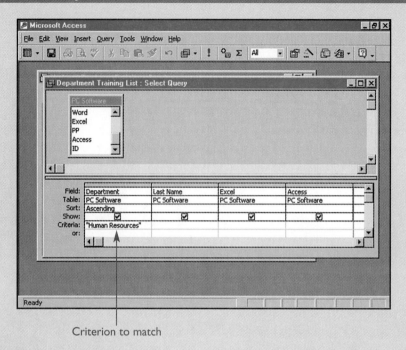

Criterion to match

▦▾ ③ **Click the View button.**
You see the results of the query. Notice that the dynaset now includes only
the staff members in the Human Resources Department (see Figure 4.16).

Figure 4.16
The query now lists all
the people in Human
Resources who are
listed in our Training
table.

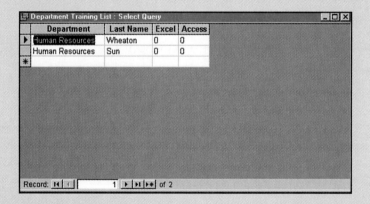

④ **Click the View button again.**
This returns you to the design grid so you can make a change to the query.

⑤ **Move to the box immediately below the Criteria box where you
previously typed Human Resources. This is the or: row. Click
this box.**

❌   If the window for the dialog box is not large enough to display more
than one line of criteria, the window may scroll the list automatically.
This results in some of the criteria disappearing from view. Maximize
this window before proceeding, if necessary.

If you want to match more than one condition, use this row to specify the second value. For this example, you might want to specify staff members in Human Resources or Accounting who have received training.

6 **Type Accounting and press ⏎Enter.**
When the entry you want to match is one word and contains no punctuation, as in this example, you don't have to type quotation marks. Access adds them automatically.

 7 **Click the View button.**
You see the results of the query. Notice that the dynaset now includes trained staff members from Human Resources and Accounting (see Figure 4.17). Keep the Department Training List query open. In the next lesson, you save the query with a new name.

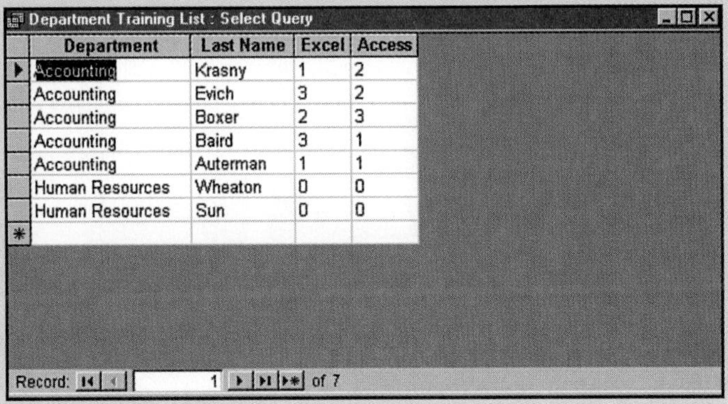

Department	Last Name	Excel	Access
Accounting	Krasny	1	2
Accounting	Evich	3	2
Accounting	Boxer	2	3
Accounting	Baird	3	1
Accounting	Auterman	1	1
Human Resources	Wheaton	0	0
Human Resources	Sun	0	0

Record: ⏮ ◀ 1 ▶ ⏭ ▶* of 7

Figure 4.17
The query now lists all of the people in Human Resources and Accounting.

 Resolving Query Errors
If you see a blank dynaset when you switch to Datasheet view, it means that Access found no matching records. Be sure that you typed the value you are trying to match exactly as you entered it in the database table. For example, you can't type "Humans Resources" to match "Human Resources." Check your typing, and try again.

If Access displays a syntax error message when you are entering text into the Criteria rows to make a match, it means that you did not type the entry in the correct format. Remember that if the text entry contains punctuation, you must supply quotation marks.

Other Query Types and Criteria
Access has many types of queries you can use. For example, you can match a range of values, as you would if you asked Access to display all staff members who received training in Excel at a level 2 or above. You can also create other types of queries, such as a query to display all duplicate records in a table.

There are other types of criteria that may be used besides a direct match. You can use comparisons such as <, which means less than, or >, which means greater than. If you use < to make a comparison in a text field, it uses alphabetical order. For example, if your criteria was <Jones, you would get all the names that came before Jones in the alphabet. Similarly, if you use <1/1/95 in a date field, you would get all the dates before January 1, 1995. For more examples of different criteria, use the Access Help index to look up help for Criteria; then explore some of the different categories.

Lesson 7: Saving the Query with a New Name and Opening Multiple Queries

In some cases, you may modify a query and then want to keep both versions of the query—the original and the modified query—for future use. In this lesson, you learn how to save a query with a new name.

You can also open a query from the database window, and you can have more than one query window open at a time. This lesson explains how to open multiple queries.

To Save the Query with a New Name and Open Multiple Queries

1 In the Department Training List query, open the File menu option and choose the Save As command.

The Save As dialog box is displayed, with the current name listed in the Save Query 'Department Training List' To: text box (see Figure 4.18).

Figure 4.18
The Save As dialog box is displayed with the current query name as the default name.

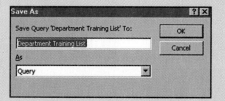

2 Type HR and Accounting.

This is the name you want to use for the new query. Accept Query in the As text box.

3 Click the OK button.

Access saves the query with the new name, and the new name is displayed in the title bar. The original query remains unchanged in the database.

4 Click the Close button in the query window.

This returns you to the database window. The Queries object button should be selected. The two queries are displayed in the Queries list (see Figure 4.19).

Figure 4.19
More than one query is displayed for the Updated Employee Training database.

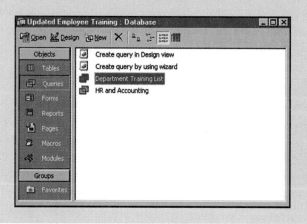

5 **Select the Department Training List query, and click the Open button.**

This step opens the query. Notice that the query displays all departments, not just the ones for Human Resources and Accounting, because you did not save the criteria.

 6 **Click the Database Window button on the toolbar.**

7 **Select and open the HR and Accounting query.**

This opens your modified query. Now both queries are open onscreen, as well as the database window.

8 **Open the Window menu and choose Cascade.**

This step arranges the windows so that you can see which windows are currently open (see Figure 4.20). You can work on more than one query at a time by moving between windows.

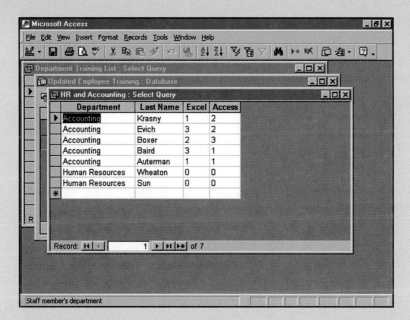

Figure 4.20
The open windows are placed on top of each other with the title bars displayed.

9 **Close both query windows and the database.**

If you have completed your session on the computer, exit Access. Otherwise, continue with the "Checking Concepts and Terms" section.

Copying and Opening a Query

You can also make a copy of a query in the database window by selecting the query, clicking the Copy button, and then clicking the Paste button. A Paste As dialog box opens so you can give the query copy a new name.

Once a query has been saved, you can open it in Design view instead of in Datasheet view. To open a query in Design view, click the query to select it, and then click the Design button.

Summary

This project focused on extracting a subset of information from a table. You learned how to create a query in Design view, select the appropriate fields, and save your query. You changed the fields and structure of the query, and had the query display only records that met conditions that you set. Finally, you duplicated a query and saved it with a different name.

You can expand your understanding of the use of queries by looking at the help available in the Office Assistant on some of the features that make queries more powerful. For example, you might want to type **How do I enter criteria** in the Office Assistant, look through the various help topics, and find examples of criteria expressions. These will give you a better idea of the many criteria features available in an Access query.

Checking Concepts and Terms

True/False

For each of the following, check *T* or *F* to indicate whether the statement is true or false.

__T __F **1.** You must include at least one field in a query. [L2]

__T __F **2.** You define the conditions of a query in the design grid. [L6]

__T __F **3.** The data for a dynaset is stored on disk separately from its source table. [L3]

__T __F **4.** You cannot include spaces or punctuation in a query name. [L3]

__T __F **5.** If you see a blank dynaset when you run a query, Access found no matching records. [L6]

__T __F **6.** The first time you save a query, the Save As dialog box appears. [L3]

__T __F **7.** You must include all fields in a query, even though they may not be displayed. [L2]

__T __F **8.** If you accidentally delete a field from the query, you can click the Undo button to restore the field. [L4]

__T __F **9.** A query can use only one table. [L1]

__T __F **10.** As you drag a field name from the field list to the query, the mouse pointer changes to an arrow with a little box attached. [L5]

Multiple Choice

Circle the letter of the correct answer for each of the following questions.

1. Which of the following can you do to add a field to the query? [L2]

a. Double-click the field name in the field list.

b. Use the drop-down list in the Field row of the design grid.

c. Drag the field name from the field list to the design grid.

d. all of the above

2. Which of the following is not a way to run a query when you are working in the query Design view? [L2]

a. Click the Run button.

b. Click the Go button.

c. Open the Query menu and choose the Run command.

d. Open the View menu and choose the Datasheet view command.

3. What is the lower half of the query window called? [L2]

a. field list

b. design grid

c. criteria box

d. query area

4. How should you enter criteria for text fields if the criterion contains punctuation? [L6]

   a. in all uppercase

   b. in all lowercase

   c. in bold

   d. within quotation marks

5. In what order are fields included in a query? [L5]

   a. the order in which you add them

   b. the order in which they appear in the table

   c. alphabetical order

   d. numerical order

6. What is the column selector? [L4]

   a. a dialog box listing all active columns

   b. a drop-down list that appears when you click the down arrow in a column field

   c. a shortcut list of columns activated by pressing the right mouse button

   d. a gray box on top of the column that enables you to highlight the entire column

7. How do you change the order of the fields in a query? [L5]

   a. Select one field, select a second field while pressing Ctrl, and choose Swap from the Edit menu.

   b. Select the field's column selector and then drag it to the new location.

   c. Drag the field from the field list to the new location. The other reference in the query will automatically be deleted.

   d. You can't change the order of the fields. They must appear in the same order as in the field list.

8. What can you do with queries? [Intro]

   a. sort data, limit fields, limit records

   b. save them to use over and over again

   c. create a dynaset

   d. all of the above

9. Which of the following is not a way of creating another query? [L7]

   a. altering the current query and saving it with a new name

   b. selecting New on the Query dialog box and building a query from scratch

   c. selecting Duplicate from the Edit menu and saving the duplicate query with a new name

   d. copying the query in the database window and renaming the copy with a new name

10. How long can a query name be? [L3]

   a. 64 characters

   b. 255 characters

   c. 8 characters

   d. any length

Screen ID

Label each element of the Access screen shown in Figure 4.21.

Figure 4.21

A. Field list

B. View button

C. Show check box

D. Sort order

E. Run button

F. Criterion

G. Source table of field

H. Field name

I. Column selector

J. Design grid

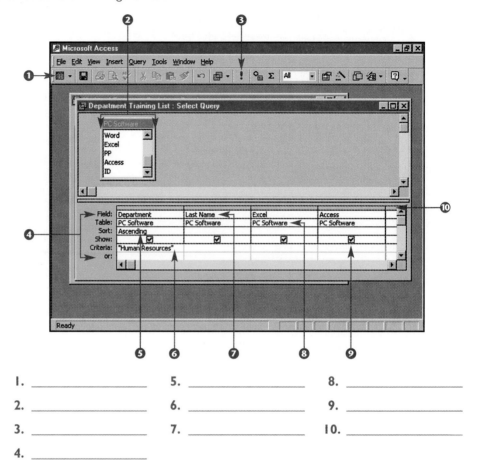

1. _____	5. _____	8. _____
2. _____	6. _____	9. _____
3. _____	7. _____	10. _____
4. _____		

Discussion Questions

1. You have created a home inventory using the following fields: room, category (for example, furniture, appliances, clothes), description, year purchased, serial number, and cost. What fields might you use queries on?

2. In the home inventory example in question 1, let's assume that some of your possessions are fairly valuable, and you want to submit a list of them to your insurance company. Which field would you set a criterion for, and which fields would you include in the query?

3. You have developed a table for an automobile parts store, containing fields for the make of the car, part name, description, number sold year-to-date,

quantity in stock, retail price, sale price, and cost. You now want to create a query or queries that might be used repeatedly. What queries would you create, and what fields would each contain?

4. For the automobile parts store table in Step 3, can you think of a query that might include a field that you don't show in the dynaset (in other words, turn off the Show check box)?

5. You can sort data in either a table or a query using different procedures. Which procedure is easier if you are sorting on a single field? Which sort procedure is easier if you want to sort on multiple, non-adjacent fields?

Skill Drill

Skill Drill exercises reinforce project skills. Each skill reinforced is the same, or nearly the same, as a skill presented in the project. Each exercise includes a brief narrative introduction, followed by detailed instructions in a step-by-step format.

You have created a database and table to store the information on your vast collection of history books. They are divided into four categories: United States, Ancient, World, and England & British Empire. There are fields for Author, Title, Year (either written or published), Pages, and Category. You would like to be able to sort your query and also view information by category.

1. Creating a Simple Query

You would like to create a query from which you can build other queries. First, you need to create a basic query.

1. Find the AC1-0402 database file on your CD-ROM, send it to drive A, remove the read-only status, and name it **History Books**. Select and <u>O</u>pen the History Books table, and look at the fields. Click the Close button to close the table.

2. Click the Queries object button, and click <u>N</u>ew to create a new query.

3. Choose Design View and click <u>A</u>dd to add the History Books table. <u>C</u>lose the Show Table dialog box.

4. Double-click the Author field to add it to the design grid.

5. Drag the Title field down to the design grid as the second field.

6. Add the Year and Category fields to the design grid, but do not add the Pages field.

7. Click the View button to see the results of your query.

8. Close the query, and save it as **All History Books**.

2. Editing Your Query

In your All History Books query, you have decided that you would really like to see the number of pages in the books, but don't care to see the Year of publication.

1. Select the All History Books query and click the <u>D</u>esign button.

2. Click the Pages field in the field box and drag it on top of the Year field. The Pages field should be between the Title field and the Year field.

3. Click the View button to view the results; then click the View button again to return to Design view.

4. Click the Show button for the Year field to hide the field in this query.

5. Click the View button to see the results of your change.

6. Close the query and save your changes.

3. Changing the Field Order in a Query

You have decided that you really should display the Year field, but you want to change the order of the fields.

1. Select the All History Books query and click the <u>D</u>esign button. Notice that the Year field has disappeared from the query, because it was not shown or used for anything (sorting or criteria).

2. Double-click the Year field to add it to the end of the fields in the design grid.

3. Click the Year column selector. Let go of the mouse button, then click the column selector again and drag the field to the right of the Title field.

4. Use the same procedure to move the Category field to the first field position. The order of fields should now be: Category, Author, Title, Year, Pages.

5. Click the View button to view the new query layout. Close the query, and save your changes.

4. Sorting the Query and Saving with a New Name

You want to look at your history books in a couple of different orders. The query design grid makes it easy to do this.

1. Select the All History Books query and click the Design button.

2. Click the Sort box for the Pages field in the design grid.

3. Click the list arrow in the Pages Sort box and select Descending to look at your largest books first.

4. Click the View button to see a list of your books from largest to smallest.

5. Click the View button to return to Design view.

6. Click the list arrow in the Pages field to turn off the sorting on this field.

7. Click the list arrow on the Title field Sort box, and select Ascending order.

8. Click the View button to see a list of your books in alphabetical order by title.

9. Choose File, Save As from the menu. Save the query as **Sorted by Title**. Close the query.

5. Matching a Single Criterion

You have divided your history books into four categories, and you frequently want to look at the books by category. It would be good to have a query for each one.

1. Select the All History Books query, and click the Design button.

2. Type **Ancient** in the Criteria box of the Category field.

3. Choose File, Save As from the menu. Save the query as **Ancient History Books**.

4. Delete Ancient from the Criteria box, and type **United States** in its place. Choose File, Save As from the menu. Save the query as **United States History Books**.

5. Delete United States from the Criteria box and type **World** in its place. Choose File, Save As from the menu. Save the query as **World History Books**.

6. Delete World from the Criteria box and type **England & British Empire** in its place. Choose File, Save As from the menu. Save the query as **England & British Empire History Books**.

7. Close the query. Highlight each of the four new queries and open them to make sure you typed the Criteria information correctly. If one of the queries does not work, select it and go to Design view to re-enter the criterion.

6. Matching More Than One Criterion

Now you want to try using more than one criterion.

1. Select the All History Books query and click the Design button.

2. Type **United States** in the Criteria box of the Category field.

3. Type **1977** in the Criteria box of the Year field.

4. Click the Run button to run the query.

5. Close the query, but don't save your changes. Close the database unless you are planning to move on to the Challenge section.

Challenge

Challenge exercises expand on or are somewhat related to skills presented in the lessons. Each exercise provides a brief narrative introduction followed by instructions in a numbered step format that are not as detailed as those in the Skill Drill section.

The database you will be using for the Challenge section is a modified version of the same database of history books you used in the Skill Drill section.

1. Creating a Query Using a Wizard

You have decided to try some of the more advanced query features on your history books database, but just to be safe, you decide to create a second database with the same data. The first feature you want to try out is the Simple Query Wizard. Make sure you read each wizard screen and read the directions.

1. Copy the AC1-0402 database file to drive A:, remove the read-only status, and rename it **History Books 2**. This is the same file you used in the Skill Drill section.
2. Select Simple Query Wizard from the New Query dialog box.
3. Select all of the fields for this query. Display all of the fields in the query.
4. Call your query **History Book Collection** and close the query.

2. Sorting on Multiple Fields

It would be very convenient to use a query to sort the data in the table on more than one field. In this case, you want to first sort by category, then sort alphabetically by title within each category.

1. Open the History Book Collection query in Design view.
2. Move the Category field to the first field in the design grids.
3. Move the Title field to the right of the Category field.
4. Select both the Category and the Title field at the same time.
5. Sort in ascending order.
6. Save the query as **Sorted by Category and Title**. Close the query.

3. Limiting Records by Looking for Parts of Text Fields

For years you have been compiling a special collection of books on Michigan history. You have given them special titles—all of the titles begin with "Michigan:" followed by the title of the book or pamphlet. All of these special titles are saved in the United States category. You would like to create a query to separate the titles in your Michigan history collection from the rest of the United States history books.

1. Open the History Book Collection query in Design view.
2. Use the available help features, on your computer or online, and find instructions on entering text criteria in a query.
3. In the Criteria box of the Title field, type in the expression used to find all titles that begin with **Michigan:**.
4. Run the query to make sure only the books beginning with "Michigan:" are included. (Hint: There should be 184 records in this query.)
5. Save the query as **Michigan History Books**. Close the query.

[?] 4. Limiting Records by Setting Limits to Numeric Fields

In the previous Challenge, you limited the records by setting a criterion that included only part of the Title field. It would also be nice to be able to set beginning and end limits to a numeric field, such as the Year field in the current database.

1. Open the History Book Collection query in Design view.

2. Use the available help features, either on your computer or online, to find instructions on entering number criteria in a query.

3. In the Criteria box of the Year field, type in the expression used to find all titles that were published between World War I and World War II. (Note: World War I ended in 1918 and World War II began for the U.S. in 1941. Your query should include books published between 1919 and 1940. Both 1919 and 1940 should be included.)

4. Sort on the Year field in ascending order.

5. Run the query to make sure only books published from 1919 to 1940 are included. (Hint: There should be a total of 59 books when you successfully set up the query.)

6. Save the query as **Books Published Between the Wars**. Close the query.

[?] 5. Including or Excluding Records by Searching for Words Anywhere in a Text Field

In an earlier Challenge, you found all of the titles beginning with "Michigan:." You might also like to be able to find words or phrases anywhere in a field. You might find it useful to be able to exclude all records with a certain word in the title. In this case, you look for the word "revolution" anywhere in the title.

1. Open the History Book Collection query in Design view.

2. Use the available help features, either on your computer or online to find instructions on entering text criteria in a query.

3. In the Criteria box of the Title field, type in the expression that will find records that have the word "revolution" in them.

4. Run the query to make sure all of the books include the word "revolution." (Hint: There should be a total of 17 books when you successfully set up the query.)

5. Go back to your help source, and figure out how to exclude those 17 records that have the word "revolution" in them. Type in the expression to remove those 17 records from your list of books. (Hint: You should have 1,136 records that don't include that word.)

6. Change the Criteria box in the Title field back to include only those books with "revolution" in the title.

7. Save the query as **Books About Revolution**. Close the query, and close the database unless you are going to proceed to the Discovery Zone.

Discovery Zone

Discovery Zone exercises help you gain advanced knowledge of project topics and application of skills. These exercises focus on enhancing your problem-solving skills. Numbered steps are not provided, but you are given hints, reminders, screen shots, and references to help you reach your goal for each exercise.

1. Creating a Crosstab Query

Crosstab queries are very powerful tools for summarizing data from large databases. They summarize the relationship between two or more fields. For example, if you sent out a survey with ten questions, you would enter each person's responses in a single record. If you got 1,000 responses, you would have 1,000 records, each with a numeric response (e.g., a 1-to-5 rating scale) to the ten questions. Counting the number of times each response was given for each question would take a long time. A crosstab query can give you a table of responses in seconds.

Goal: Create a crosstab query that counts the books published each year by category of book, then sort the crosstab in descending order.

Use the AC1-0402 file to create a new database called **History Books 3** on your disk. Use help from your computer or online to understand how crosstab queries work and how they are built. Save the query as **Category by Year Crosstab**.

> Hint #1: Put the years from the Year field down the left side of the crosstab table, and use the categories from the Category field as column headers. If you do it the other way, it will be extremely difficult to read.
>
> Hint #2: Have the program count the instances, not add them up!
>
> Hint #3: You will not perform the sort until you have built and run the crosstab.

2. Using Queries to Delete Records from Tables

Queries can be used for more than just creating dynasets of tables. They can also be used to directly affect the information in tables. They can be used to append records to existing tables, to update the information in tables, and even to delete records in tables. These must be used with care! Any time you are going to use one of these special query types, always back up your database first, just in case you change more than you intended.

Goal: Use a query to delete records from a table.

Use the History Books 3 database you used in the first Discovery Zone exercise. (If you did not do the first exercise, copy AC1-0402 and create a new database on your disk.) Create and run a Delete Query that removes all titles beginning with "Michigan:" from the History Books table. Do not save the query.

> Hint #1: Look for the Query Type button on the Design view toolbar.
>
> Hint #2: Use what you learned in the Challenge section to identify those records that begin with "Michigan:"
>
> Hint #3: Run the query from the Design view window.
>
> Hint #4: You'll know you're on the right track when you run the query and the program warns you that you are about to delete 184 rows and won't be able to get them back.

Creating and Using Forms

Objectives

In this project, you learn how to

➤ **Create an AutoForm**

➤ **Enter and Edit Data Using a Form**

➤ **Save, Close, and Open a Form**

➤ **Create a New Form from Scratch**

➤ **Add Fields to Forms**

➤ **Move and Resize Fields in Forms**

➤ **Add a Form Header and Label**

Key terms introduced in this project include

- AutoForm
- control
- field label
- field text box
- form
- Form Detail
- Form Footer
- Form Header
- label
- Selection handles
- Tab Order

Why Would I Do This?

When you enter records in a table, each record is displayed in a row, and all records are displayed. If the table has many fields, you may not be able to see all of the fields in the table onscreen, and you might find it difficult to find the record you want with all the records displayed. A *form* is used to display one record at a time, and you can place the fields anywhere on the screen. Even if a record has many fields, you may be able to see them all on one screen. You can move the fields around and add text to the form so that it resembles paper forms that are already in use. It is often easier for people to transfer data from paper forms to a form on the screen that looks the same.

Using a form offers the following advantages:

- You can select the fields you want to include in the form, and you can arrange them in the order you want.

- You can display only one record at a time, which makes it easier to concentrate on that record.

- You can make the form more graphically appealing.

Access provides an *AutoForm* that you can create quickly without a great deal of work. The AutoForm is a wizard that sets up an input screen that includes all of the fields in the table. If this form isn't what you need, you can also create a form from scratch. In this project, you use both methods to create forms.

Visual Summary

When you have completed this project, you will have created a form that looks like Figure 5.1:

Figure 5.1
Forms make it easy to enter data.

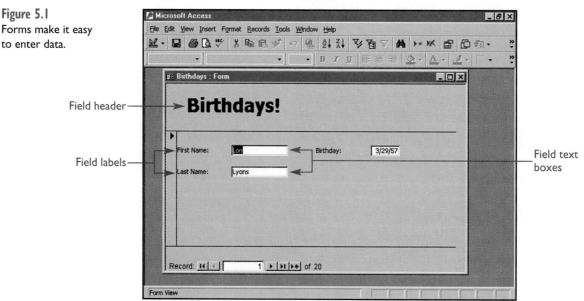

Lesson 1: Creating an AutoForm

If you want a simple form that lists each field in a single column and displays one record at a time, you can use one of the Access Form Wizards to create an AutoForm. The Form Wizards look at the structure of your database table and then create a form automatically. You simply choose the commands to start the Wizards.

To Create an Autoform

1 **Launch Access. Click OK to open an existing file.**
Make sure you have a disk in drive A:.

2 **Find the AC1-0501 file on your CD-ROM, right-click on it, and send it to the floppy drive. Move to drive A:, remove the read-only status, and rename the file New Address List. Open the new database.**
In this project, you use a version of the Address database you worked with in Project 1, "Getting Started with Access." You should see the database window, listing the Contacts table.

3 **Click the Forms object button.**
No forms are listed, because you have not yet created or saved any (see Figure 5.2).

Forms object button →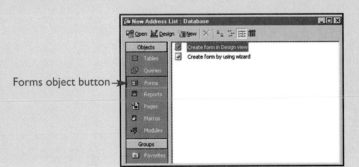

Figure 5.2
No forms are listed, because you have not yet created any.

4 **Click the New button.**
The New Form dialog box is displayed. First, you have to select a table to use with the form. Then you must decide whether you want to use one of the Form Wizards or start with a blank form.

5 **Click the down arrow in the box labeled Choose the table or query where the object's data comes from:.**
You see a list of the tables and queries available in the database (see Figure 5.3). You can base a form on either a query or a table. You must select the Contacts table, even though it is the only table or query available.

continues ▶

To Create an Autoform   (continued)

Figure 5.3
From the drop-down list, choose the table or query on which you want to base the form.

←Select a table from the list

⑥ Click Contacts.
This step selects the table you want to use.

⑦ Click the AutoForm: Columnar option, and then click OK.
The Form Wizard creates the form. This step may take several seconds. The status bar displays the progress so that you can see that Access is working. After the AutoForm is built, Access displays the table's first record. Notice that the fields are displayed in a column in the form. Your screen may not have the same background settings. The navigation buttons are displayed at the bottom of the form to enable you to move through the records (see Figure 5.4). Keep this form onscreen as you continue to the next lesson, where you learn more about the navigation buttons.

Figure 5.4
An AutoForm containing all fields displayed in a single column.

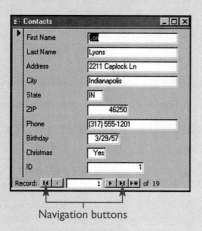

Navigation buttons

⚠️ Other Ways to Create a New Form
You can also create a new form by clicking the drop-down arrow to the right of the New Object button on the toolbar in the database window. When you are in the table Datasheet view, you can click the New Object list button and select either the Form button or the AutoForm button to create a new form.

Lesson 2: Entering and Editing Data Using a Form

Forms often make it easier to enter and edit data. Before you save the form, you may want to try some data entry to be sure that you like the structure of the form. If you don't like how the form is set up, you can change it or create a new one, as you learn later in this project.

You can use the same tools to enter, find, sort, and display records in a form that you use in a table. In this lesson, you will add and edit a record using a form.

To Enter and Edit Data Using a Form

1 The AutoForm based on the Contacts table should still be on your screen from the previous lesson. Click either one of the New Record buttons.

New Record buttons are located both on the toolbar and with the navigation buttons on the bottom of the form window. This step adds a new record, and a blank form is displayed (see Figure 5.5).

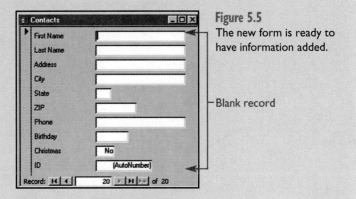

Figure 5.5
The new form is ready to have information added.

Blank record

2 Type the following data, pressing `Tab` after each entry to move to the next field.

Janet

Eisenhut

455 Sheridan

Indianapolis

IN

46204

(317) 555-6588

3/29/60

Yes

Notice that when you type the phone number, Access automatically provides parentheses around the area code, moves you over so that you can type the exchange, and provides a hyphen after the exchange.

You may have to scroll down to see all the fields in the form. When you reach the last field—the ID field—you do not have to enter a value, because it is a counter field. Also, remember that when you move to another record, Access automatically saves the record you just entered. Keep in mind that the record is saved in the underlying Contacts table. You don't have to worry about updating the table separately.

3 Click the First Record button.

This moves you to the first record in the table.

continues ▶

To Enter and Edit Data Using a Form   (continued)

▶ ❹ **Click the Next Record button to scroll through the records until you see the record for Shelli Canady.**
This is the record you want to edit. Notice that the Birthday field is blank.

✗ If you can't find the record that you want to edit by scrolling, you can open the Edit menu and use the Find command. (Refer to Project 3, "Entering and Editing Data," for more information on searching records.)

❺ **Click in the Birthday field.**
This action moves the insertion point to the field you want to edit.

❻ **Type 11/4/65.**
This enters a birthday for Shelli.

◀◀ ❼ **Click the First Record button.**
This moves you back to the first record and saves the change to the record you just edited. Keep the form open on your screen as you continue to the next lesson.

Undoing Editing Changes
If you make an editing change and want to undo it, open the Edit menu and choose the Undo command or press the Undo button. This will undo your last change.

Keyboard Navigation
Besides using the navigation buttons, you can use the keyboard to move among records and fields. Press `Tab↹` or `↓` or `→` to move to the next field; `⬆Shift`+`Tab↹` or `↑` or `←` to move to the previous field; `PgUp` to scroll to the previous record; and `PgDn` to scroll to the next record. `Ctrl`+`Home` will move the insertion point to the first field in the first record and `Ctrl`+`End` will move the insertion point to the last field in the last record.

Lesson 3: Saving, Closing, and Opening a Form

If you use the form and like how it is organized, you can save the form so that you can use it again later. If you try to close the form without saving, Access reminds you to save. You don't have to save the form; you should save it only if you intend to use it again. If you accidentally close the form without saving it, you can simply re-create it (follow the steps in Lesson 1 of this project).

As with the other objects you have created, you are prompted to type a name the first time you save the form. You can type up to 64 characters, including spaces. After you have saved the form, you can close it and open it again when you want to use it.

To Save, Close, and Open a Form

 1 The AutoForm that uses the Contacts table should still be open on your screen. Click the Save button.
The Save As dialog box is displayed (see Figure 5.6). The default name, Contacts, is the name of the table on which the form is based.

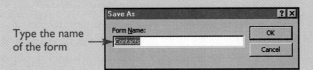

Type the name of the form

Figure 5.6
Give the form a name before you save it.

2 Type Contacts AutoForm, then click the OK button.
Access saves the form.

3 Click the Close button in the upper-right corner of the form window to close the form.
The form window closes, and you see the database window again. Notice that your new form is now included in the Forms list (see Figure 5.7).

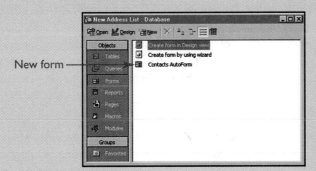

New form

Figure 5.7
The name of your form now appears in the Forms list.

4 Double-click Contacts AutoForm to open it.
Access displays the first record in the table on which the form is based. You can add, modify, or delete records. When you are finished working in the form, close it again. As you move from field to field, Access automatically saves any changes you make.

5 Click the Close button to close the form.
Access closes the form. Keep the New Address List database open and continue to the next lesson.

Other Ways to Save a Form
You can choose File, Save from the menu or press Ctrl+S to save the form instead of using the Save button.

Lesson 4: Creating a New Form from Scratch

Sometimes the Form Wizards do not create exactly the form you want. When that happens, you can start from a blank form and create one that better suits your needs. The form can include any text, fields, and other **controls** you want to incorporate. Controls are any objects selected from the toolbox, such as text boxes, checkboxes, or option buttons.

A form consists of several different elements. Each part of the form is called a section. The main, or **Form Detail**, section is the area in which records are displayed. You can also add **Form Headers** (top of form) or **Form Footers** (bottom of form). Anything you include in the section will be displayed onscreen in Form view when you use the form. You can also add page headers and page footers, which are not visible onscreen in Form view but will appear if you print the form.

The rest of this project covers some of the common features you can use when you create a form from scratch. Keep in mind, however, that Access offers other form features, such as drop-down lists, groups of option buttons, graphic objects, and much more.

In this lesson, you create a new, blank form.

To Create a New Form from Scratch

1 **In the New Address List database window, click the Forms object button (if necessary); then click the New button.**
You see the New Form dialog box. Before you choose whether you want to use the Form Wizard or start with a blank form, you should select the table you want to use for the form.

2 **Click the down arrow in the drop-down list in the New Form dialog box, and select the Contacts table.**

3 **Select the Design View option from the top of the list, and click OK.**
The form is displayed in Design view. To work on a blank form, it is useful to have the rulers turned on and the Field List and Toolbox windows open. If they were used the last time the program was in the form Design view, they will be displayed. Examine your screen and compare it to Figure 5.8. Perform the following steps as needed.

4 **If the list of fields does not appear on the screen, click the Field List button on the Form Design toolbar.**

5 **If the Toolbox does not appear on the screen, click the Toolbox button.**
The Toolbox appears in the size, shape, and location it was last used on your computer. It may even be docked along the bottom, top, or side of the screen.

6 **If the Ruler does not appear on the screen, choose View, Ruler from the menu bar.**
The Design view should now include the Ruler, Toolbox, and Field List.

7 **Drag the two windows to the right of the Form Design window as shown.**
The blank form is displayed with the rulers, Field List, and Toolbox (see Figure 5.8). Keep this blank form open on your screen. In the next lesson, you learn how to add fields to a form.

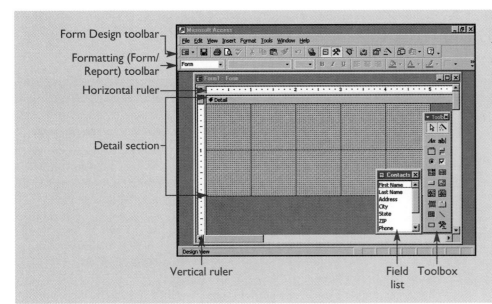

Form Design toolbar

Formatting (Form/ Report) toolbar

Horizontal ruler

Detail section

Vertical ruler

Field list

Toolbox

Figure 5.8
The blank form should display the Field list and the Toolbox.

 Controls Tied to the Table Fields
Some controls are bound to the fields in the table. If you create a text box for a field and enter data in the field in the form, for example, the field in the table is updated. Other controls are not tied to the table but, instead, are saved with the form. For example, you may want to add a descriptive title to the form. This type of text is called a *label* and is not bound to the underlying table.

Lesson 5: Adding Fields to Forms

You decided it would be a good idea to send birthday greetings to your customers to help maintain good relations. You added a birthday field to your Contacts table, but you have entered only the birthdays of contacts who are your customers. To make sure that birthday greetings are sent to your customers, you want to create a simple form that lists just the person's name and his or her birthday. This form will include three fields—Last Name, First Name, and Birthday—and will also include a label in the form's header.

When you want to set up or change the structure of a form, you must use Design view. Access includes the following items to help you design the form:

- **Toolbar.** Use the toolbar to access some form design commands. You can click the Save button to save the form, the View button to view the form, and so on. If you place the pointer on a button, the button name appears directly under the button.

- **Toolbox.** Use the toolbox to add items, such as labels or images, to the form. As with the toolbar, you can place the mouse pointer over a toolbox button to see its name. The Toolbox may not be displayed when you create a new form. If it is not, click the Toolbox button to display it.

- **Field list.** Use the field list to add fields to the form. The field list box may not be displayed when you create a new form. If it is not, click the Field List button in the toolbar.

- **Rulers.** Use the rulers to help position controls on the form.

In this lesson, you use the field list to add fields to the form. The new, blank form you are creating for the Contacts table should still be on your screen from the preceding lesson. Try adding fields to the form now.

To Add Fields to Forms

1 **Click and drag the First Name field from the field list to the Detail section of the form.**

As you drag, your pointer becomes a small, boxed field name. You can use this to help place the field onscreen. The *field text box*, which holds a place for the contents of the field you have selected, is placed where you release the box.

2 **Release the mouse button and drop the field at approximately the 1-inch mark on the horizontal ruler, and down about 1/4" from the top of the detail area.**

This places the field text box and *field label*, which is the field name, on the form (see Figure 5.9). The label box will be placed to the left of the text box, so you need to leave space for it.

X If you see only one field box when you drag the field from the field list, you may have placed the field too far to the left (beyond the 1-inch horizontal mark, for example), or the field text box and field label may be on top of one another. You have to move or resize the field so that you can see both the field label and the field text box.

You can delete the field and start again if you run into problems. To delete a field, click it to select it and then press (Del). This will remove the field from the form, but it will not delete the field or its contents from the table.

Figure 5.9
You add a field to the form by dragging it from the field list.

Field label

Field text box

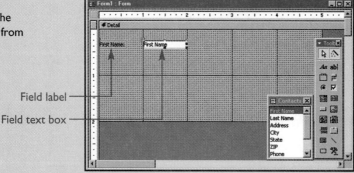

3 **Drag the Last Name field to the form; place this field below the First Name field at the same horizontal location (the 1-inch mark) and about 1/4" below the First Name field.**

This step adds a second field to the form. As you drag and drop the field, try to align the field with the field above it. Make sure that you leave enough room between the two fields—don't drop the fields on top of one another.

4 **Drag the Birthday field to the form. Place this field below the Last Name field (also at the 1-inch horizontal mark).**

Your form now includes three fields (see Figure 5.10). You can save and name the form so that these changes won't be lost.

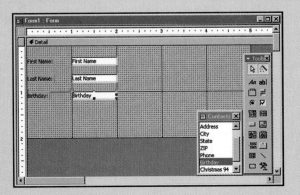

Figure 5.10
The new form contains three fields.

5 **Open the File menu and choose the Save command.**

You see the Save As dialog box, in which you can assign a name for this new form.

6 **Type Birthdays and click OK.**

Access saves the form and returns to Design view. You can continue building the form, or you can display it.

7 **Click the View button on the toolbar.**

The form is displayed as it will appear when you use it (see Figure 5.11). You can see whether you need to make any adjustments, such as adding a label or resizing the fields. Keep the Birthdays form open, and continue with the next lesson.

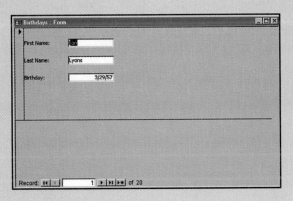

Figure 5.11
Your new form is displayed in Form view.

 Creating Other Forms; Modifying Forms

In addition to creating a blank form, you can use the Form Wizard to create other types of forms, such as columnar, tabular, charts, and pivot tables.

To modify an existing form, click its name in the database window; then click the Design command button. Alternatively, you can open the form and change to Design view by clicking the View button.

Lesson 6: Moving and Resizing Fields in Forms

When you create your form, you may find it difficult to get the fields in the right place the first time. That's okay; you can move or resize the fields after you have added them to the form. You can drag and place them visually, using the ruler as a guide. Otherwise, you can have Access align the fields with an underlying grid—making them an equal distance apart.

In this lesson, you move the Birthday field up next to the First Name field.

To Move and Resize Fields in Forms

1 In the Birthdays form, click the View button to return to Design view.

To make changes to the form design, you must return to Design view. You cannot make changes in Form view.

2 If the Birthday field is not selected, click the field text box.

Selection handles appear around the borders (see Figure 5.12). Selection handles are small squares that appear at the corners and on the sides of boxes. They can be used to change the size of the box. Notice that both the field label and the field text box are selected, because these two items are attached. However, handles only appear all the way around the object on which you clicked. The other one (in this case, the field label) has one large handle in the upper-left corner. Most of the time you want to keep the two together, such as when you want to move them.

Figure 5.12
You must click a field to select it before you can move it.

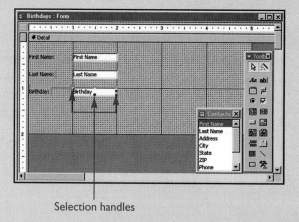

Selection handles

3 Place the mouse pointer on one of the borders, but not on one of the handles.

When the pointer is in the correct spot, it should resemble a small hand (see Figure 5.13). If you see arrows rather than the hand, the pointer isn't in the correct spot. Move it around until you see the hand.

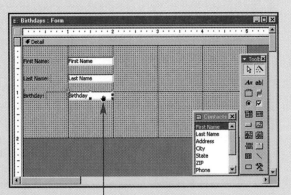

Figure 5.13
To move the field, the pointer must look like a hand.

The pointer appears as a hand

④ **Drag the Birthday field up next to the First Name field and place it so that the left edge of the Birthday field label is at approximately the 2 1/2-inch mark on the horizontal ruler.**

Notice as you drag that you can see the outline of both the field label and the field text box. When you release the mouse button, Access moves the field up next to the First Name field. (You may need to drag the field list box out of the way so that you can see where you are positioning the Birthday field.)

⑤ **Move the pointer to the right side of the Birthday field and place it on the center handle. The pointer turns into a two-headed arrow (see Figure 5.14).**

The birthday field is longer than necessary, so you are going to change the size to approximately 1/2" wide.

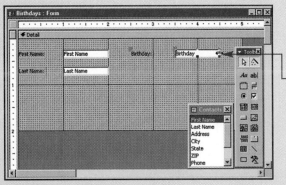

Figure 5.14
Use the selection handles to resize a field.

The pointer appears as a two-headed arrow

⑥ **Make the field smaller by dragging the right side of the field to the left. Stop at the 4" mark on the horizontal ruler so that the field is about 1/2" wide.**

The Birthday field is now about the right size to contain a date.

⑦ **Click the View button to return to Form view to verify that the date will fit in the new box.**

⑧ **Click the Save button.**

This step saves the form with the changes you just made. Keep the Birthdays form open. In the next lesson, you add a Form Header to the form.

If you see arrows in the form and begin to drag, you will resize the field. If you resize by accident, click the Undo button to undo the change.

When you want to move a field, be sure to place the pointer on the edge of the field and wait until it changes to a hand. Don't place the pointer on one of the selection handles.

Moving the Label Box or Text Box
If you want to move the label box separately from the text box, point to the larger square in the upper-left corner of the label box. When the pointer turns into a pointing finger, you can click and drag the label box to a new location. The text box can move independently from the label box by using the same technique. Point to the larger box in the upper-left corner of the text box until the pointer turns into a pointing finger, then click and drag the text box to the desired location.

Changing Tab Order
When you enter data into a form, the insertion point jumps from one box to the next each time you press (Tab⇆). This is called the **Tab Order**. When you move fields around in a form, you may need to change the Tab Order. In Design view, select View, Tab Order from the menu and a list of fields will be displayed. Click once on the field to select the one that you want to move, then click and drag it to the desired position on the list. You can also click the Auto Order button, which often (but not always) sets the tab order the way you want it.

Lesson 7: Adding a Form Header and Label

The final step for this form is to add a Form Header that will appear at the top of the form and to include a label showing the name of the form. Form Headers show up at the top of every form. Form footers are similar to Form Headers, but they appear at the bottom of every form.

In this lesson, you first add a new section to the form—the Form Header section—and then you add a label to the form. In addition to adding the label, you can change the font and font size of the text so that the form label stands out.

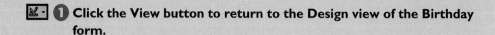
To Add a Form Header and Label

① Click the View button to return to the Design view of the Birthday form.

② Choose View, Form Header/Footer from the menu.
Access adds two sections to the form, a Form Header and a Form Footer (see Figure 5.15). You want to include the form label in the header, but the section is too small. Therefore, you need to adjust the size of the section.

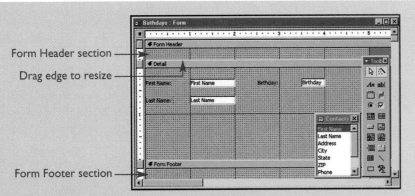

Form Header section —

Drag edge to resize —

Form Footer section —

Figure 5.15
Form Header and Form
Footer sections can be
added to the form.

3 **Place the mouse pointer on the bottom edge of the Form Header section (the top edge of the Detail section bar).**
The pointer should change to display a thick horizontal bar with a two-sided arrow crossbar (see Figure 5.16). This pointer shape indicates that you are about to resize this section.

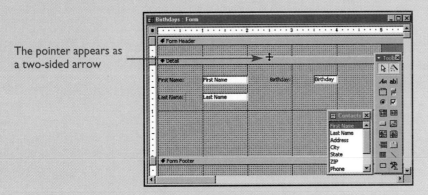

The pointer appears as
a two-sided arrow

Figure 5.16
The two-sided arrow
pointer indicates that
you are about to resize
the Form Header area.

4 **Drag down until the Form Header is about an inch tall.**
You can use the rulers along the left edge of the form's Design view to gauge the size of the section. Don't worry if the size isn't exact. Now that the header is a little bigger, you can add a label to the form.

5 **Click the Label button in the toolbox.**
The Label button has an uppercase and lowercase "A" on it. Remember that you can place your pointer on a button to see its name.

6 **Position the crosshairs of the pointer near the upper-left corner of the Form Header section. Drag to the right and down to draw a box. Make the box approximately 2 inches wide and 1/2 inch tall.**
The pointer should appear as a small crosshair with an "A" underneath while you are positioning it (see Figure 5.17). When you release the mouse button, you see a label box with the insertion point inside.

continues ▶

To Add a Form Header and Label   (continued)

Figure 5.17
The Label pointer is used to place and size the label box.

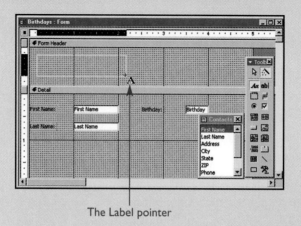

The Label pointer

> ❎ If you make the label box too small, you can always resize it. Click the box to select it. Then place the pointer on one of the selection handles and drag to resize.

7 Type Birthdays!
This is the text you want to include as the label. As you can see, the text is fairly small, but you can change it.

8 Click outside the text area to end the text-editing mode.

9 Click inside the box to select it.
Notice that the formatting toolbar displays the font and font size in the Font and Font Size drop-down lists. You can use these lists to change the font and the font size (see Figure 5.18).

Figure 5.18
You can change the font and font size of a label using the Formatting toolbar.

Font list box

Font Size list box

Selected label

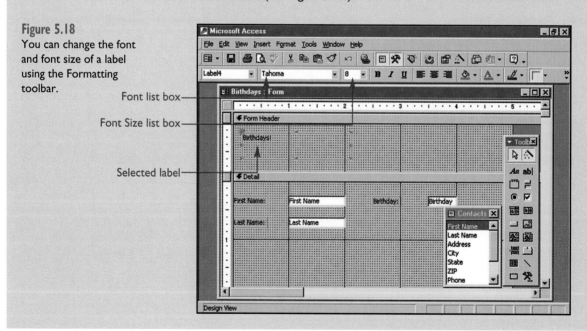

⑩ Click the down arrow next to the Font Size box. Click 24 (or the next largest size available on your system).
This changes the font in the label box to 24-point type. You don't have to change the actual font, but you can make the text bold.

[B] ⑪ Click the Bold button on the toolbar.
Access makes the text bold.

[💾] ⑫ Click the Save button on the toolbar.
The form is saved with the changes you have made.

⑬ Click the View button on the toolbar.
This switches you to Form view so that you can see the form you just created (see Figure 5.19).

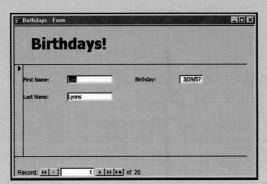

Figure 5.19
The Form view shows the results of your design changes.

⑭ Close the Birthdays form and then close the New Address List database.
In Project 6, "Creating and Printing Reports," you use a different database to create a report.

Printing Forms and Selected Records
The purpose for creating forms is to make it easy for users to input and read data onscreen. Should you need to print a form, you can view it first by clicking the Print Preview button. If you click the Print button, all records in the database will be printed in a continuous form. If you want to print one record per page, click the Page Break button in the Toolbox and drag the small Page Break symbol onto the form.

If you want to print a selected record, move to that record and select File, Print to see the print menu. Choose the Selected Record(s) option button on the Print menu. Choosing this option prints the current record.

If you have completed your session on the computer, exit Access and Windows before you turn it off. Otherwise, continue with the "Checking Concepts and Terms" section of this project.

Summary

This project focused on the use of the various form features built into Access. You learned how to create an AutoForm from a table and how to create a new form in Design view. You entered and edited information in a form and modified the form structure by adding fields, moving and resizing fields, and adding form headers and labels.

To enhance your ability to create effective forms, look for help on adding page headers and footers. Pay particular attention to the procedure for adding current information, such as the date, time, or page numbers to headers and footers.

Checking Concepts and Terms

True/False

For each of the following, check *T* or *F* to indicate whether the statement is true or false.

__T __F   **1.** AutoForm creates a form with all the fields in your table. [L1]

__T __F   **2.** When you use a form to enter data, that data is saved in the form. You also have to update the table. [L2]

__T __F   **3.** You must save a form if you want to use it again. [L3]

__T __F   **4.** You can have only one section in a form. [L4]

__T __F   **5.** To delete a field from a form in Form Design View, click once on the field to select it and then press (Del). [L5]

__T __F   **6.** By pressing (Ctrl)+(Alt) in Form view, you can use the mouse to make changes to the form without switching to Design view. [L5]

__T __F   **7.** If you accidentally close a form without saving it, you can simply click the Undo button to restore the form. [L3]

__T __F   **8.** In the toolbox of form Design view, the Label button has both an uppercase and a lowercase "A" on it. [L7]

__T __F   **9.** When a field text box is selected, its associated label is also selected. [L6]

__T __F   **10.** After you generate a form, you cannot change it. You must generate a new form in Design view. [L6]

Multiple Choice

Circle the letter of the correct answer for each of the following questions.

1. How do you create a new record using a form? [L2]
   a. Scroll to the last record and then edit it.
   b. Edit the first record displayed.
   c. Click the New Object button on the toolbar.
   d. Click the New Record button on the Navigation bar and enter data into the empty form.

2. Which key(s) can you use to move from field to field in a form? [L2]
   a. (Tab)
   b. (Shift)+(Tab)
   c. (→) or (←)
   d. all of the above

3. Which type of section includes the record information? [L4]
   a. Detail
   b. Page Header
   c. Page Footer
   d. Form Header

4. Which of the following is a way to select a field in Design view? [L5]
   a. Choose File, Select Field.
   b. Click it once.
   c. Point to it.
   d. Click the Select Field button on the toolbar.

5. What should the pointer look like to move a field? [L6]

   a. a hand

   b. a white cross

   c. a two-headed arrow

   d. a crosshair

6. Which of the following is not a part of a form? [L4]

   a. Form Header

   b. Page Footer

   c. Detail Area

   d. Format Area

7. To save data to the table after you have entered several records using a form, you must do which of the following? [L2]

   a. Choose <u>S</u>ave from the <u>F</u>ile menu.

   b. Choose <u>U</u>pdate from the <u>F</u>ile menu.

   c. Click the Save button on the toolbar.

   d. none of the above (because data is saved automatically)

8. Which of the following is a fast way to create a form based on the current table? [L1]

   a. Use the QuickForm.

   b. Use an AutoForm.

   c. Open a blank form and drag the fields onto it from the Field List window.

   d. Click NewForm on the Toolbox.

9. You can generate all the following by using the Form Wizard, except what? [L5]

   a. columnar forms

   b. charts

   c. pivot tables

   d. spreadsheets

10. How can you add the toolbox to the Design View window if the toolbox is not already present? [L4]

   a. Select Open <u>T</u>oolbox from the <u>T</u>ools menu.

   b. Choose <u>I</u>nsert, Toolbo<u>x</u> from the menu.

   c. Click the Toolbox button on the Form Design toolbar.

   d. Press ¶.

Screen ID

Label each element of the Access screen shown in Figure 5.20.

Figure 5.20

A. Label pointer

B. Toolbox

C. Field text box

D. Label button

E. Toolbox button

F. Font list box

G. Field list button

H. Field label

I. Font size list box

J. Field list

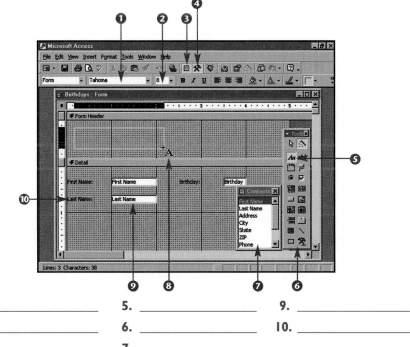

1. _____	5. _____	9. _____
2. _____	6. _____	10. _____
3. _____	7. _____	
4. _____	8. _____	

Discussion Questions

1. In Project 3, you answered a question about when you might use forms and when you might want to enter data directly into the table. Now that you have some experience with forms, has your opinion changed? Do you think you will use forms or tables (or some combination) for data entry into tables you anticipate using in the future?

2. If you have a table with a few fields (fewer than 10), what would be the advantage of using one of the form wizards to create a columnar or tabular form? Would there be any advantage to creating the form in Design view?

3. The tabular form looks a lot like the table Datasheet view. Can you think of any reason why you would ever want to create this type of form instead of simply entering the text into the table?

4. You can add form headers and footers and page headers and footers. When would you use page headers & footers? When would you use form headers and footers?

5. In what types of situations would you print out information in the form view? Can you think of any place you might have received a form view printout from a database?

Skill Drill

Skill Drill exercises reinforce project skills. Each skill reinforced is the same, or nearly the same, as a skill presented in the project. Each exercise includes a brief narrative introduction, followed by detailed instructions in a step-by-step format.

The database you will be using for these exercises contains two tables, one with information about short story books, and the other with information about the authors of these books.

1. Creating an AutoForm

Entering the data into the Book information table is not easy, because the fields scroll off the screen to the right. It would be a good idea to create a form to make data entry easier. You decide to use the AutoForm feature to create the new form.

To create an AutoForm, complete the following steps:

1. Find the AC1-0502 database file on your CD-ROM, send it to drive A:, remove the read-only status, and name it **Short Story Books**. Select and open the Book information table and look at the fields. Click the Close Window button to close the table.

2. Click the Forms object button and click New to create a new query.

3. Select the Book information table from the drop-down list.

4. Select the AutoForm: Columnar wizard, and click OK.

5. Close the Form, and save it as **Book information data input**.

2. Adding Data to the Form

You just found a short story book at the local used bookstore and can't wait to try out the new form you just created.

To add data to the form, complete the following steps:

1. Select the Book information data input form and click the Open button.

2. Click the New Record button on the toolbar.

3. Press ⏎Enter to skip the BookID field, which is entered automatically.

4. Enter **Rinehart, Mary Roberts** in the Author field.

5. Enter **Affinities and Other Stories** in the Title field.

6. Enter **1920** for the Year field, **282** for the Page field, and **Review of Reviews** for the Publisher field.

7. Close the form.

3. Editing Data in the Form

When looking more carefully at the book you just entered, you find that the publisher you listed was just a reprint house, and that the original publisher was George H. Doran. You also find out that the date of publication for *Auld Licht Idylls*, by J. M. Barrie (also the author of the children's classic *Peter Pan*) was written in 1888. You need to go into your form and change this information.

To edit data in the form, complete the following steps:

1. Select the Book information data input form and click the Open button.

2. Place the insertion point in the Title field, and click the Find button.

3. Type **Affinities** in the Find What drop-down list box, then select Start of Field from the Match drop-down list box.

4. Click Find Next. Move the Find and Replace dialog box, if necessary, and change Review of Reviews to **George H. Doran** in the Publisher field.

5. Place the insertion point in the Title field and type **Auld** in the Find What drop-down list box.

6. Click Find Next. Type **1888** in the Year field.

7. Close the Find and Replace dialog box, then close the Book information form.

4. Creating a New Form in Design View

Now that you've created a form for the Book information table, you decide that you also want one for the Author information table.

To create a new form in Design view, complete the following steps:

1. Click the Forms object button; click New to create a new form.

2. Select the Author information table from the drop-down list.

3. Select Design View, and click OK.

4. Maximize the Form window. Click the Toolbox and Field List buttons if they are not turned on. Select View, Ruler to turn the rulers on, if necessary.

5. Drag the Author field onto the form about 1/4" down and 3/4" to the right of the left edge.

6. Drag the DOB field to the 3" mark. Line it up to the right of the Author field.

7. Place the Birth City, State, and Birth Country fields under the Author field, about 1/4" apart. Use the hand pointer to adjust the field locations, if necessary.

8. Click the View button to see your form.

9. Close the form, and save it as **Author information data input**.

5. Moving and Resizing Fields

You decide that you don't like the look of the form. You'd like the last three fields to line up across the screen.

To move and resize fields, complete the following steps:

1. Open the Author information data input form in Design view.

2. Grab the State field, and move it just to the right of the Birth City field.

3. Grab the Birth Country field and move it to the right of the State field. Don't worry if the field overlaps the edge of the work area—the work area will widen automatically.

4. Click the View button to see your form.

6. Deleting Field Labels and Adding a Label

Your form still does not look right. It would look much better without the field names, and with a single label describing all three fields.

To delete field labels and add a label, complete the following steps:

1. Click the View button to return to Design view.

2. Click the Birth City field label. Handles should appear around the label on the left, but not around the field text box (which should have one large handle in the upper-left corner).

3. Click (Del) to remove the Birth City label.

4. Select and delete the field labels for the State and Birth Country fields.

5. Select all three fields in the second row and move them down about 1/2" and over to the left edge of the form. (Note: Click the Birth City field, then hold down (◆Shift) and click the State and Birth Country fields.)

7. `Place of Birth:` in the text box.

8. Click outside the text box; then click it again to select it. Click the Bold button. Resize the text box if necessary. Your Design window should look like Figure 5.21.

9. Click the View button, and click the Next Record button a few times to see how your form works. The fourth and fifth records should contain data in all five fields.

10. Close the form, and save your changes.

Figure 5.21
A single label replaces three field labels.

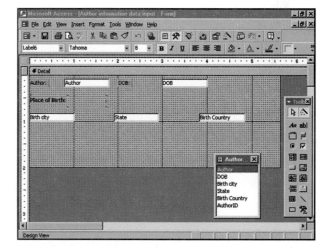

6. Click the Label button, and click and drag the crosshair pointer to place a text box above the three fields you just moved.

Challenge

Challenge exercises expand on or are somewhat related to skills presented in the lessons. Each exercise provides a brief narrative introduction followed by instructions in a numbered step or bulleted list format that are not as detailed as those in the Skill Drill section.

The database you will be using for the Challenge section is the same database of short story books and authors you used in the Skill Drill section. The Book information data input form has been modified. Before you start the Challenge exercises, spend a little time looking at the form in Form view; then look at it in Design view. Notice how it has been laid out and how some of the field labels have been deleted and replaced by other labels.

1. Adding the Date and Time to the Form Header

You have decided to make your Book information data input form more user-friendly. Because you expect to print single forms frequently, you'd also like to make the forms more informative. The first thing you want to do is to add the current date to the Form Header.

To add the date and time to a Form Header, complete the following steps:

1. Copy the AC1-0503 database file to drive A:, remove the read-only status, and rename it **Revised Short Story Books**.

2. Open the database and open the Book information data input form in Form view. Maximize the form window and examine the form layout.

3. Move to Design view and examine the layout of the form.

4. Use the Insert menu to place the date (in the 12/31/99 format) and the time (in the 11:59 PM format) in the form.

5. Click the View button. If the date and time are not in the upper-left corner of the Form Header, return to Design view and move them to that location.

6. Close the form, and save your changes.

2. Adding a Page Number to a Page Footer

You have added the date and time to the Form Header; now you want to keep track of the page numbers.

To add the page number to a Page Footer, complete the following steps:

1. Open the Book information data input form in Design view. Maximize the form window.

2. Scroll down until you can see the Form Footer area, if necessary.

3. Use the Insert menu to place the page number (in the Page N of M format).

4. Place the page number at the bottom of the page and center align it.

5. Notice that the program has added Page Header and Page Footer sections. The page number is in the Page Footer section.

6. Click the View button to look at the page number. Notice that the page number does not appear. Use your Help menu to find out why it does not show up here and what possible use this feature might be.

7. Close the form and save your changes.

3. Adding an Image to a Page Header

You have added the date and time to the Form Header and the page number to the Page Footer. Now you want to improve the appearance of your form. The first thing you want to do is to add a small graphic image to the Form Header.

To add an image to a Page Header, complete the following steps:

1. Open the Book information data input form in Design view. Maximize the form window.

2. Use the Help menu or online help to figure out how to add the **Books.wmf** image file included on your CD-ROM to your form.

3. Turn on the ruler, if necessary, and use it to help you resize the image to about 1/2" high.

4. Move the image to the top of the right side of the Form Header.

5. If necessary, click and drag the right edge of the image so it does not appear cut off.

6. Click the View button to see how the image looks on the form.

7. Close the form and save your changes.

4. Customizing the Look of the Form

You have added an image to the form. Now you would like to make some changes to the overall form design. You decide to try to change the background color of the Detail area and give the field labels and field text boxes a special effect.

To customize the look of a form, complete the following steps:

1. Open the Book information data input form in Design view. Maximize the form window.

2. Find the Fill/Back Color button and change the background color to a pale blue.

3. Select all of the field labels and field text boxes. (Hint: You can move the pointer to the vertical ruler near the top of the Detail area. It changes to a right arrow. Click and drag down below the last row of fields and release the mouse button. All of the field labels and field text boxes are selected.)

4. Use the right mouse button on any one of the selected field labels or field text boxes. Find the option that will allow you to customize these boxes, and select Sunken.

5. Click the View button to see how your changes look on the form. Your form should look like Figure 5.22.

6. Close the form, and save your changes.

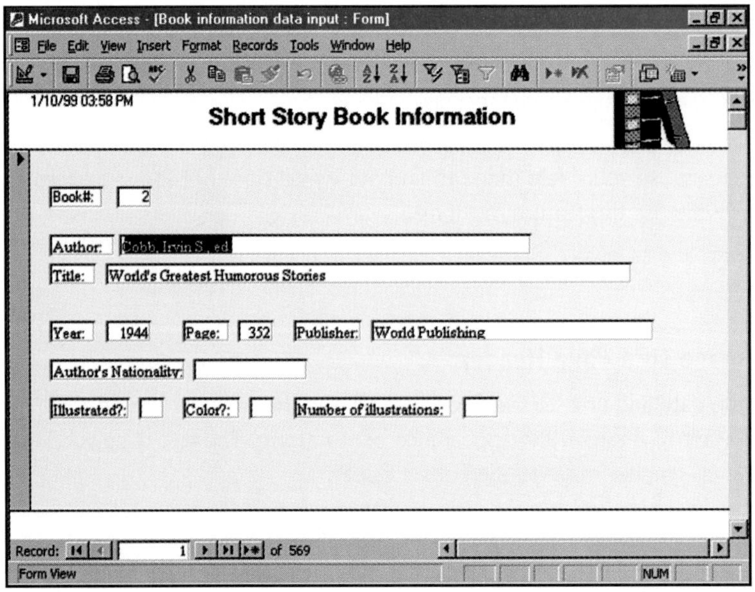

Figure 5.22
The background color and the look of the labels and text boxes have been changed.

5. Inserting a Page Break and Printing a Form

The forms will print continuously if you don't add an artificial page break in form Design view.

To insert a page break and print a form, complete the following steps:

1. Open the Book information data input form in Design view. Maximize the form window.
2. Find and click the Page Break button on the Toolbox.
3. Move the new pointer and click about 1/4" under the last row of fields.
4. Click the View button to move to Form view.
5. Choose File, Print from the menu.
6. Make sure the correct printer is selected and the printer is turned on.
7. Choose the Selected Record(s) option to print only the current record; then click OK.
8. Close the form, and save your changes.

6. Copying a Form and Basing It on a Query

Your collection includes books by a number of different publishers, but you specialize in books published by Scribner's. You would like to create a query that would show just Scribner's books, then use the new query as the source for a copy of the form on which you have been working.

To copy a form and base it on a query, complete the following steps:

1. Create a query in Design view. Add all of the fields from the Book information table. Use `Scribner's` as the Criteria in the Publisher field, then sort on Author and Title. Save the query as `Scribner's Books`.
2. Find and click the Page Break button on the Toolbox, and add a page break at the bottom of the form.
3. Move to the Forms window. Use the Access help resources to find out how to make a copy of the Book information data input form and paste it as `Scribner's information`.
4. Switch to the Scribner's information Design view. Use the Access help resources to view the Properties box for the entire form. (Hint: If you want to use the shortcut menu, the ruler must be turned on. If you want to use the menus, the whole form must be selected.)
5. Change the Record Source from the Book information table to the Scribner's Books query.
6. Switch to Form view, and scroll through a few records to make sure the only books shown are the ones published by Scribner's.
7. Close the form and save your changes.

Discovery Zone

Discovery Zone exercises help you gain advanced knowledge of project topics and application of skills. These exercises focus on enhancing your problem-solving skills. Numbered steps are not provided, but you are given hints, reminders, screen shots, and references to help you reach your goal for each exercise.

1. Adding a Drop-Down List to a Field in a Form

In many cases, you will have fields in tables that have a limited number of possible entries. An example would be a field that asks for the name of a state or a department in a company. Access has a feature that enables you to create a drop-down menu that you can use to choose from a list of choices. These drop-down menus are called Combo boxes.

Goal: Create a Combo box in the Publisher field that enables you to select from a list of the most common publishers.

Use the AC1-0504 file to create a new database called **Short Story Books with a Combo Box** on your disk. Use help from your computer or online to understand how combo boxes are set up. Then go to the Book information data input Form Design view and change the Publisher field text box to a combo box. Include the following publishers in the list:

```
Century
Colliers
Dodd, Mead
Grosset & Dunlap
Harpers
Scribner's
```

Hint #1: A shortcut menu option will help determine the type of field text box.

Hint #2: The Properties box for the Publisher field text box will be used to determine where the information for the combo box comes from. You can create a table to use as the source, or you can type the Value List in another box in the Properties box.

Hint #3: A Value List is usually best when you are working with only a few items, whereas a table is best for a larger number of items.

Your combo box should look like Figure 5.23.

Figure 5.23
A combo box has been added to the form.

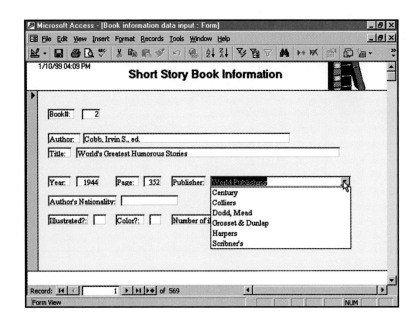

[?] 2. Using Multiple Pages with Tabs on a Form

When there are a large number of fields in a table, or if the table can be easily divided into more than one category, Access includes a feature that enables you to divide a form into pages. These pages have tabs at the top, and all you have to do to move between pages is to click on a tab.

Goal: Create two tabbed pages on a form based on a table showing the number of cars and trucks by location in the United States.

Use the AC1-0505 file to create a new database called **US Motor Vehicle Statistics** on your disk. Use help from your computer or online to understand how Tab Control works. Create the new form in Design view, and save it as **US Cars and Trucks**. Your form should have the following:

- Two pages, with the tabs labeled **Cars** and **Trucks**.
- The Location, Privately Owned Cars, and Publicly Owned Cars fields on the Cars tab.
- The Location, Privately Owned Trucks, and Publicly Owned Trucks fields on the Trucks tab.
- Identical field labels for both occurrences of the Location field (Hint: You will need to change the field name on one of them.)

    Hint #1: This is much easier than it sounds! Look in the toolbox to get started.

    Hint #2: Most of your time will be spent resizing the field labels and the field text boxes and lining them up.

Your tabbed form should look like Figure 5.24.

Figure 5.24
The US Cars and Trucks
form now has two tabs.

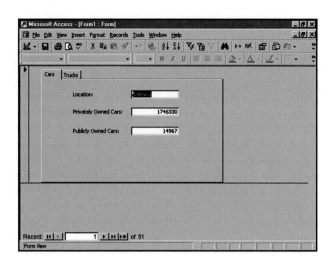

Creating and Printing Reports

Objectives

In this project, you learn how to

- ➤ **Print the Data in a Table**
- ➤ **Create a Report Using the Report Wizards**
- ➤ **Print and Rename a Report**
- ➤ **Modify a Report Design**
- ➤ **Save a Report with a New Name**
- ➤ **Add Labels to Reports**

Key terms introduced in this project include

- ■ AutoReport
- ■ expression
- ■ landscape orientation
- ■ portrait orientation
- ■ report
- ■ section

Why Would I Do This?

The information in your database can be displayed in several ways. You can print a form or print copies of tables or queries. These printouts are limited in format and flexibility. To produce flexible printouts from tables or queries, you need to learn how to use **reports**. Reports are database objects that are designed to print and summarize selected fields. They are divided into **sections** that can contain controls, labels, formulas, and even images. In this project, you learn the fundamental tasks involved in creating, modifying, saving, and printing a simple report.

Before you create a report, think about why you need the printed data. Do you want to check the entries to make sure they are correct? Do you need an address list or phone list? Do you need to pass the information along to someone else? If so, what information does that person need and in what order? If you spend a few moments determining the purpose of the report, you can design one that truly meets your needs.

Access provides many tools for creating a report—you can create an **AutoReport**, use the Report Wizards to create other common report types (single-column report, mailing labels, and so on), or create a blank report that you add information to later. You can also change the layout of an existing report design and add report labels to help make the report more self-explanatory. This project shows you how to use the report tools included with Access.

When you have completed this project, you will have created a document that looks like this:

The report name is
used at the report title

Figure 6.1
The Report Wizard
enables you to create
a report quickly.

The columnar report was
created using a wizard

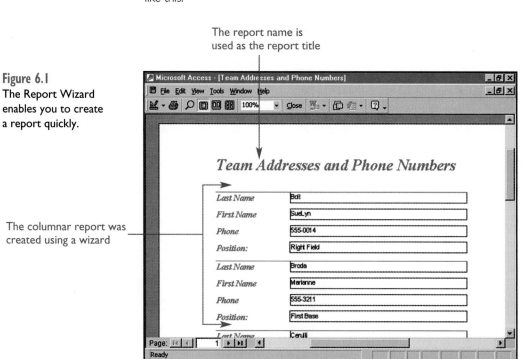

Lesson 1: Printing the Table Data

If all you need is a printout of the entire table or query, it is faster to simply print the table without using a report. For example, you may want to print the data in a table so that you can check the accuracy of the records. In this case, you don't have to create a report.

To Print the Table Data

1 **Launch Access. Click OK to open an existing file.**
Make sure you have a disk in drive A:.

2 **Find the ACI-0601 file on your CD-ROM, right-click on it, and send it to the floppy drive. Move to drive A:, remove the read-only status, and rename the file** Softball Team. **Open the new database.**
The Softball Team database includes a table of team members and a table of game information. After you open the Softball Team database, you should see the two tables displayed in the Tables list. In this project, you work with the Team table.

3 **Click the Open button to open the Team table. Maximize the Table window.**
This table is opened in Datasheet view. You may want to scroll through the table to see how it is set up. The table includes fields for the first and last name of each player, along with his or her position, phone number, address, and dues. You can print this information, but before you print, preview the printout so that you have some idea of what the printed list will look like.

4 **Click the Print Preview button.**
A preview of the printed list is displayed (see Figure 6.2). The structure of the printout is fairly simple; each record is displayed as a row in a grid. The navigation button that enables you to scroll to the next page is active, which indicates that the printout will be more than one page. This means that all of the table columns will not fit on one page width when the report is printed.

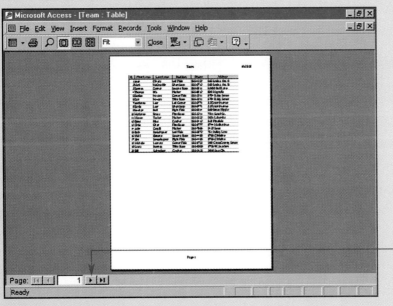

Figure 6.2
The table may be previewed before printing.

An active Next Page button means there is at least one more page

continues ▶

To Print the Table Data (continued)

▶ **5** **Click the Next Page button, which is the same as the Next Record button in a form or table.**

This step displays the second page of the printout, which shows the remaining column. This presents a problem with printing all the fields in the table. If the table is too wide by just a few columns, you can still get a usable printout by changing the orientation of the page so that Access prints across the long edge of the page, rather than down the page. Using this *landscape orientation*, you can fit more columns across the page.

6 **Choose File, Page Setup from the menu.**

The Page Setup dialog box lists options for setting margins and page layouts.

7 **Make sure the margins are all 1"; then click the Page tab to display the page orientation (see Figure 6.3).**

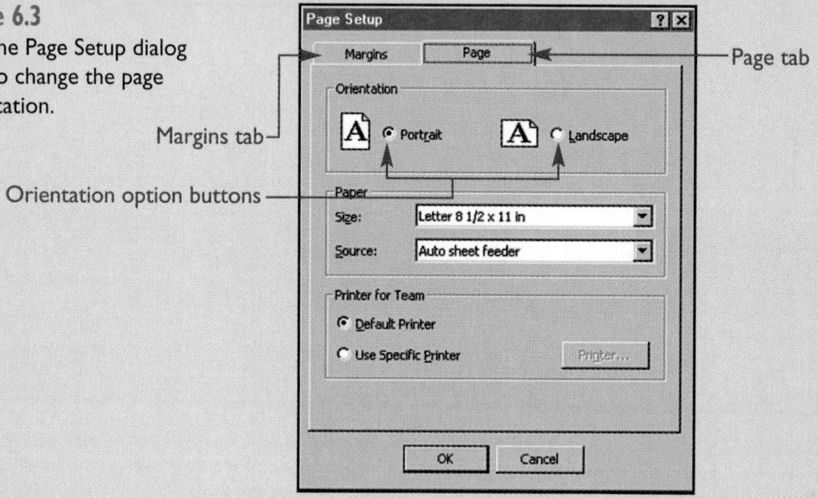

Figure 6.3
Use the Page Setup dialog box to change the page orientation.

8 **In the Orientation area, click the Landscape option button and then click OK.**

This step changes the orientation of the page to landscape, which is the horizontal orientation of a page. The standard vertical positioning of a page is called *portrait orientation*. Now, when you print the report, all the columns fit on a single page.

9 **From the File menu, choose Print.**

The Print dialog box is displayed (Figure 6.4). Here you can control which pages are printed, how many copies are printed, and select other options. The default settings are already appropriate for this one-page printout.

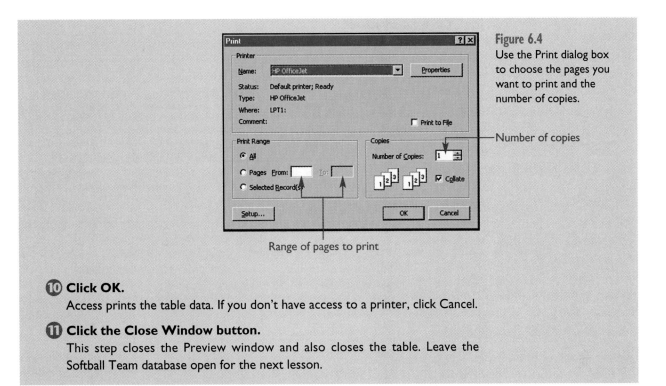

Figure 6.4
Use the Print dialog box to choose the pages you want to print and the number of copies.

Number of copies

Range of pages to print

 Click OK.
Access prints the table data. If you don't have access to a printer, click Cancel.

 Click the Close Window button.
This step closes the Preview window and also closes the table. Leave the Softball Team database open for the next lesson.

Previewing the Printout
You don't have to preview the printout, but previewing is a good idea. You can print directly from Datasheet view. Simply click the Print button on the toolbar or open the File menu and choose the Print command. Access then prints the table. The keyboard shortcut for the Print command is Ctrl+P.

Fitting Data on the Page
If the data doesn't quite fit on the page, there are several things you can do to make them fit. You can reduce the width of the columns. If this cuts off some of the data, you can reduce the font size using Format, Font from the menu.

Lesson 2: Creating a Report Using the Report Wizards

Simple table printouts are limited in what they can do. Access provides several reporting options to make it easy to create more sophisticated reports. Using the New Report feature, you can create the reports described in Table 6.1.

Table 6.1 Common Report Creation Options

Type of New Report	Description
Design View	Opens a design window where you can add fields or text. This option does not use the wizards.
Report Wizard	Guides you through the process of creating a report. The Report Wizard has several options for the layout and grouping of data.

continues ▶

Table 6.1   continued

Type of New Report	Description
AutoReport: Columnar	Places all the fields in a table in a single-column report.
AutoReport: Tabular	Places all the fields in the table in a row-and-column format similar to the layout of a spreadsheet.
Chart Wizard	Guides you through the process of selecting fields that you want to summarize in a graphical form. The Chart Wizard enables you to choose from several chart types, such as pie, line, and bar.
Label Wizard	Enables you to set up and print mailing labels in more than 100 different label styles.

A report wizard leads you step by step through the process of creating a report, asking you which fields to include in the report, which sort order to use, what title to print, and so on. After you make your selections, the wizard creates the report.

In this lesson, you create a columnar report for your Team table in the Softball Team database. This report works well as an address list.

To Create a Report Using the Report Wizards

1 **Click the Report object button.**

No reports are listed, because you haven't created any at this point (see Figure 6.5).

Figure 6.5
No reports are listed in the Report object window.

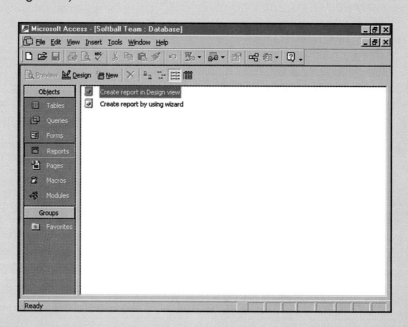

2 **Click the New button.**

The New Report dialog box is displayed (see Figure 6.6). You will need to select the method of creating the report and the table or query on which you want to base the report. This is exactly the same procedure you used to create a form.

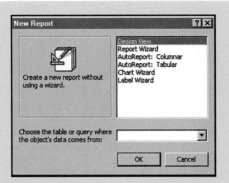

Figure 6.6
You choose the method you want to use to create a new report and the table or query on which to base the report.

③ Select Report Wizard and choose the Team table as a source. Click OK.

The first Report Wizard dialog box is displayed.

④ In the Available Fields list, click the First Name field. Then click the Add button.

The Wizard removes the field from the Available Fields list and places the field in the Selected Fields list (see Figure 6.7). The fields will appear in the report in the order you select them. The First Name field, for example, will be the first field listed in the current report.

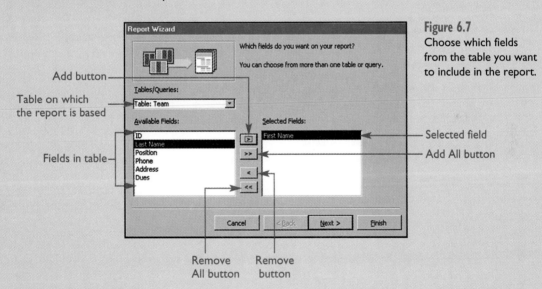

Figure 6.7
Choose which fields from the table you want to include in the report.

⑤ Highlight and add the Last Name, Address, and Phone fields to the Selected Fields list.

Your report now includes four fields. They are all the fields you want to include for this lesson.

⑥ Click the Next button.

The second Report Wizard dialog box is displayed. You could use this step to group similar records together, such as grouping the team by position played. In this example, however, we have not included any fields that need to be listed together as a group.

continues ▶

To Create a Report Using the Report Wizards   (continued)

7 **Click Next again.**
The third Report Wizard dialog box enables you to sort the data on one or more fields.

8 **Click the down arrow next to the first sort selection to reveal the available fields. Select Last Name to sort on. Click Next.**
The fourth Report Wizard dialog box enables you to select the layout, orientation, and fit (see Figure 6.8).

Figure 6.8
Select the layout and orientation options.

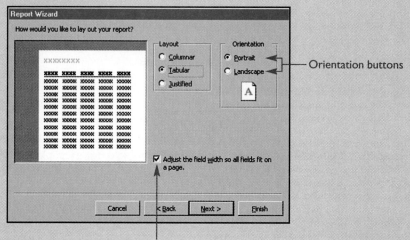

Orientation buttons

Fit-to-page check box

9 **Select a Columnar layout, Portrait orientation, and the checkbox labeled Adjust the field width so all fields fit on a page. Click the Next button.**
The fifth Report Wizard is displayed. In this dialog box, you select a report style.

10 **Select the Corporate style report, and click the Next button.**
The final Report Wizard dialog box is displayed. In this screen, you enter the title for the report. By default, the Wizard uses the table name as the title, unless you change it.

> ❌ If you make a mistake or change your mind about an option anywhere in the Wizard, you can back up by clicking the Back button in the Wizard dialog box.

11 **Type Team Addresses and Phone Numbers to change the title of the report, then click the Finish button.**
A preview of the report is displayed (see Figure 6.9) showing the title you entered. You can print, zoom, and save the report, as you learn in the next lesson. Keep the report open for the next lesson, where you print and rename a report.

The report name is used as the default label

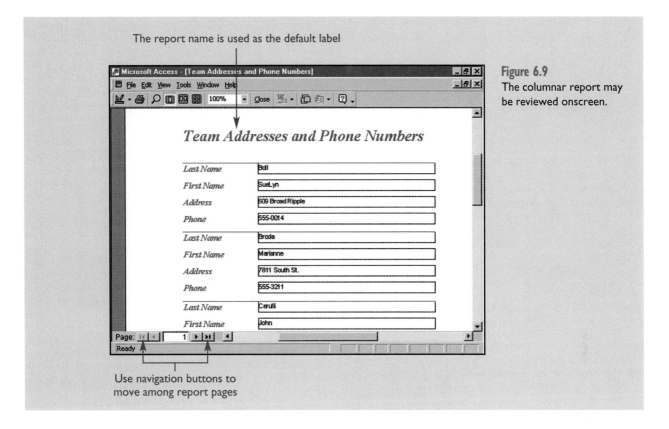

Figure 6.9
The columnar report may
be reviewed onscreen.

Use navigation buttons to
move among report pages

 Using AutoReport Wizard
In Project 5, "Creating and Using Forms," you used the Form Wizard to create
an AutoForm quickly. You can also create an *AutoReport* using the Report
Wizards. An AutoReport includes all the fields from the table in the report.
The report is in either a one-column or tabular format with as many records on
the page as possible. The report also includes a header with the table name and
current date and a footer with the page number. To create this type of report
from the Reports page, choose one of the two AutoReport options in the New
Report dialog box.

Lesson 3: Printing and Renaming a Report

The next step is to print your report. However, before you print, it's always a good idea
to preview the report. In the Print Preview mode, you can use the navigation buttons to
check for unexpected additional pages, check the font, the font size, and the actual data in
the report. Then, if you click the Zoom button on the toolbar, you can view the entire
report to determine how the printed report will look on the page. If you do not like how
the report is set up, you can make changes before you print it. This strategy can save you
some time and paper.

You can also rename a report in the database window to ensure that it's not confused
with other database objects with the same name.

To Print and Rename a Report

1 **With the Preview window still active, click the pointer anywhere on the report.**

Access displays a full-page view of the report, so that you can see the entire page (see Figure 6.10).

Figure 6.10
The full-page view may be used to preview the report.

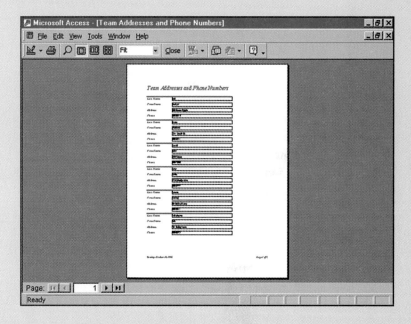

2 **Click on the report again.**

Access zooms in so that you can read the text of the report. It will center on the spot you clicked, so you may need to use the scrollbars to get back to the section you want to see. Now you are ready to print.

3 **Click the Print button on the toolbar.**

Access prints the report. If you do not have access to a printer, skip this step.

> **X** This report is three pages long. If you are restricted to printing one page, select File, Print from the menu, then choose to print from pages 1 to 1 in the Print Range section.

4 **Click the Close button on the toolbar to close the Preview window.**

The program returns to the report Design view.

5 **Click the Close button to close the report.**

The new report is shown in the database window under the Reports list. You may decide that the name you gave the report could be improved.

6 **Right-click on the Team Addresses and Phone Numbers report, and select Rename from the shortcut menu.**

The name changes to edit mode, in which it can be changed.

7 **Type the name Team Roster.**

8 **Press ⏎Enter or click outside the name box to save the change.**

The report name is now Team Roster. Keep the database open for the next lesson, where you modify a report design.

Lesson 4: Modifying a Report Design

Once you have created a report, you may decide that you want to modify it. The finished report may not be exactly what you intended. Rather than start over with a wizard or a blank form, you can modify the report design so that the report includes the information you want.

When you look through the report in Design view, you will notice some unusual things in the Page Footer. These are **expressions**, which are predefined formulas that perform calculations, display built-in functions, or set limits.

Suppose that you need a phone list in addition to the team roster. You can modify the Roster report to create this new report. Start by deleting the Address field, which you don't need in your phone list. Then add the position field so you have a list that includes the name, phone number, and position played by each member of the team.

To Modify a Report Design

1 **Select the Team Roster report and open it in Design view.**
The report is displayed in Design view (see Figure 6.11). This view is similar to the Design view you used when you created a form. The same tools are available onscreen. You can use the ruler to place items on the report, the toolbox to add controls, and the field list to add fields.

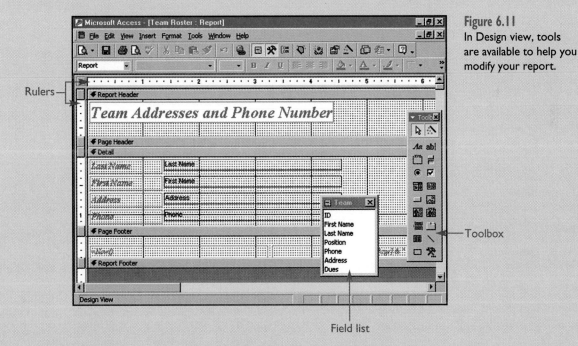

Rulers —

— Toolbox

Field list

Figure 6.11
In Design view, tools are available to help you modify your report.

Formatting Report Titles Using Size to Fit
You may have noticed that the title of the report in the design view appears to be truncated, whereas it is fully displayed in the print preview. When the title was entered, the program automatically applied the size to fit the format for this label. You can test this by selecting the title label and choosing F̲ormat, S̲ize, To F̲it from the menu. The size of the label box remains the same, because it is large enough to enable the title to print.

continues ▶

To Modify a Report Design   (continued)

② Click the scroll arrows to scroll through the report and see how it is structured.

Notice that the report includes a Page Footer with the date and page number. The expression **=NOW()** inserts the current date (see Figure 6.12). An expression is similar to a function in spreadsheet software. Access provides many expressions that you can include in your report.

The expression **="Page" & [Page] & "Of" & [Pages]** on the right side of the Page Footer prints the current page and the total number of pages. Remember that you placed this expression in the form in Project 5.

The Detail section includes four fields: First Name, Last Name, Address, and Phone.

Figure 6.12
Expressions add calculations or functions to a report.

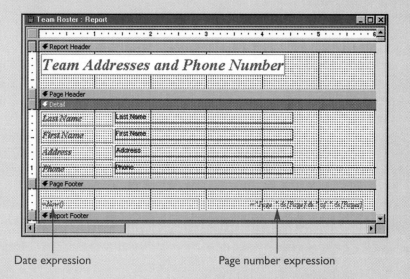

Date expression   Page number expression

③ Maximize the window and click the Address field text box.

The field label is on the left, and the field text box is on the right. If you click on the Address field text box, handles will appear at the sides and corners of the field text box and in the upper left corner of the field label box.

④ Press Del.

Access removes the field and its label from the report. Now you have a gap between two of the fields. To fix this gap, you can move the Phone field up.

⑤ Click the Phone field to select it.

Position the pointer on the field so that it turns into an open hand.

⑥ Drag the Phone field so that it is directly under the First Name field.

The Phone field is now closer to First Name. Now you will add the position field to the report.

⑦ In the field list box, click the Position field and drag it to the detail section of the report, directly below the Phone field text box, and release the mouse.

The pointer turns into a small field box when you are dragging the field onto the report. As soon as you release the mouse, the field text box is positioned under the Phone text box and the field label for the new field is added to the left of the field. (see Figure 6.13). Next, you need to format the new field to match the ones on the report.

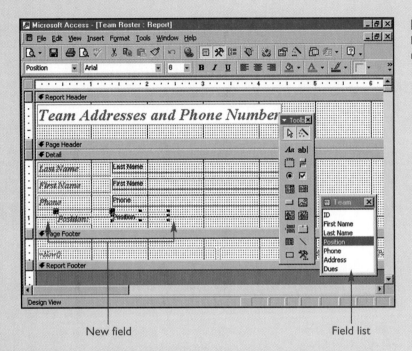

Figure 6.13
Fields may be added to a report using the field list.

New field   Field list

⑧ **Point to the Phone field text box above the new Position text box. Hold down ⬆Shift) and click. The Phone and Position boxes should both be selected.**

⑨ **Choose Format, Size, To Widest to match the length of the two boxes.**

⑩ **Choose Format, Size, To Tallest to match the height of the two boxes.**

⑪ **Choose Format, Align, Left to match the alignment of the two boxes.**

⑫ **Click in an unused space in the Detail area to deselect the boxes.**

⑬ **Select the field label box for Position. Grab the center handle on the left edge of the field label box and drag to the left until it is lined up with the left edge of the Phone field label box.**

⑭ **Click the Print Preview button on the toolbar.**
The new field should now match the other boxes in size and alignment. However the other field text boxes have a border. Next you add the border to the Position text box.

⑮ **Click the View button to return to Design view, then click the Position field text box to select it.**

⑯ **Click the down arrow to the right of the Line/Border Width button on the Formatting toolbar (see Figure 6.14).**

continues ▶

To Modify a Report Design   (continued)

Line/Border
Width Option #1

Down arrow on
Line/Border button

Figure 6.14
The Line/Border Width
button is used to add a
border or to change the
color of a border to a
selected control.

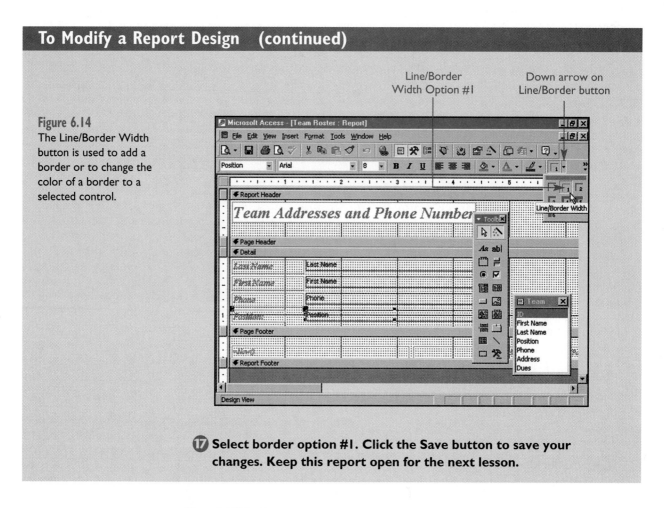

 Select border option #1. Click the Save button to save your changes. Keep this report open for the next lesson.

Modifying Wizard Reports
The Report Wizards are used to give you all of the necessary elements of a report and to place these elements in their proper locations. The wizards will save you time, but will seldom provide finished reports. You will almost always need to modify field lengths, add or format labels, modify the spacing between fields, and change locations of some of the elements. If you are asked to create a report using a wizard, make sure you use the Print Preview feature to scan through the data and look for fields that may have been cut off and need to be modified.

Lesson 5: Saving the Report with a New Name

As you modify a report, you may decide that you want to keep the original report as well as your modified version. If this is the case, you can save the modified report with a new name. Doing so enables you to use both reports.

In addition to saving the report with a new name, you should change the Report Header so that it reflects the purpose of the new report.

To Save the Report with a New Name

1 **With the Team Roster report still on-screen, choose File, Save As from the menu.**
The Save As dialog box is displayed with the original name listed (see Figure 6.15).

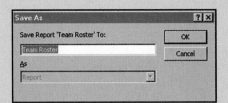

Figure 6.15
When you choose Save As/Export, Access displays the original name in the report name box.

2 **Type Phone List; then click OK.**
The report is saved with a new name.

3 **Click the label box in the Report Header section.**
Here, you want to replace the existing text with a more descriptive title.

4 **Drag across the existing text to select it; then type Phone List.**
The new text replaces the selected text.

 5 **Click the Save button**
This step saves your changes to the Phone List report by writing over the report with that name. Keep the Phone List report open and continue to the next lesson, where you add labels to a report.

(i) **Another Way to Copy a Report**
You can also create a duplicate report from the database window. With the Reports tab selected, right-click on the report name and select Copy from the shortcut menu. Right-click again in an open area of the window and select Paste from the shortcut menu. Give the duplicate report a new name when prompted.

Lesson 6: Adding Labels to Reports

When you create a report using a wizard, the labels tend to be short and non-descriptive. Once you have modified the report, as you did in Lesson 4, you will often find that additional labels are necessary to explain exactly what is on the report. Access gives you an easy way to add labels to either the Report Header or the Page Header. Labels added to the Report Header will show up on the first page of the report, whereas labels added to the Page Header area will appear on the top of every page. In this lesson, you add the team name to the Page Header area.

To Add Labels

1 **With the Phone List report open in Design view, point to the top edge of the Detail section divider. When the mouse pointer changes to a two-headed arrow, click and drag down to make the Page Header area about 1/2" high.**
You will use this space to place the new text label.

2 **Click the Label button in the Toolbox.**
When you move the pointer over an open area of the design window, the pointer turns into a large "A" with a crosshair attached.

3 **Click at the upper left corner in the Page Header section and drag down and to the right until you have a text box about 2" wide and 1/4" high.**
This label box is where you enter your text (see Figure 6.16).

Figure 6.16
The Label button in the Toolbox enables you to add new labels.

Label box

4 **Type The Oakville Tigers in the label box.**
If the text is too long for the box you created, you can select the box and resize it to fit.

5 **Click in an open area of the Page Header.**
This will turn off the text edit.

6 **Click the Print Preview button.**
The original title and the new title you just added are displayed at the top of the report (see Figure 6.17).

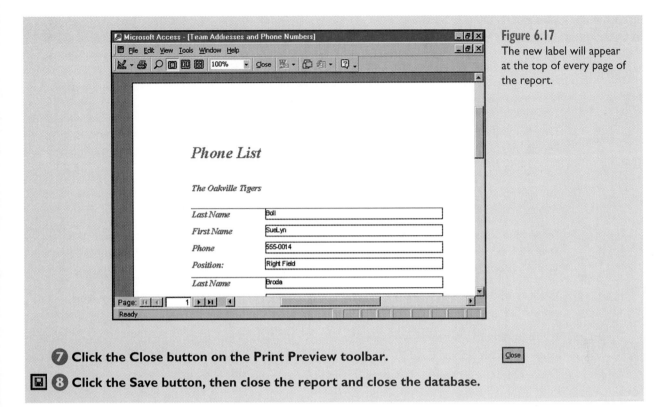

Figure 6.17
The new label will appear at the top of every page of the report.

7 Click the Close button on the Print Preview toolbar.

 8 Click the Save button, then close the report and close the database.

Where Header and Footer Labels Appear
Remember, labels that are placed in the Report Header area will only appear on the first page, and labels that are placed in the Report Footer area will only appear on the last page of the report. Labels added to the Page Header and Page Footer areas will appear on every page of the report.

If you have completed your session on the computer, exit Access and Windows before you turn off the computer. Otherwise, continue with the "Checking Concepts and Terms" section of this project.

Summary

The main output component of Access is the report. Although you can print a table, as you did in this project, reports are designed to be printed for presenting information to others. In this project, you created a report using the Report Wizard. You printed the report and renamed it after it had been created. You then learned some of the techniques that can be used to modify a report, including how to add and resize fields. After modifying a report, you saved it with a new name using the Save as command. Finally, you used the label tool to add a label to the report.

Several different report styles and options can be used, as you noticed when you used the wizard. To expand your knowledge, create a report and explore the different options that are displayed in the wizard to see what alternatives are offered. Use Help and read the topic, "Reports: What they are and how they work." Also review the topic, "Print a report." Continue with the exercises at the end of this project to practice creating and modifying reports.

Checking Concepts and Terms

True/False

For each of the following, check *T* or *F* to indicate whether the statement is true or false.

__T __F **1.** To print table data, you have to use a Report Wizard. You can't just print directly from the table. [L1]

__T __F **2.** You can modify the report layout in Print Preview mode. [L4]

__T __F **3.** To rename a report in the database window, click once on the report name and type the new name. [L3]

__T __F **4.** You cannot add new fields to an existing report. [L4]

__T __F **5.** To add a label to a report, you use the Label tool in the Toolbox. [L6]

__T __F **6.** When you drag a field name into a report, the mouse pointer turns into a small field box. [L4]

__T __F **7.** To save a report with a new name, select Save As from the File menu. [L5]

__T __F **8.** If you delete a field text box, its label box will be deleted also. [L4]

__T __F **9.** The expression [#Pages] in the footer will insert page numbers in the Page x of y format in your report. [L4]

__T __F **10.** If the data in a report is too wide to fit in Portrait orientation, it may fit in Landscape orientation. [L3]

Multiple Choice

Circle the letter of the correct answer for each of the following questions.

1. Which of the following choices is not one of the selections when you select New from the Reports window? [L2]

a. Report Wizard

b. Double-column

c. AutoReport: Tabular

d. AutoReport: Columnar

2. To change the orientation of the report, which command do you use under the File menu? [L1]

a. Print Setup

b. Print Orientation

c. Page Setup

d. Printer Setup

3. If you make a mistake and want to go to the previous screen in a Wizard, which button do you use? [L2]

a. Next

b. Back

c. Previous

d. Go Back

4. Which report design tool helps you precisely position controls on the report? [L4]

a. the toolbox

b. the toolbar

c. the field list

d. the ruler

5. How do you delete a control from a report? [L4]

a. Click it and press Del.

b. Drag it off the report.

c. Double-click it and press Del.

d. Press +Backspace.

6. If you have entered all the information you need on the Report Wizard, you can complete the process by selecting which button? [L2]

a. Finish

b. Complete

c. Done

d. OK

7. To make a group of text boxes the same dimensions from top to bottom, select Format, Size, then which command? [L4]

　a. Tallest

　b. Highest

　c. Height, Tallest

　d. Largest

8. In Print Preview, what do you click to switch between a full-page view and a close-up view of the report? [L3]

　a. the PageUp button

　b. anywhere on the report

　c. the View button

　d. the Full Page button

9. An AutoReport includes which of the following? [L2]

　a. all non-automatic fields in the table

　b. all fields in the database

　c. the fields you designate in the third dialog box

　d. all fields in the source table

10. Finished reports include all the following except what? [Intro]

　a. labels

　b. find buttons

　c. sections

　d. controls

Screen ID

Label each element of the Access screen shown in Figure 6.18.

Figure 6.18

A. Expression

B. Label button

C. Field label

D. Ruler

E. Field list box

F. Print Preview button

G. Field List button

H. Toolbox button

I. Field text box

J. Label

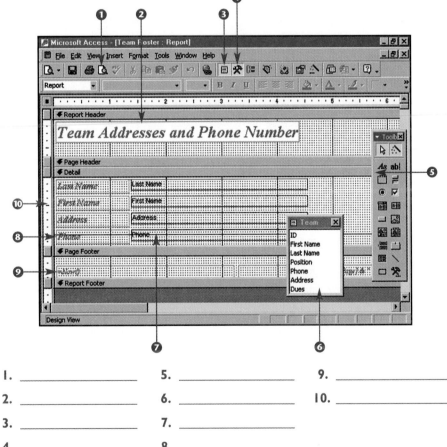

1. _____   5. _____   9. _____

2. _____   6. _____   10. _____

3. _____   7. _____

4. _____   8. _____

Discussion Questions

1. Why do companies produce reports? What are some of the goals or purposes of reports that are created from databases?

2. In databases that you use, what reports are produced? How are they organized? How are they sorted?

3. What formatting has been applied to reports you use that make them easier to read and understand? What techniques have you seen in Access reports that are comparable to the formatting in the reports you use?

4. If you were to redesign a report that you currently receive, how would you organize the information? Think about bank statements, utility bills, and other bills you receive. These statements are reports to customers.

5. Look for an example of a report that you think is well done and share it with class members, pointing out what makes this easy to use.

Skill Drill

Skill Drill exercises reinforce project skills. Each skill reinforced is the same, or nearly the same, as a skill presented in the project. Each exercise includes a brief narrative introduction, followed by detailed instructions in a step-by-step format.

The database you will be using for these exercises contains tornado data for the state of Arizona. These records cover a 45-year time span, and include all of the confirmed sightings during that period. The records are an abbreviated form of records produced by the National Oceanic and Atmospheric Administration (NOAA). The fields included in this sample table include the year, date, time of day, number of people killed, number of people injured, a damage scale, the county, and the F-scale (a measure of tornado intensity). Many of the fields are blank because there were no casualties or damage, or because the F-scale was not recorded.

1. Printing Data from a Table

You just want a quick printout of the tornadoes in Arizona over the past 45 years. The layout is not important, and because there are not a lot of fields, you decide to print out the information directly from the table.

To print data from a table, complete the following steps:

1. Find the AC1-0602 database file on your CD-ROM, send it to drive A:, remove the read-only status, and name it **Arizona Tornadoes**. Select and open the Arizona Tornadoes table, and examine the fields. Notice that the records are displayed in chronological order.

2. Click the Print Preview button to make sure the fields will fit across the page in portrait orientation.

3. Click the View button to return to Datasheet view.

4. Select File, Print from the menu.

5. Print only the second page.

6. Close the table.

2. Creating a Report Using the Report Wizard

Printing directly from the table allowed you to scan the data quickly but did not give you any real control over the final product. You decide to use the Report Wizard to build a more useful, attractive report.

To create a report using the report wizard, complete the following steps:

1. Click the Reports object button.
2. Click the New button.
3. Select the Arizona Tornadoes table, and choose the Report Wizard.
4. Select all of the fields.
5. Group on the County field.
6. Sort on the Year field first. Sort on the Date field second.
7. Choose the Block layout.
8. Select the Soft Gray style.
9. Maximize the print preview window, and scroll down to look at your new report. Leave the report open for the next exercise.

3. Printing a Report

Reports are created with one thing in mind—publishing, to either paper or the Web. You decide you would like to see how your report looks on paper.

To print a report, complete the following steps:

1. Click on the preview window to see the whole page. Notice that the report is not centered.
2. Select File, Page Setup from the menu.
3. Change the Left margin to 1.25" and the Right margin to 0.75".
4. Select File, Print from the menu.
5. Print only page 1. Leave the report open for use in the next exercise.

4. Modifying a Report

The form you created using the wizard looks pretty good, but the title is not terribly descriptive. You decide to add the period of time covered by the report.

To modify a report, complete the following steps:

1. Click the View button to move to the report Design view.
2. Click once on the title in the Report Header to select it.
3. Grab the center handle on the right edge of the title and drag it to the 6" mark. (If your rulers are not turned on, choose View, Ruler from the menu.)
4. Modify the title so that it reads `Arizona Tornadoes, 1951-1995`.
5. Click the View button to see your changes.
6. Close the report and save your changes.

5. Changing Character Formatting in a Report

The report is looking better and better, but a few more changes would make it really easy to read. First, the text in the Detail area is a little small, and second, the names of the counties could be emphasized a little more.

To change character formatting in a report, complete the following steps:

1. Open the Arizona Tornadoes, report in Design view.
2. Move the pointer to the ruler to the left of the Detail area until it changes to an arrow pointing right.
3. Click once to select all of the fields in the detail section.
4. Click the Font Size list box, and change the font size from 11 points to 12 points.
5. Click in an open area to deselect the fields, then click the County field to select it.
6. Click the Bold and Italic buttons to add character formatting to the county names.
7. Click the View button to see the changes to your report. Leave the report open for the next lesson.

6. Adding a Label to a Report

One last thing is needed to finish the report—a subtitle to show where the information came from. It is always good form to give your sources, even when the sources are public domain.

To add a label to a report, complete the following steps:

1. Click the View button to return to Design view.

2. Click the Label button and draw a label box about 1/4" high and 3" wide just below the title in the Report Header.

3. Type `National Oceanic and Atmospheric Administration (NOAA)` in the text box. Notice what happens when you get to the end of the text box.

4. Click in an open area to deselect the label, then click the label box to select it again. Handles should appear around the label.

5. Click the Italic button.

6. Click the Font/Fore Color button and select white to change the color of the font to match the title.

7. Click the View button to see the results of your changes. Your report should look like Figure 6.19.

Figure 6.19
The finished Arizona Tornadoes, report should look like this.

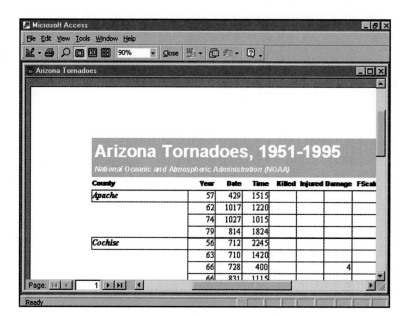

8. Close the report and save your changes.

Challenge

Challenge exercises expand on or are somewhat related to skills presented in the lessons. Each exercise provides a brief narrative introduction followed by instructions in a numbered step or bullet list format that are not as detailed as those in the Skill Drill section.

The database you will be using for the Challenge section is a modified version of the one you used in the Skill Drill section, including the changes you made.

1. Creating a Report Using the AutoReport: Columnar Option

You have not yet tried several other ways to create reports. You decide to experiment with a couple of them just to see what they look like. The first one you try is the AutoReport: Columnar option.

To create a report using the AutoReport: Columnar option, complete the following steps:

1. Copy the AC1-0603 database file to drive A:, remove the read-only status, and rename it `Arizona Tornadoes 2`.
2. Switch to the Reports window and create a new report.
3. Create an AutoReport: Columnar report based on the Arizona Tornadoes table.
4. Scroll down and look at the layout of the report. Move to Design view and examine the structure of the report.
5. Close the report and save it as `Column Report`.

2. Creating a Report Using the AutoReport: Tabular Option

You've tried the AutoReport: Columnar option and can't figure out how you'd ever use it. Maybe the AutoReport: Tabular option will produce better results.

To create a report using the AutoReport: Tabular option, complete the following steps:

1. Create a new report.
2. Create an AutoReport: Tabular report based on the Arizona Tornadoes table.
3. Scroll down and look at the layout of the report. Move to Design view and examine the structure of the report. Which of the two AutoReports do you think would be most useful the majority of the time?
4. Close the report and save it as `Tabular Report`.

3. Summarizing Data in a Report

As you create reports in the future, you will often want to summarize the data grouped in a field. Access enables you to print all of the data along with summaries, or just the summaries themselves. In this exercise, you create a report that summarizes tornado data by county.

To summarize data in a report, complete the following steps:

1. Create a new report based on the Arizona Tornadoes table using the Report Wizard.
2. Select all of the fields and group by county. Don't sort the records, but click the Summary Options button on the sorting page of the wizard.
3. In the Summary Options dialog box, choose to Sum the Killed and Injured fields, and Avg (average) the Damage and FScale fields.
4. In the same dialog box, choose to display the Summary Only.
5. Use the Outline 2 layout and the Portrait orientation. Select the Bold style.
6. Name the new report `County Summaries`. Notice that some of the categories are empty, and some are shown with seven decimal places. A part of the second page is shown in Figure 6.20.

Figure 6.20
This is how the county summaries will appear.

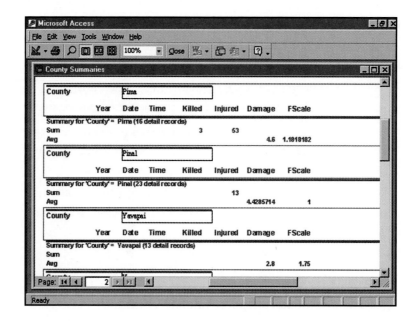

7. Leave the report open for the next exercise.

4. Formatting the Numbers on Reports

The numbers of decimal places in the Damage and FScale fields are inconsistent. You would like to fix them so that both fields display the results to one decimal place.

To format the numbers in a report, complete the following steps:

1. In Design view, select both the Damage and the FScale summary fields in the County Footer area.
2. Click the Properties button in the Report Design toolbar.
3. Use the help menu to figure out how to set the numbers to a fixed format and the decimal places to 1.
4. Click the View button to make sure you set both formatting options.
5. Close the report and save your changes.

5. Changing the Report Sort Order

The Tornado date has been grouped by county, and sorted by year and date. You decide that you'd like to change it to sort on the FScale field in descending order.

To change the report sort order, complete the following steps:

1. Open the Arizona Tornadoes report in Design view.
2. Locate and click the Sorting and Grouping button.
3. Use the help options available to you to help you delete the Year and Date fields from the sorting area. Add the FScale field and sort in descending order.
4. Look at a preview of your report.
5. Close the report and save your changes.

⟦?⟧ 6. Draw Lines in a Report

Looking at the report entitled Tabular Report that you created earlier in this Challenge section, you decide that you would like to try adding a line under the title.

To draw lines in a report, complete the following steps:

1. Open the Tabular Report in Design view.

2. Click the Line button and draw a straight line under the title in the Report Header. (Hint: To draw a straight line, hold down ⟦◆Shift⟧ while you click and drag the line.) Notice that the line is not continuous, but consists of dots and dashes.

3. Use the available help to figure out how to change the line to a solid line. (Hint: The line style is a property of the line.)

4. Change the line color to red.

5. View your changes, then close and save the report.

Discovery Zone 🌐

Discovery Zone exercises help you gain advanced knowledge of project topics and application of skills. These exercises focus on enhancing your problem-solving skills. Numbered steps are not provided, but you are given hints, reminders, screen shots, and references to help you reach your goal for each exercise.

⟦?⟧ 1. Changing the Grouping of Report Data and Keeping the Groups Together

When you finally get your report finished, you may decide that you want to change its focus. You might also consider copying and pasting the report to save the work of creating another one. You can then use this copy to display the data in a different manner. For example, in the Arizona Tornadoes report you grouped the data on the County field and sorted on the Year and Date fields. Suppose you also wanted to be able to examine the data by year, and you wanted to make sure the tornadoes of one year did not overlap from one page to the next.

Goal: Change the grouping field in an existing report and have the report keep the data from the grouped field together (on the same page) in the report.

Use the AC1-0604 file to create a new database called `Arizona Tornadoes by Year` on your disk. Use help from your computer or online to understand how to change the grouped field and how to keep the data together for each of the grouped items. You will modify the Arizona Tornadoes report. To modify this report, you should:

- Change the grouping to the Year field, rather than the County field.
- Change the sort field to the Date field only.
- Change the character formatting to bold for the Year field and remove the bold formatting from the County field.
- Swap the location of the County field and the Year field.
- Have the county name show in every record; however, the year should be displayed only when it changes (that is, each year should be displayed only once).

Hint #1: There is a button on the Report Design toolbar that will lead you to a way to make several of the changes.

Hint #2: You can eliminate duplicate years in the Properties box.

Your tabbed form should look like Figure 6.21.

Figure 6.21
The Arizona Tornadoes report is modified now to sort by year.

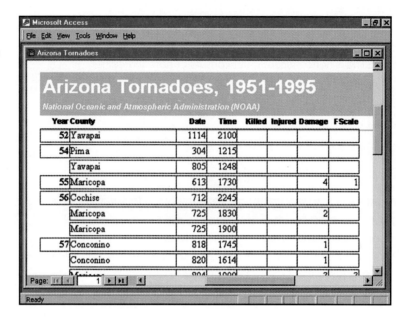

? 2. Creating Mailing Labels Using the Label Wizard

If you are creating a database for a business, church, or organization, one of the most common reports will be used to create mailing labels. Mailing labels are usually printed on special sheets that contain ready-to-use labels in various sizes. The Avery company specializes in making labels that fit every need, from folder labels to nametags. Each of the different types of labels have their own "Avery number." When you set up your mailing label, you will need to know which Avery label you are using. The wizard asks for the Avery number and then automatically sets the page up for you.

Goal: Create a report using the Label Wizard that will generate mailing labels from a table of addresses.

Use the AC1-0605 file to create a new database called **Address Labels** on your disk. Read through the Access help on mailing labels to understand how the wizard works. Also, carefully read the help provided on each of the wizard screens. Use the following guidelines:

- The report should use Avery #5160 labels.
- The font should be normal (no special character formatting) and 10 point.
- The first row should contain the First Name and Last Name fields with a space between them.
- The second row of each label should contain the Address field.
- The third row of each label should contain the City field, followed by a comma and a space; then the State field and a space; and finally, the ZIP field.
- Name your report **Contact Mailing Labels**.

Preview the page, then print the labels. Your report should look like Figure 6.22.

Figure 6.22
This form is ready to be
printed on Avery #5160
labels.

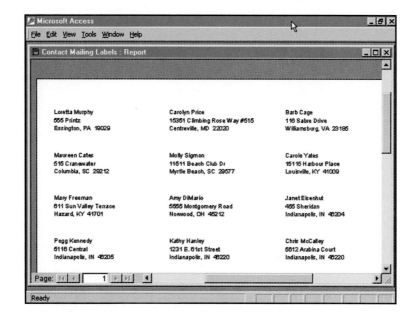

Project 7

Project

Customizing Fields and Tables

Objectives

In this project, you learn how to

➤ **Modify a Table Design**

➤ **Enter a Default Value**

➤ **Change a Field Type and Select a Format**

➤ **Change a Field Size**

➤ **Work with More Than One Table**

➤ **Create Table Relationships**

➤ **Create a Multiple Table Query**

Key terms introduced in this project include

- enforce referential integrity
- Input masks
- join
- one-to-many

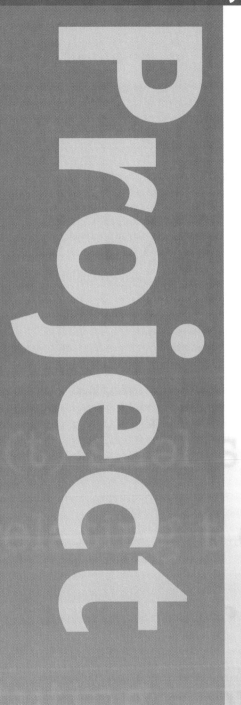

Why Would I Do This?

Access provides many features to help you customize your database table. You can select the field size, enter a default value, or select how data in that field is displayed.

When you first create a database, you may not be sure which of these options you want to use. After you have entered several records, however, you may find that you need to make changes, and you can make them by modifying the table design. You can add fields to the table or delete fields. You can also change the field properties, which are the defining attributes of a field, of the table entries. In this project, you learn how to modify a table design and change some of the field properties.

Another way you can customize tables is by connecting two or more tables together. Access is a relational database, which means that data is stored separately in tables and then connected or related by common fields in each table. Connecting tables enables you to set up a sophisticated database system and makes managing the information easier.

The connection between the two tables is called a relationship. The most common type of relationship is called a **one-to-many**. If two tables have a one-to-many relationship, it means that each record in the first table can be related to more than one record in the second table. Records in both tables must share a field that can be used to relate them. Other types of relationships are possible. For instance, in a one-to-one relationship one record from a table is related to one record in another table through a common field.

The advantage of using two tables can be demonstrated by a database designed for a small company. The company sells supplies to 20 different retail outlets. Each month, the company sends several orders to each outlet. The company wants to record the mailing address of each of the outlets and information about each order. If a single table is used with all the fields in it, the company will have to enter all of the address information of the outlet every time an order is sent. If the database is designed with two tables, the mailing address information can be entered once for each outlet in one table, and the specific order information can be entered in a second table.

This project examines some of the relational features of a database.

Visual Summary

When you have completed this project, you will have created a query that looks like Figure 7.1:

Figure 7.1
The query consists of fields from two tables.

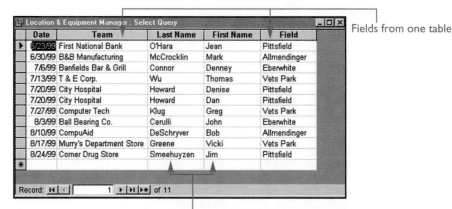

Fields from one table

Fields from a second table

Lesson 1: Modifying a Table Design

It is a good idea to spend some time planning your database structure—thinking about which fields to include and in which order. If you had only one chance to get the database table right, however, you probably would get frustrated quickly, because it is difficult to anticipate all of the features that need to be included in a table.

Fortunately, Access lets you make changes to a table design even after you have created the table. Consequently, you can add fields, delete fields, or modify field properties as the need arises.

If the field already contains data and you make a change to the field, the data will be affected. Sometimes the change doesn't cause any problems. For example, if you have already entered numbers in a field and then decide you want to format them as currency, you won't lose any data.

However, if you enter a note in a field and then change that field type to a Yes/No field, you will lose most of the data in the field when Access reformats it to the new type. Just be sure that you understand the changes you are making and that you realize how they will affect your data. Back up your database before you change data types.

You begin this lesson by modifying the Team table of the Softball database by adding a few new fields.

To Modify a Table Design

① Launch Access. Click OK to open an existing file.
Make sure you have a disk in drive A:.

② Find the AC1-0701 file on your CD-ROM, right-click on it, and send it to the floppy drive. Move to drive A:, remove the read-only status, rename the file Softball2, and open the new database.
The Softball Team database includes a table of team members and a table of game information. After you open the Softball database, you should see the two tables displayed in the Tables list. In this lesson, you work with the Team table.

③ Click the Team table, and then click the <u>D</u>esign button. Maximize the Design window.
The Team table opens in Design view so that you can make changes (see Figure 7.2). When you first created the table, you didn't include the city, state, or ZIP code for the players, because most of them live in the same city; you didn't think you needed to track this information.

After using the database for some time, however, you have decided that you want to include the city, state, and ZIP Code in the table so that you can have complete addresses for mailings. Now you want to add these three fields to the table, and you want to place them after the address field.

continues ▶

To Modify a Table Design   (continued)

Figure 7.2
Open the table in Design
view so that you can
modify its design.

Row selector ——

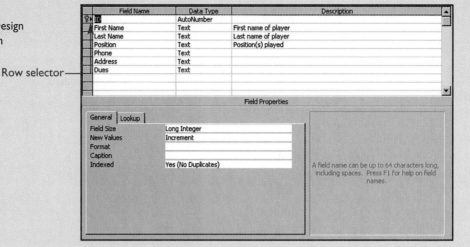

4 Click the row selector next to the Dues field and click the Insert
Rows button three times.

Access inserts three rows in which you can enter the City, State, and
ZIP Code fields. You can also insert a row by selecting the Insert menu and
choosing the Rows command.

5 Click in the first empty Field Name column box, and type `City`.
Press Tab⇄ three times.

This enters the field name, accepts Text as the field type, skips the
Description column, and moves you to the next row.

6 Repeat this step to enter the State and ZIP Code fields.

When you have finished, you will have inserted three new fields (see Figure 7.3).

Figure 7.3
You can add new fields to
a table by inserting new
rows.

New fields ——

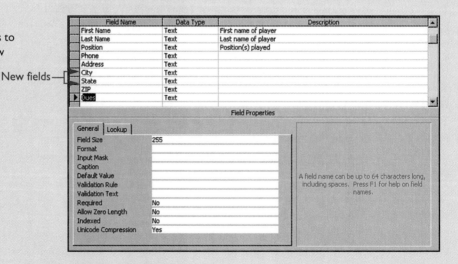

7 Click the Save button on the toolbar, and close the table. Leave the
Softball2 database open.

The Team table is saved with the modifications you have made.

8 Click the Games table to select it; then click Design.

Notice that the table has a counter field that is used as the Primary key. Because the team never plays more than one game on any given day, the Date field can serve as the Primary key field.

9 Click the row selector for the Date field, and then click the Primary Key button on the toolbar.

The Primary key icon is now displayed on the row selector button next to the Date field.

10 Click the row selector button for the ID field and press the Delete Rows button on the toolbar.

A warning message will appear that tells you all data in this field will be deleted permanently (see Figure 7.4).

Field to be deleted

New primary key field

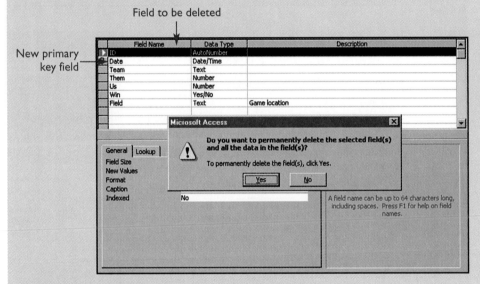

Figure 7.4
Access asks you to confirm that you want to make the deletion.

11 Click Yes to confirm the deletion of the fields. Close the table and save your changes.

Keep the database open for use in the next lesson, where you learn to enter a default value.

Lesson 2: Entering a Default Value

At times, you may want a particular value to appear in a specific field for most of the records in your table. In the three new fields you entered in the preceding lesson, for example, you want to use the same city, state, and ZIP Code for nearly all the records. You can type the entry over and over again for each record, or you can enter a default value.

When you enter a default value, Access automatically uses that field entry for all new records. (All records you entered previously, however, are not affected.) If you are entering a record with a different value, simply type over the default value.

Creating Small Database Fields
One of the rules of database design is to create the smallest usable fields. In this table, the Address field contains the street number and the street name. This practice reduces the number of fields in the table but it also reduces your options for sorting the data. For example, if you wanted to sort the addresses by street name, it would be difficult because the street number comes first in the field.

Another illustration would be to use a single field for a person's name. If you entered names with the last name followed by a comma and the first name (**Preston, John**), they would sort properly, but you would have trouble when you wanted to print mailing labels, because the last name would always be listed before the first name. Once again, two fields are best.

In general, do not group two types of data into the same field unless you are confident that the need to use them separately is unlikely to occur. It is difficult to change this decision once the data has been entered.

To Enter a Default Value

① Select the Team table and click Design. Click in the record selector next to the City field.
This step selects the field you want to modify. When a field is selected, you see the appropriate field properties for that field type in the lower half of the window. The available properties vary, depending on the data type. In this area, you can enter a default value (see Figure 7.5).

Figure 7.5
You can enter default values in the property boxes in the Field Properties area.

Selected field →

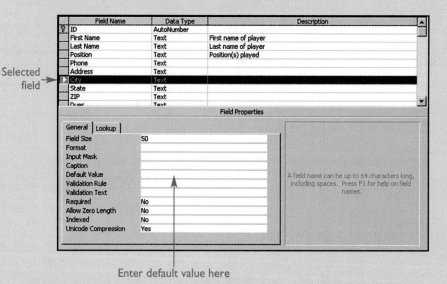

Enter default value here

② Click the Default Value property box in the Field Properties area. Type Ann Arbor and press ↵Enter.
Notice that Access has placed quotation marks around the default value. They are automatically added to all text entries.

All records you add to the table from here on will default to Ann Arbor in the City field. Typing in the city name will overwrite this field.

> **X** In some cases, you must surround the default value with quotation marks, or Access may display an error message if the entry is mistaken for a command. For example, when you type only IN as the default value for the state field, Access thinks you are creating an expression (formula) rather than entering a default value for Indiana. Quotation marks indicate to Access that this is not an expression.
>
> If you see a syntax error message, it means that you forgot to type the quotation marks around the default value in the table design. Click the OK button, and then edit the entry in Design view to include the quotation marks.

3 Click in the row selector next to the State field.
This selects the next field you want to modify.

4 Click the Default Value property box for this field, and type MI.
Here is where you enter the value you want to use for all new records.

5 Click the row selector next to the ZIP Code field.
This selects the ZIP Code field and displays its properties.

6 Click the Default Value property box for this field and type 48103.

7 Click the Save button.
This saves the changes you have made to the table design. Now try adding a new record.

8 Click the View button on the toolbar. Then click the New Record button.
This switches you to Datasheet view and moves the insertion point to a new row so that you can enter a new record.

9 Press Tab to skip the Counter field; then type the following entries, pressing Tab after each one.
Steve
Rasche
First Base
555-8177
8409 Evanston
Notice that when you get to the City, State, and ZIP Code fields, the values have already been entered (see Figure 7.6).

continues ▶

To Enter a Default Value (continued)

Figure 7.6
Your default values are
entered automatically.

Last Name	Position	Phone	Address	City	State
Wu	Pitcher	555-8812	890 Magnolia		
Howard	Center Field	555-2211	6704 Daisy Street		
Howard	Third Base	555-2211	6704 Daisy Street		
Lear	Left Center	555-6771	33 Eaton Avenue		
Lear	Short Stop	555-6771	33 Eaton Avenue		
Boll	Right Field	555-0014	609 Broad Ripple		
Broda	First Base	555-3211	7811 South St.		
Tucker	Pitcher	555-6322	9001 Labomba		
Klug	Catcher	555-5412	623 Pittsfield		
Chan	First Base	555-8777	8744 Marilyn Ave		
Cerulli	Pitcher	555-7666	5422 Seed		
DeSchryver	Left Field	555-9872	751 Kelley Lane		
Greene	Second Base	555-4460	8766 Christine		
Smeehuyzen	Right Field	555-4460	8766 Christine		
Leonard	Center Field	555-8733	98A CrossCountry Street		
Kenney	Third Base	555-8999	8756 W. Stadium		
Schneider	Catcher	555-9126	9010 Sue City		
Rasche	First Base	555-8177	8409 Evanston	Ann Arbor	MI
				Ann Arbor	MI

Record: |◄| |◄| 21 |►| |►I| |►✱| of 21 |◄|

City, State, and ZIP are
entered automatically

🔟 **Press** Tab↹ **three times to move past the three fields that have
default values and type 50 in the Dues field. Press** Tab↹ **to move back
to the first field.**

This record is saved when you press Tab↹ to move to the next record. Keep
the Team table open, and continue with the next lesson.

Lesson 3: Changing a Field Type and Selecting a Format

In addition to adding fields to the table, you can also modify existing fields. Suppose
that when you first added fields to your table, you were unfamiliar with the other data
types, so you used Text as the data type for all your fields. A Text field type is the most
common type and works well in many cases.

Now you have a better understanding of the various field types, and you want to change a
particular field type so that it more accurately reflects the format of the data being
entered. In this case, you can modify the table design and change the field type.

In this lesson, you change the Dues field to a Number data type and then select a format
to display the number as currency. The format controls how the data in that field is
displayed and what kind of data can be entered.

To Change a Field Type and Select a Format

🖾▾ ❶ **With the Team table still open, click the View button to return to
Design view.**

Remember that you can't make changes to the structure of the table in
Datasheet view; you must switch to Design view.

2 Click in the Data Type column of the Dues field.

This is the field you want to change. You see a down arrow, and the field properties for this field are listed in the lower half of the window. This field currently has a Text field type, but you have entered numbers in this field. You can change it to a Number field.

3 Click the down arrow.

A drop-down list appears, showing the available data types (see Figure 7.7).

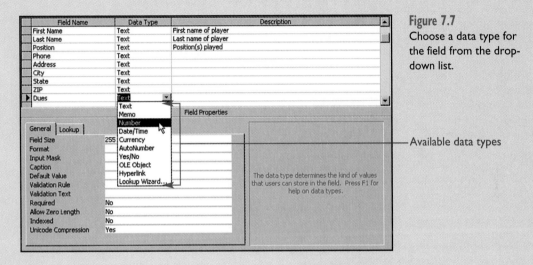

Figure 7.7
Choose a data type for the field from the drop-down list.

—Available data types

4 Click Number in the list.

This selects Number as the data type. You could have selected Currency; however, this method will show you several other options for formatting numbers as well as currency.

5 Click the Format property box in the Field Properties area.

A down arrow is displayed in the text box.

6 Click the down arrow.

A drop-down list appears showing the available display formats (see Figure 7.8). The listed formats vary depending on the data type of the selected field.

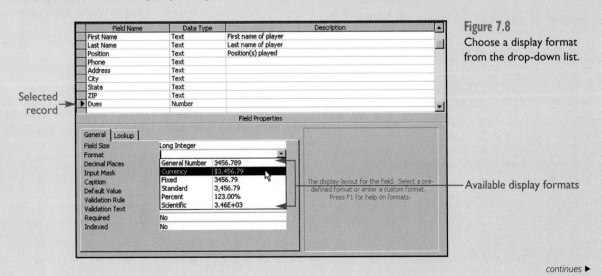

Figure 7.8
Choose a display format from the drop-down list.

Selected → record

—Available display formats

continues ▶

To Change a Field Type and Select a Format   (continued)

7 **Click Currency in the list.**

This selects Currency as the display format for the selected field.

🖫 **8** **Click the Save button on the toolbar.**

This saves the changes you have made to the table design. To take a look at how these changes affected your table, switch to Datasheet view.

🖼▾ **9** **Click the View button on the toolbar.**

Scroll to the Dues column and notice how the data is now formatted (see Figure 7.9). Keep the Team table open, and continue to the next lesson, where you learn how to change a field size.

Figure 7.9
The Dues column is now displayed using the Currency display format.

	Address	City	State	ZIP	Dues	
▶	565 Louisa, Apt. A				$50.00	
	560 Louisa, Apt. B				$50.00	
	6910A Bull Lane				$50.00	
	890 Magnolia				$50.00	
	6704 Daisy Street				$50.00	
	6704 Daisy Street				$50.00	
	33 Eaton Avenue				$50.00	
	33 Eaton Avenue				$50.00	
	609 Broad Ripple				$50.00	
	7811 South St.				$50.00	
	9001 Labomba				$50.00	
	623 Pittsfield				$50.00	
	8744 Marilyn Ave				$50.00	
	5422 Seed				$50.00	
	751 Kelley Lane				$50.00	
	8766 Christine				$50.00	
	8766 Christine				$50.00	
	98A CrossCountry Street				$50.00	
	8756 W. Stadium				$50.00	

Record: ◀◀ ◀ 1 ▶ ▶◀ ▶◀ of 21

Field with Currency display format

Setting Decimal Places and Currency Signs
The Field Properties area is also the place to choose the number of decimal points to use for a number field. The default is Auto, which works well if you are using currency with two decimal places. If you wanted a field displaying dollar signs and commas every third number, but with no cents, you would use the drop-down menu in the Decimal Places box and choose 0.

Lesson 4: Changing a Field Size

Another property of your table that you may want to change is the field size. When a field is added to a form or report, the size of the field's text box is determined by the field size. Setting field sizes in the table for fields such as State will reduce the modifications you will have to make to forms and reports later.

Be careful that you do not choose a field size that is too small; doing so limits what you can enter in that field. In the State field, for example, you want to type the two-letter state abbreviation. You can change the field size and then add a description to the field so that anyone who uses this table is aware of this restriction.

To Change a Field Size

1 **With the Team table still open on your screen, click the View button.**
This switches to Design view, which is where you have to be to change the table.

2 **Click the Description column for the State field.**
This is the field you want to change. The field properties for this field are listed in the lower half of the window.

3 **Type Enter two-letter abbreviation.**
This description will appear in the Status bar in Datasheet view when the insertion point is in the State field.

4 **Click the Field Size property box in the Field Properties area.**
The default for text fields is 50, which will be too long for many fields.

5 **Delete 50, and type 2.**
The new field size is large enough for a two-letter abbreviation for the state (see Figure 7.10).

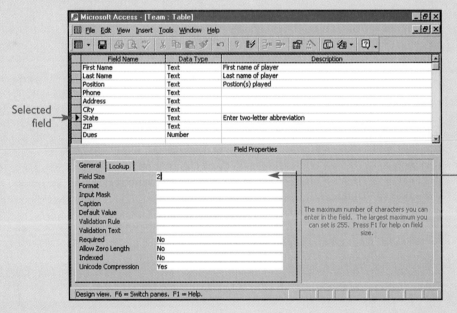

Selected field

Type a new field size here

Figure 7.10
Use the Field Size property box to change the field size.

6 **Click the Save button.**
Access prompts you to let you know that you may lose some data by reducing the field size (see Figure 7.11). In this case, none of the entries is longer than two characters, so it is safe to proceed.

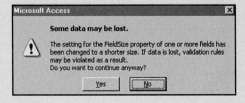

Figure 7.11
The program warns you that reducing the field size could result in loss of data.

continues ▶

To Change a Field Size (continued)

7 **Click Yes to confirm the change in field size.**
Now when you enter a state in the table, you will be able to type only two characters. Keep the Team table open, and continue with the next lesson, where you work with more than one table.

(i) **Effect of Column Width on Field Size**
Remember that changing the column width in Datasheet view has no effect on the field size. To change the field size, you must change the field property.

Lesson 5: Working with More Than One Table

Rather than lumping all the information you want to maintain in your Access database into one large table that may be difficult to manage, you can keep your data in more than one table. You can create separate tables and connect them by setting relationships.

In order to relate tables, the tables must share at least one common field. The data type for the common field must be the same for both tables. You cannot, for example, relate a Text field to a Date/Time field. Once the relationship is established, you can take advantage of it by creating queries that use data from several tables at the same time.

In the rest of this project, you first add a common field you can use to relate two tables; then you enter the data, set the relationships, and use the two tables to create a query.

For this lesson, you want to relate the Games table to the Team table to see who is responsible for the equipment at each game. So that one person doesn't have to be responsible for the equipment all season, the job is rotated to a new player for each game. Start by adding a new field called Equipment Date. This field shows the date on which a specific player acts as equipment manager. This date field will then be related to the date field in the Games table.

To Work with More Than One Table

 1 **With the Team table still open on your screen, click in the row selector next to the Dues field. Click the Insert Rows button.**
Access inserts a new row in which you can enter the new field information.

2 **Click in the Field Name column, and type** `Equipment Date`. **Press** `Tab⇆`.
The field name is entered, and Access moves you to the Data Type column.

3 **Click the down arrow.**
A drop-down list appears, showing the available data types.

4 **Click Date/Time in the list.**
This selects a Date data type for the Equipment Date field (see Figure 7.12).

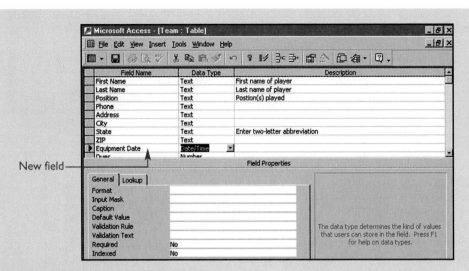

New field—

Figure 7.12
A field has been added
that will be used to relate
the tables.

5 Click the Save button.

This saves the changes you have made to the table design. Next, you need to
enter values in the field you just added.

6 Click the View button.

Access displays the table in Datasheet view so that you can enter values into
the new field.

There is a problem with entering the Equipment Dates. The new field is several
columns away from the column with the players' names.

**7 Point to the field selector for the first column. Click and drag across
the first three columns (ID, First Name, and Last Name) to select
them.**

8 Select Format, Freeze Columns from the menu.

This will keep these columns on the screen while you scroll through the other
columns.

**9 Click anywhere in the table to deselect the columns, and scroll the
table columns until you can see the name columns and the
Equipment Date column at the same time (see Figure 7.13).**

continues ▶

To Work with More Than One Table   (continued)

Figure 7.13
The names and equipment date fields are onscreen at the same time to simplify the addition of the dates.

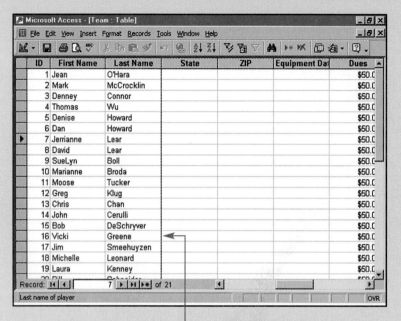

Heavier line indicates that columns are frozen

🔟 **Enter the following dates for the appropriate team players.**

Player	Equipment Date
O'Hara	6/23/99
McCrocklin	6/30/99
Connor	7/6/99
Wu	7/13/99
Howard, (Denise)	7/20/99
Howard, (Dan)	7/20/99
Klug	7/27/99
Cerulli	8/3/99
DeSchryver	8/10/99
Greene	8/17/99
Smeehuyzen	8/24/99

These dates match the dates in the Date field of the Games table. Notice that Dan and Denise Howard are sharing the responsibility on July 20, because they ride to the game together (see Figure 7.14). Access saves your entries automatically as you type an entry and move to the next row.

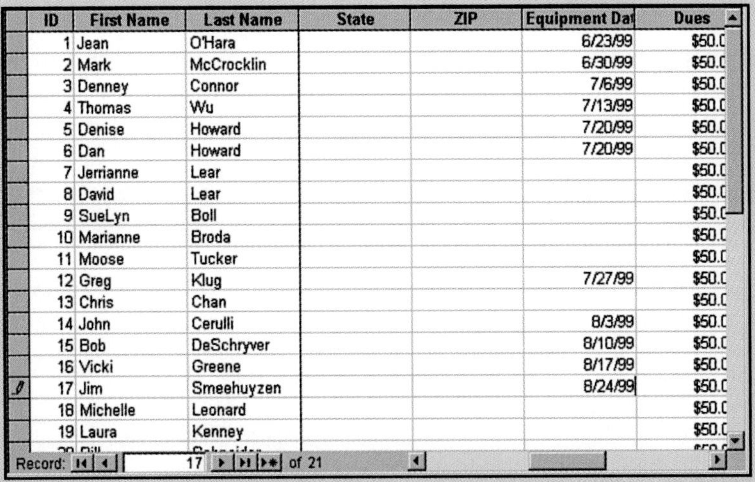

ID	First Name	Last Name	State	ZIP	Equipment Dat	Dues
1	Jean	O'Hara			6/23/99	$50.0
2	Mark	McCrocklin			6/30/99	$50.0
3	Denney	Connor			7/6/99	$50.0
4	Thomas	Wu			7/13/99	$50.0
5	Denise	Howard			7/20/99	$50.0
6	Dan	Howard			7/20/99	$50.0
7	Jerrianne	Lear				$50.0
8	David	Lear				$50.0
9	SueLyn	Boll				$50.0
10	Marianne	Broda				$50.0
11	Moose	Tucker				$50.0
12	Greg	Klug			7/27/99	$50.0
13	Chris	Chan				$50.0
14	John	Cerulli			8/3/99	$50.0
15	Bob	DeSchryver			8/10/99	$50.0
16	Vicki	Greene			8/17/99	$50.0
17	Jim	Smeehuyzen			8/24/99	$50.0
18	Michelle	Leonard				$50.0
19	Laura	Kenney				$50.0

Record: 17 of 21

Figure 7.14
The equipment dates have been added to the table.

⓫ Close the table by clicking the Close button in the upper-right corner of the table window (not the Access window).
Confirm that you want to save your changes to the layout. This preserves the Freeze Columns feature.

The table closes and the database window is displayed. From this window, you can set the relationship between the tables, which you do in the next lesson.

Relating a Number Field to a Counter Field
There is a possibility that the two fields that are used to relate the tables may be different. When the primary key in one table is a counter field and it is used as one of the related fields, it must be related to a number field stored as a long integer in the other table. Counter fields are actually stored as long integers, so this exception still conforms to the "same data type" rule, but it isn't obvious.

Creating Common Fields Among Tables
Setting up common fields among tables that you want to relate is an idea you should consider when you are creating a new database. You can always edit the table to include a linking field, if necessary, and you can use an existing field if it is an appropriate data type.

Lesson 6: Creating Table Relationships

When you want to relate two tables, you choose a field in each table that contains the same values. For example, in the Team table, you now have a list of game dates in the Equipment Date field. These are the same dates contained in the Date field of the Games table.

Often the fields have the same name, but that isn't a requirement for establishing a relationship between the two. The fields must, however, be the same data type.

You can create various types of relationships. In this lesson, you create a one-to-many relationship between the dates in the Games table to the dates in the Team table.

A one-to-many relationship requires that the field in the table on the "one" side of the relationship does not contain any duplicate values. The Date field that is used as the primary key for the Games table has this property. The field that will be on the "many" side of the relationship may use the same date more than once. In this example, Dan and Denise Howard are both assigned to take care of the equipment on the same game date.

To Create Table Relationships

1 Click the Relationships button on the Database toolbar.
You can also select the Tools menu and choose the Relationships command. The Show Table dialog box is displayed (see Figure 7.15). The first step in the process is to choose the tables you want to relate.

Figure 7.15
In the Show Table dialog box, you choose the tables you want to relate.

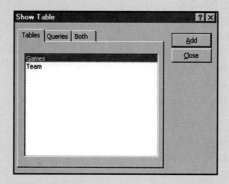

In some cases, such as after you have deleted relationships, the Show Table dialog box will not be displayed when you click the Relationships button. If this happens, click the Show Table button in the Relationship toolbar.

2 Click the Games table, and then click the Add button.
Access adds the table to the Relationships window; the dialog box remains open.

3 Click Team, and then click the Add button.
Access adds the Team table to the Relationships window. (The Team table will probably be hidden behind the Show Table dialog box.)

4 Click the Close button in the Show Table dialog box.
This closes the dialog box and displays both tables listed in the Relationships window.

5 Place the pointer on the bottom border of the Team field list and drag down until all the fields are visible (see Figure 7.16). Do the same thing to the Games field list.
The primary key fields of each table are displayed in boldface type.

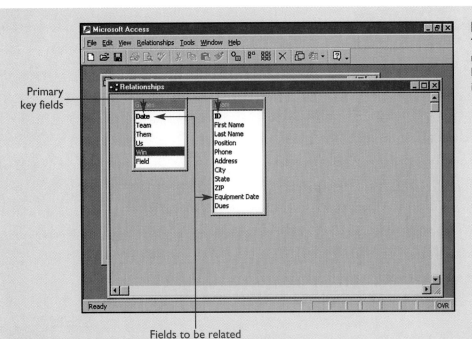

Primary
key fields

Figure 7.16
The Relationships window
may be used to establish
links between similar fields
in two or more tables.

Fields to be related

**6 Click the Date field in the Games table and drag it to the
Equipment Date field in the Team table.**
When you release the mouse button, the Relationships dialog box is displayed
(see Figure 7.17). In this dialog box, you can confirm that the relationship is
correct. You can also set other options, such as the type of relationship you
want. For this lesson, the default settings are acceptable.

Tables

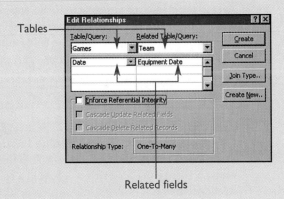

Related fields

Figure 7.17
Use the Relationships
dialog box to confirm
whether you have
selected the correct
fields for the relationship.

(i) Referential Integrity
When you create a one-to-many relationship, you can elect to *enforce
referential integrity*. This is used to ensure that each record in the
related table is connected to a record in the primary table. This helps
prevent orphan records. It also prevents you from adding records that
are not connected to an existing record in the primary table.

---

7 Click the Create button.
Access creates the relationship. A line connects the two fields (see Figure 7.18).

continues ▶

To Create Table Relationships (continued)

Figure 7.18
A line connects the fields
you have chosen to relate.

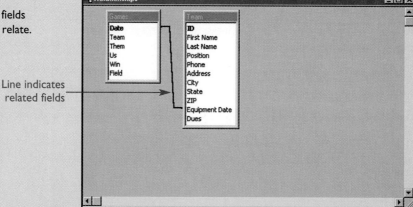

Line indicates
related fields

 8 Click the Save button on the toolbar.
This saves the relationship you just created; the Relationships window remains open.

9 Close the Relationships window.
You return to the database window. Keep the Softball2 database open as you continue to the next lesson, where you create a multiple-table query.

Deleting or Changing a Relationship
To delete a relationship, click the line connecting the two tables and press [Del]. Access prompts you to confirm the deletion. Click the OK button. Once the relationship has been deleted, the relationship can be re-created by dragging the field name from one table onto the field name in the second table.

If you want to change the relationship options, right-click on the line, then choose Edit Relationship from the shortcut menu. This option is also available in the Relationships menu choice.

 Changing the Field Size of a Joined Field
You cannot change the field size of a field that is part of a relationship. If you want to change the field size of a field in a relationship, you need to remove the relationship first.

Lesson 7: Creating a Multiple-Table Query

After you have established a relationship between tables, you can create forms and queries using data from both tables. When you have defined a relationship, Access automatically knows how to relate the data in the two tables and creates a *join*.

When you create a query that involves two or more tables, Access gives you a choice of three types of joins. The most commonly used join includes only those records with matching values in the common field in both tables. For example, your Games table includes the dates for all the Softball matches. Access uses these dates to create the join and pulls only the records with matching date entries from the Equipment Date field of the Team table. The other two types of joins include all the records from one table and just the matching records from the other table.

In this lesson, you create a query that lists three fields from the Games table: Date, Team, and Field; and one field, Equipment Manager, from the Team table.

To Create a Multiple-Table Query

1 **Click the Queries object button in the Softball2 database window, and click the New button.**
The New Query dialog box is displayed, showing the different query design options.

2 **Select Design View and click OK.**
The Show Table dialog box is displayed with the Query window in the background.

3 **Click the Games table, and then click the Add button.**
This adds the Games table to the query window.

4 **Click the Team tables, and then click the Add button.**
This adds the Team table to the query window.

5 **Click the Close button.**
Notice that the relationship between the two tables is displayed. Also displayed are field lists for each table; you will need to scroll the list of Team fields to see the related field (see Figure 7.19).

Relationship line

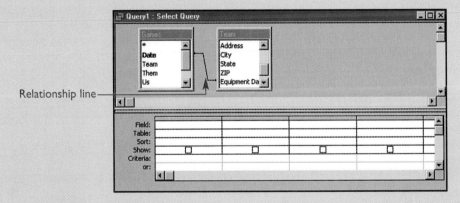

Figure 7.19
Related tables are displayed in the Design window.

6 **From the Games field list, drag the Date field to the first column in the design grid. Then drag the Team field from the Games field list to the second column.**
The Date and Team fields are added to the query.

7 **Drag the Last Name field from the Team field list to the third column in the design grid.**
The Last Name field is added to the query.

8 **Drag the First Name field from the Team field list to the fourth column in the design grid.**
The First Name field is added to the query.

continues ▶

To Create a Multiple-Table Query   (continued)

9 **Drag Field from the Games field list to the fifth column of the design grid.**

You may have to scroll down the field list and scroll to the right to find the fifth column. You now have added all the fields you want to include in the query (see Figure 7.20). Check the results of the query.

Figure 7.20
Five fields have been added to the query from two tables.

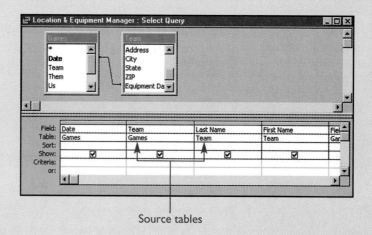

Source tables

10 **Click the View button on the toolbar.**

The results of your query are displayed (see Figure 7.21). The query lists the game date, team played, equipment manager's last and first name, and playing field location. You can save this query.

Figure 7.21
Here is your completed multiple-table query.

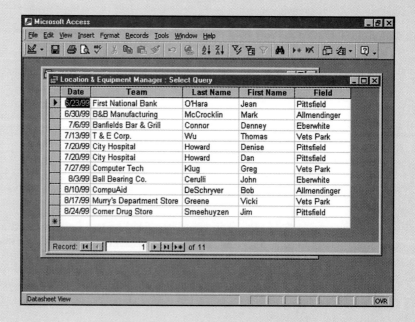

11 **Click the Save button.**

The Save As dialog box is displayed.

12 **Type Location & Equipment Manager and click the OK button.**

This step saves the query with the name Location & Equipment Manager.

13 **Close the query so that you are back in the Softball2 database window; then close the database.**

If you have completed your session on the computer, exit Access. Otherwise, continue with the "Checking Concepts and Terms" section in this project.

Removing Joins Between Tables in a Query
You can also remove the joins between tables in a query. To do this, click on the line that joins the field lists. The line becomes much thicker, indicating that the relationship has been selected. Press (Del). The line (and the relationship) is removed. This does not affect any relationships between the tables other than in this one query.

Summary

You can use the field properties in a table to help control the data that is entered. In this project, you learned how to modify a table by changing the field size, type, and format. You also learned how to work with more than one table by creating a relationship between tables and by using more than one table in a query.

To expand your knowledge, examine some of the other property options in the table design view. Notice how the properties that are available depend on the data type of the field that is selected. Use Help to look for information on table field properties. Use the Field Properties Reference page, select a property that is of interest to you, and read how it works. Some of the properties are set in the table; others are set in a form or report.

Checking Concepts and Terms

True/False

For each of the following, check *T* or *F* to indicate whether the statement is true or false.

__T __F **1.** To relate two fields, they must be the same data type. [L5]

__T __F **2.** The properties for a field are always the same, no matter what the data type. [L2]

__T __F **3.** You can change the field size by adjusting the column width in Datasheet view. [L4]

__T __F **4.** To create a relationship between two tables, the two tables must have at least two pairs of similar fields. [L6]

__T __F **5.** To create a relationship, the matching fields must have the same name. [L6]

__T __F **6.** You can't make changes to the structure of a table in Datasheet view. [L3]

__T __F **7.** Using the Format, Freeze Columns menu selection, you can freeze columns onscreen so that they will always be visible. [L5]

__T __F **8.** Click the Show Table button if you open the Relationships dialog box and the Show Table dialog box is not displayed. [L6]

__T __F **9.** If you change the data type for a field that already contains data, you always lose the data you have already input. [L1]

__T __F **10.** When you enter a default value in a field for a table that already contains data, Access inserts the default value in all the existing records. [L2]

Multiple Choice

Circle the letter of the correct answer for each of the following questions.

1. Which button do you use to insert a new field into a table in Design view? [L1]
   a. Insert Rows
   b. Insert Fields
   c. New Record
   d. Field Design

2. What is the default field size for text fields? [L4]
   a. 100
   b. 50
   c. 20
   d. 25

3. How are related tables displayed in the relationship or query window? [L6]
   a. Related fields are in boldface.
   b. Related fields are underlined.
   c. Related fields are connected by a line.
   d. Related fields are aligned next to each other.

4. When you define a default value for a field, how or when is that value used? [L2]
   a. for all existing records
   b. only for new records
   c. only for records that contain a blank field
   d. only when you select a special command

5. In which view can you modify the structure of a table? [L3]
   a. any view
   b. Datasheet view
   c. Design view
   d. Query view

6. Which of the following is the most commonly used relationship? [L6]
   a. one-to-one
   b. one-to-many
   c. many-to-one
   d. many-to-many

7. Why must you be careful about how you designate the information you use as default values? [L2]
   a. You can't use default values.
   b. The information must be used for every new record that follows.
   c. Even though you designate the information, you must Paste it each time you are in that field.
   d. Some words are reserved for Access commands and must be enclosed by quotation marks.

8. After you have defined a field in a table, which of the following can you change? [Intro]
   a. the size
   b. the data type
   c. the default value
   d. all of the above

9. Where are default values entered? [L2]
   a. in the dialog box that appears when you select the Properties button on the toolbar
   b. in the Default Value box in the Field Properties area of the table Design view window
   c. in the Default Value box next to the Data Type box in the field definition area of the Table Design view window
   d. in the dialog box that appears when you select Default Values from the Edit menu

10. The currency data type: [L3]
    a. must always use two decimal places
    b. is the default data type for numbers
    c. displays a dollar sign and commas when necessary
    d. is a property of a text field

Screen ID

Label each element of the Access screen shown in Figure 7.22 and Figure 7.23.

Figure 7.22

A. Insert Rows button

B. Delete Rows button

C. Field selector indicator

D. Primary key indicator

E. View button

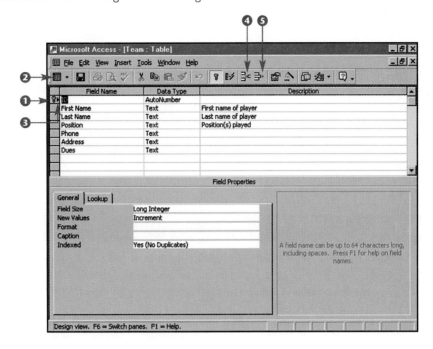

Figure 7.23

F. Source tables

G. Relationship line

H. Primary key field

I. Show Table button

J. Table name

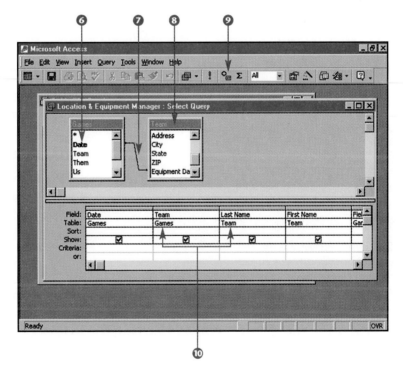

1. _____	4. _____	7. _____
2. _____	5. _____	8. _____
3. _____	6. _____	9. _____
		10. _____

Discussion Questions

1. In the databases with which you are familiar, how is data integrity maintained? What steps and procedures are used?

2. In the databases with which you are familiar, are there controls that restrict the type of data that can be entered in each field? How does this help to ensure that good data is entered? What are some of these controls?

3. When would it make sense to use a default value for a field? When would you not use a default for a field?

4. If you were a sales representative for a company and you had an assigned list of customers you were responsible for, what kind of information would you want to maintain about your customers?

5. In the above example, how might the company use a relational database to keep track of their sales force and their customers? How would these two sets of records be related?

Skill Drill

Skill Drill exercises reinforce project skills. Each skill reinforced is the same, or nearly the same, as a skill presented in the project. Each exercise includes a brief narrative introduction, followed by detailed instructions in a step-by-step format.

The database you will use in the Skill Drill exercises contains a short table of suppliers for a small swimming pool, spa, and sauna company. It also contains a table containing a list of swimming pool parts.

1. Adding a Field to a Table

For billing purposes, you find that you need the tax number of your suppliers. There is no field for a tax number, so you will need to create one. It will need to go between the Phone field and the Billing field.

To add a field to a table, complete the following steps:

1. Find the AC1-0702 database file on your CD-ROM, send it to drive A:, remove the read-only status, and name it **Pool Store**. Select the Parts Suppliers table and click the Design button.

2. Click anywhere in the Billing field and click the Insert Rows button to insert a row between the Phone field and the Billing field.

3. Add a new field called **Tax Number**.

4. Accept Text as the Data Type.

5. Close the table and save your changes.

2. Adding a Default Value

There is a field in the Parts Supplier table that contains billing data. The various suppliers give you 30, 45, or 60 days to pay for your orders. Most of the suppliers use 30 Day billing, so to save time, you decide it would be a good idea to add a default value to the field.

To add a default value, complete the following steps:

1. Select the Parts Supplier table and click the Design button.

2. Click anywhere in the Billing field.

3. Click in the Default Value box in the Field Properties area.

4. Enter **30 Day** for the Billing default value.

5. Close the table and save your changes.

3. Changing the Field Type

Because both the Price and Sale Price fields are dollar amounts, you would like to add dollar signs and decimal places to the fields. The easiest way to do this is to change the field types.

To change the field type, complete the following steps:

1. Select the Pool Parts Inventory table and click the Design button.

2. Move to the Data Type column of the Price field.

3. Click the drop-down arrow and select Currency from the drop-down list.

4. Move to the Data Type column of the Sale Price field.

5. Click the drop-down arrow and select Currency from the drop-down list.

6. Click the View button to switch to Datasheet view. Save your changes when prompted. Look at the two fields you just changed.

7. Close the table.

4. Changing the Field Size

All of the fields in the Parts Supplier table are text fields, and most of them are too large.

To change the field size, complete the following steps:

1. Select the Parts Suppliers table and click the Design button.

2. Click anywhere in the Contact field.

3. Delete the Field Size in the Field Properties area and type 30 to change the field size to 30 characters.

4. Repeat the above procedure to change the field size of the City field to 20 characters.

5. Change the Phone, ZIP, and Billing fields to 10 characters and the State field to 2 characters.

6. Close the table and save your changes.

5. Creating Table Relationships

You want to eventually be able to create a query that shows the contact person for each of the pool parts. The first step in this process is to create a relationship between the tables. The only fields that contain the same information are the Name field in the Parts Supplier table and the Distributor field in the Pool Parts Inventory field.

To create table relationships, complete the following steps:

1. From the Database window, click the Relationships button. If the Show Table dialog box is not displayed, click the Show Table button.

2. Select the Parts Suppliers table and click the Add button.

3. Select the Pool Parts Inventory table and click the Add button.

4. Click the Close button to close the Show Table dialog box.

5. Click the Name field in the Parts Suppliers field list and drag it on top of the Distributor field in the Pool Parts Inventory field list.

6. Click the Create button to create the relationship.

7. Close the Relationships window and save your changes.

6. Creating a Multiple-Table Query

You want to be able to print out a list of pool parts along with the names and telephone numbers of the contact person at the company that sells the parts. To do this, you need to create a query that is based on both tables in the Pool Store database.

To create a multiple-table query, complete the following steps:

1. Click the Queries object button, then click the Design button.

2. Select the Parts Suppliers table in the Show Table dialog box, and click the Add button.

3. Select the Pool Parts Inventory table and click the Add button.

4. Click the Close button to close the Show Table dialog box.

5. Click the Contact field from the Parts Suppliers field list, and drag it into the first empty field of the query design table.

6. Click and drag the Phone field from the Parts Suppliers field list into the next empty field.

7. Click and drag the Part Name field from the Pool Parts Inventory field list into the next empty field.

8. Click and drag the Description field from the Pool Parts Inventory field list into the next empty field.

9. Click the View button to see the results of your query in Datasheet view.

10. Close the query, and save it as `Contacts and Parts`.

Challenge

Challenge exercises expand on or are somewhat related to skills presented in the lessons. Each exercise provides a brief narrative introduction followed by instructions in a numbered step or bulleted list format that are not as detailed as those in the Skill Drill section.

You will be using two databases for the Challenge exercises. The first is a modified version of the one you used in the Skill Drill exercises. The two tables could benefit from a few modifications, such as lists and drop-down boxes for fields with common entries. They could also use an input format for telephone number entry.

The second database contains some information you are becoming familiar with—tornado data. You will use this database to link three tables together. You will also create both a report and a form that draw information from more than one table.

1. Formatting Fields Using Input Masks

Input masks are special formatting features that make data entry easier. For example, when typing in a phone number, it helps to have the various parts set up in a (999)000-0000 format. Other types of data that can benefit from input masks are Social Security numbers, 9-digit ZIP Codes, dates, and time. In the Parts Suppliers table, the phone number has been entered as a long string of numbers. You will add an input mask to the Phone field.

To format a field using an input mask, complete the following steps:

1. Copy the AC1-0703 database file to drive A:, remove the read-only status, and rename it `Pool Store2`.

2. Open the Pool Store2 database and open the Parts Suppliers table in Design view.

3. Select the Phone field, and click in the Input Mask box of the Field Properties area.

4. Click the Build button (the one with three dots) on the right edge of the Input Mask box.

X You may get a message that Access can't start this wizard. This feature is not installed as part of the standard installation. You will be asked if you want to install it now. Check with your instructor for directions if you are in a computer lab. If you are using your own machine, insert the CD-ROM that came with your software and choose Yes.

5. Select the Phone Number input mask from the Input Mask Wizard dialog box.

6. Accept the defaults in the other wizard dialog boxes.

7. Switch to Datasheet view to look at the results of your new input mask.

8. Close the table.

2. Creating a List Box

When there are only a few choices that can be made in a field, you can place a list on the screen from which the user can choose. This is called a list box. List boxes have the advantage of making sure that data that is entered is entered consistently and with no typographical errors. Nothing can be entered into the field except those items shown in the list box. List boxes can also be added to forms.

To create a list box, complete the following steps:

1. Open the Parts Suppliers table in Design view.

2. Click anywhere in the Billing field, and click the Lookup tab in the Field Properties area.

3. Use the Display Control drop-down arrow to select List Box.

4. Select Value List from the Row Source Type drop-down menu.

5. In the Row Source box, type "30 Day";"45 Day";"60 Day" exactly as shown. The quotation marks identify each item in the list, and the semicolons separate the list items.

6. Switch to Datasheet view to observe the results of your changes.

7. Close the table.

3. Creating a Drop-Down (Combo) Box

A second useful list type is called a combo box. This creates a list arrow and a drop-down list of choices for a field. The advantages of combo boxes are that they take up no more room than a standard field text box, and you can type in an item that is not included on the list. Combo boxes can also be added to forms.

To create a combo box, complete the following steps:

1. Open the Pool Parts Inventory table in Design view.

2. Select the Distributor field, and click the Lookup tab in the Field Properties area.

3. Change the Display Control to Combo Box.

4. Change the Row Source to the Parts Suppliers table.

5. Switch to Datasheet view, and click in the Distributor field in the empty record at the end of the table.

6. Click the drop-down arrow to see your combo box.

7. Close the table; then close the Pool Store2 database.

4. Linking Three Tables Together

It is possible to link more than two tables at a time. The database you will be working with in the next three exercises contains three tables—one with county names, one with state names, and one with tornado data and codes for the county and state names. The last two exercises involve creating queries and reports using all three tables. The first thing you must do is to create a relationship between the three tables.

To link three tables together, complete the following steps:

1. Copy the AC1-0704 database file to drive A:, remove the read-only status, and rename it **Five Year Tornado Data**.
2. Open the Relationships window; then show the list of tables.
3. Add all three tables to the Relationships window.
4. Increase the size of the 5 Year US Tornado field list so that you can see all of the fields.
5. Move the field lists around in the Relationships window so that the 5 Year US Tornado field list is in the middle.
6. Create a relationship between the CountyID field in the 5 Year US Tornado table and the CountyID field in the County Names table.
7. Create a relationship between the StateID field in the 5 Year US Tornado table and the State field in the County Names table.
8. Close the Relationships window, and save your changes.

[?] 5. Creating a Query Using Fields from Three Tables

Now that you have created a relationship between the three tables, you can create a query that eliminates the code numbers for the counties and states and replaces them with the actual county and state names. This will make the data easier to read and understand.

To create a query using fields from multiple tables, complete the following steps:

1. Use the available help features to create a query containing fields from all three tables in the database. Use the Simple Query Wizard.
2. Include all of the fields from the 5 Year US Tornadoes table except the StateID, CountyID, and County fields.
3. Include the State Name field from the State Names table.
4. Include the County Name field from the County Names table.
5. Save the query using the default name.
6. Move the State Name field so that it is displayed in the first column, and display the County Name field in the second column.
7. Sort on four fields in the following order: State Name, County Name, Year, and Date. Preview your query.
8. Close the query, and save your changes.

[?] 6. Creating a Report Using Fields from Multiple Tables

A report can be produced in two ways. You can base it directly on the tables that contain the data, or you can base it on a query, where the work of selecting the tables, fields, criteria, and sort order has already been done.

To create a report using fields from multiple tables, complete the following steps:

1. Use the available help features to create a report based on the 5 Year US Tornadoes query. Use the Report Wizard.

2. Accept all of the defaults.

3. Fix any labels or data that are cut off.

4. Put your name in the center of the page footer, then print page 70 of the report.

5. Close the report. Close the database and exit Access unless you are going to try the Discovery Zone exercises.

Discovery Zone

Discovery Zone exercises help you gain advanced knowledge of project topics and application of skills. These exercises focus on enhancing your problem-solving skills. Numbered steps are not provided, but you are given hints, reminders, screen shots, and references to help you reach your goal for each exercise.

[?] 1. Creating Your Own Input Mask

Access has pre-set input masks for phone numbers, Social Security numbers, 9-digit ZIP Codes, and several other common data structures. You may have a data structure that is common in your business. Perhaps you would like to create an input mask for that data. You added a Tax Number field to the Parts Suppliers table in the Pool Store database earlier in this project. This field could use an input mask to aid in data entry, because all tax numbers have the same structure.

Goal: Create a new input mask and add it to the list of input masks available in Access.

Use the AC1-0705 file to create a new database called **Pool Store3** on your disk. Use any available help from your computer or online to understand how to add an input mask to the Tax Number field. There should be a dash after the second character in the tax number and a dash before the last character. For example, the tax number for the Compaq Spa and Pool should read **2A-436234-C**. Your input mask should:

- Require the entry of the two letters as letters.
- Require the entry of the all seven numbers as numbers (0 through 9).
- Automatically change any letters entered into the input mask to uppercase.
- Insert a dash after the second character and before the last character.
- Use the underscore character as a placeholder for blanks while data is being entered.
- Store the dashes along with the letters and numbers.
- Show the Compaq Spa and Pool tax number (2A-436234-C) as the sample number in the Input Mask wizard.
- Save the new input mask so that you can use it in future databases.

Hint #1: You can make the input mask work by typing it into the Input Mask box in the Field Properties area of the Tax Number field, but in order to do the last two steps, you will need to use the Tax Number Build button.

Hint #2: You do not want to replace an existing input mask. When you are creating the input mask, no input mask should be displayed.

Enter a new record with the following data (these are in the order of the fields in your Parts Suppliers table): `Twinhead Chemicals`, `William McMahon`, `4722 Edison Lane`, `Port Huron`, `MI`, `48060`, `(810) 986-0000`, `1B-7536222-Z`, `30 Day`. When you enter the tax number, enter lowercase letters to see if the program automatically changes them to uppercase.

[?] 2. Creating Validation Rules and Validation Error Messages

All of your suppliers come from Michigan or northern Ohio, which means that all of the ZIP Codes you enter will begin with the number 4. You are also using just the five-digit ZIP Code rather than the nine-digit ZIP Code. To help avoid typographical errors in the future, you would like to have the program automatically detect when an incorrect ZIP Code is added, and include a message on the screen to help the user.

Goal: Create a validation rule for a ZIP Code field and add an error message to be displayed when an incorrect number is entered.

Use the Pool Store3 file that you created in the first exercise of the Discovery section. If you did not do the first exercise, use the Proj0705 file to create a new database called `Pool Store3` on your disk. Read through the Access help on validation rules and validation text to understand how validation works. Use the following guidelines:

- The validation rule should restrict entry to five-digit numbers beginning with the number 4.
- The error message that appears when an incorrect entry is made should say `The ZIP code must be a 5-digit number beginning with the number 4`.

   Hint #1: The ZIP field is a text field, but that does not matter in this case. The procedure would be the same for a text field containing numbers or a numeric field.

   Hint #2: You will need to build an expression for the validation rule so that you test the entry to make sure it is between two numbers.

Add a new record, and try to type in a number that does not meet your conditions to make sure your validation rule and validation text work the way you want.

Project 8

Integrating Access with Other Sources of Data and the Internet

Objectives

In this project, you learn how to

> Convert a Database from a Previous Version of Access
> Link an Access Table to a Form Letter in Word
> Merge an Access Table with a Form Letter
> Import a Table from Excel
> Save a Form as a Data Access Page
> Use a Browser to Interact with the Database

Key terms introduced in this project include

- browser
- data access page
- delimiter
- import
- mail merge

Why Would I Do This?

As you have seen, the data in a database may come from another source—another database, a spreadsheet, or even the Internet. The files you interact with may be on your computer or on a computer anywhere in the world. The Tornado information that you used in an earlier project, for example, was obtained over the Internet from the U.S. Storm Data Center. You can also use the power of Access in combination with Microsoft Word to produce form letters that can send information to people individually.

The reports, queries, and forms you create may need to be seen by others. Access is capable of placing information on the World Wide Web so that it can be accessed from anywhere in the world.

Visual Summary

When you have completed this project, you will have created a document that merges data from a table of addresses, imported a table of data from a non-Access source, and set up the database for use on the Internet. The merged document, the imported table, and a form as a Web page look like this:

Figure 8.1
You can merge Access fields with a Word document.

Insert Access fields by clicking this button

Access fields

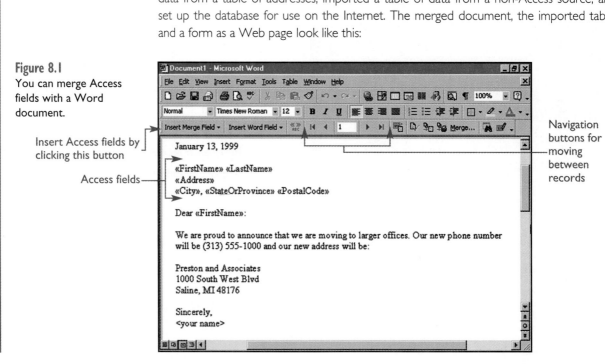

Navigation buttons for moving between records

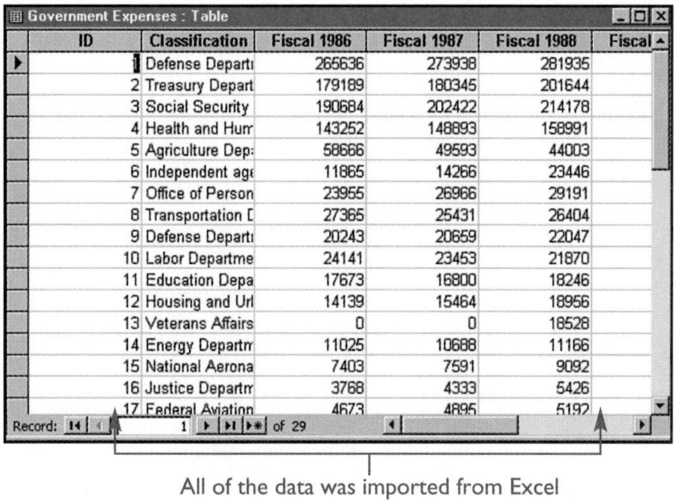

Figure 8.2
The data in this Access table was imported from an Excel spreadsheet.

All of the data was imported from Excel

Web browser

Figure 8.3
Access forms can be saved as Web pages.

Record from an Access table

Web navigation buttons

Lesson 1: Converting a Database from a Previous Version of Access

Access has changed its basic file structure to conform to an international standard that supports several languages. Databases stored using previous versions of Access will be converted automatically to the new version. Older versions of Access cannot read this data structure, and there is no program provided at this time to convert entire Access 2000 databases into older versions of Access. Access does not have a Save As option like the other Office products.

In this lesson, you convert a database from the Access 97 format to the Access format.

To Convert a Database from a Previous Version of Access

1 **Launch Access. Click OK to open an existing file.**

Make sure you have a disk in drive A:.

2 **Find and select the AC1-0801 file on your CD-ROM. Click Open.**

The Convert/Open Database dialog box is displayed (see Figure 8.4).

Figure 8.4
The Convert/Open
Database dialog box
enables you to convert
databases created in older
versions of Access.

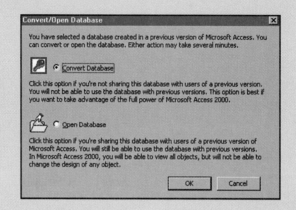

3 **Select the Convert Database option button and click OK.**

The Convert Database Into dialog box is displayed.

4 **Choose 3 1/2 Floppy (A:) in the Save in drop-down list box. Change the name to Associates in the File name text box.**

The window should look like Figure 8.5.

Figure 8.5
The Convert Databases
Into dialog box enables
you to select a file location
and rename the file.

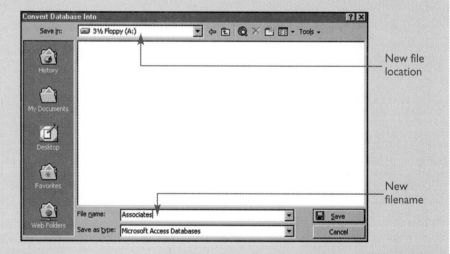

New file
location

New
filename

5 **Click Save.**

The file is converted and placed on your disk. The process may take a while, depending on the speed of your computer. When it is done, the file will open automatically.

Leave the Associates database open to use in the next lesson.

Opening an Older Database Without Converting
The Convert/Open Database window also enables you to use the database without updating it to Access 2000. If you want to open the database without converting it, choose the Open Database option button. This is particularly important if you are sharing the database with someone who is still using an older version of the program. The limitation is that you cannot change the design of any of the objects in the database using Access 2000 until the database has been converted to this version. If structural changes are to be made, they have to be done by the person using the older version.

Lesson 2: Linking an Access Table to a Form Letter in Word

Databases that contain names and addresses can be merged with Microsoft Word documents to create a series of documents in which each document contains data that is unique to that individual. This feature is known as **mail merge**. We have all received mail that has a label attached with our names and addresses on it, and most of us have received letters that have our names, birthdays, addresses, or phone numbers embedded in the text. These are examples of how an organization can communicate with its members. Such mailings are not limited to postal services—you can also create mailings for fax or email.

In this lesson, you create a letter to notify your business associates that you are moving and will have a new address and phone number.

To Link an Access Table to a Form Letter in Word

1 **If it is not already highlighted, select the Addresses table in the database window. Click the list arrow to the right of the OfficeLinks button on the Standard toolbar.**
A list of links to other Microsoft Office programs is displayed.

2 **Select Merge It with MS Word.**
The Microsoft Word Mail Merge Wizard dialog box is displayed (see Figure 8.6).

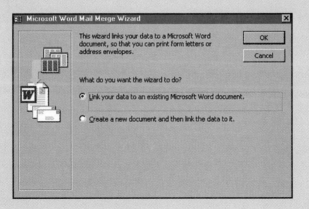

Figure 8.6
The Microsoft Word Mail Merge Wizard dialog box enables you to link to an existing document or create a new one.

continues ▶

To Link an Access Table to a Form Letter in Word   (continued)

③ Click the option button labeled <u>C</u>reate a new document button and then link the data to it. Click OK.

Microsoft Word is launched and a new document opens. Notice that the Mail Merge toolbar is displayed (see Figure 8.7).

Figure 8.7
A new Microsoft Word document opens with the Mail Merge toolbar displayed.

The Mail Merge toolbar

New document

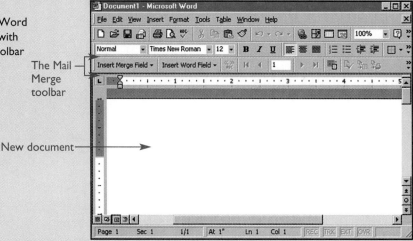

> ❌ The Mail Merge toolbar should open. It may be above or below the formatting or standard toolbar. If it does not open, you can open it by choosing <u>V</u>iew, <u>T</u>oolbars from the menu and then click Mail Merge to open the toolbar.

④ Maximize the Word window, change the Zoom to 100%, and set the Font Size to 12, if necessary.

⑤ Type today's date in the first line, and press ⏎Enter twice.

Notice that when you begin typing the date, Word automatically suggests the month, then the date. You can press ⏎Enter to accept the month, then press Spacebar. Press ⏎Enter again when today's date appears and the date will be completed for you. Press ⏎Enter twice more to move the insertion point down two lines.

⑥ Click the Insert Merge Field button on the Mail Merge toolbar.

A list of fields from the Addresses table in the Associates database is displayed. You select one field at a time from this list to create the inside address for a letter.

⑦ Click FirstName. Press Spacebar.

The name of the field is placed in the document and is followed by a space.

⑧ Click the Insert Merge Field button again, and click LastName.

The LastName field is placed after the FirstName field.

⑨ Press ⏎Enter to move to the next line of the address. Refer to the Figure 8.8 to create the rest of the document.

Type your name in the last line rather than <your name>. Be sure to include the comma after the City field and spaces as appropriate. If the Office Assistant opens, just click Cancel to close it.

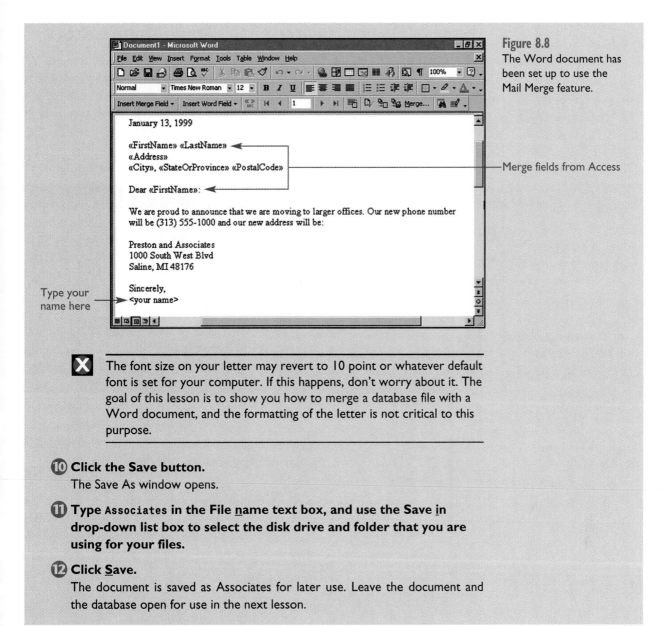

Merge fields from Access

Type your name here

The font size on your letter may revert to 10 point or whatever default font is set for your computer. If this happens, don't worry about it. The goal of this lesson is to show you how to merge a database file with a Word document, and the formatting of the letter is not critical to this purpose.

---

10 Click the Save button.
The Save As window opens.

11 Type Associates in the File name text box, and use the Save in drop-down list box to select the disk drive and folder that you are using for your files.

12 Click Save.
The document is saved as Associates for later use. Leave the document and the database open for use in the next lesson.

Using a Query-Based Mail Merge
You can also use the mail merge feature with a query. This is useful when you need to include a calculated field in the letter, restrict the mailing to clients who meet a certain criteria, or use fields from more than one table.

Naming an Access Database to Match a Word Document
Microsoft Word documents are automatically saved with a file extension of .doc, and Access databases are saved with an .mdb extension. You can use the same name for the Word document and the Access database, because they will have different extensions, even though the extensions may not appear on your screen.

Lesson 3: Merging an Access Table with a Form Letter

Once you have linked the database field names into a Word document, you can create a series of documents that each contain the data from a record in the database table. This process creates a file of the merged, personalized letters. You also learn how to print a few of the letters to ensure that they do not contain errors before you send the rest of them to the printer.

In this lesson, you merge the database file into the letter and print two of the documents.

To Merge an Access Table with a Form Letter

1 Click the View Merged Data button on the Mail Merge toolbar in Word.

The data from the first record in the Addresses table is inserted into the document (see Figure 8.9).

Figure 8.9
The Word document displays the data from the first record in the table.

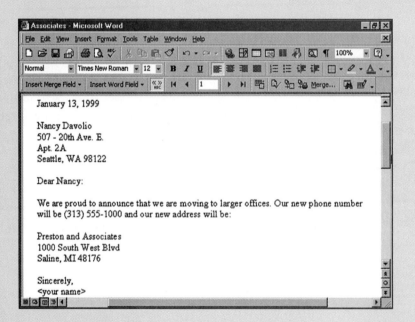

2 Click the Next Record button.

The data from the second record is displayed. Notice that the address of the first person takes two lines, whereas the second person's address takes only one line. Word adjusts for multiple line addresses and for empty fields.

3 Click the **M**erge button on the Mail Merge toolbar.

The ScreenTip for this button displays Start Mail Merge. When you click it, the Merge dialog box is displayed.

4 Click the list arrow next to the Me**r**ge to drop-down list box.

Notice that you can send this letter electronically by email as well as by traditional postal service (see Figure 8.10). If your system is set up to use a fax, it will also be displayed as an option.

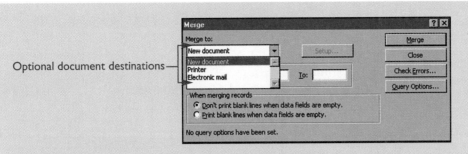

Optional document destinations —

Figure 8.10
The Mail Merge document
can be sent by fax or to
email addresses.

5 **Select Printer. Click the From text box in the Records to be merged section, and type 1. Type 2 in the To text box.**

6 **Click the Merge button to print the letters to the first two people in the Addresses table.**
The Print dialog box is displayed.

7 **Click OK.**
The first two letters are printed.

8 **Close the Associates Word document.**
Save any changes when prompted. Close Microsoft Word. Leave the Associates database open for use in the next lesson.

Creating the Main Document Using Word
The mail merge process can start with Word rather than Access. You can open Word, use the mail merge procedures for Word to create a document, and then tie it to the Access database that contains the records of the names and addresses for your letter.

Lesson 4: Importing a Table from Excel

Excel has some database management features, such as the capability to sort and filter data. Therefore, many people use Excel as a simple database management program. Often, however, the amount of data that needs to be maintained becomes too cumbersome to do effectively in Excel. When this happens, you will need to **import** data that is stored in an Excel spreadsheet and use it with an Access database. When you import data, the rows of data are treated as records and are copied into Access. Each column of information in Excel is identified as a field in Access.

In this lesson, you will import an Excel spreadsheet that contains budget information for the U.S. Government into the Associates database that is open from the previous lesson. The Associates database is being used for convenience—the information being imported in the next three lessons is not related to the address table in the database.

To Import a Table from Excel

1 **Launch Excel and open AC1-0802 from the CD. Scroll down the rows, and examine the data.**

Notice that each row is a record of a type of government expense. The column headings will become field names (see Figure 8.11).

Figure 8.11
The Excel column headings will become Access field names.
Column headings —

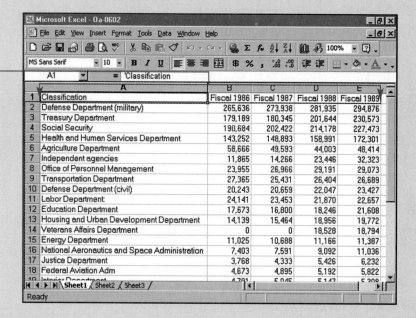

2 **Close the file, and close Excel.**

Switch to Access and the Associates database.

3 **Choose File, Get External Data, Import.**

The Import dialog box is displayed.

4 **Click the list arrow next to the Files of type drop-down list box, and select Microsoft Excel. Locate and select the AC1-0802 Excel file on the CD.**

Your Import dialog box should look like Figure 8.12.

Figure 8.12
You must specify the file type you want to import.

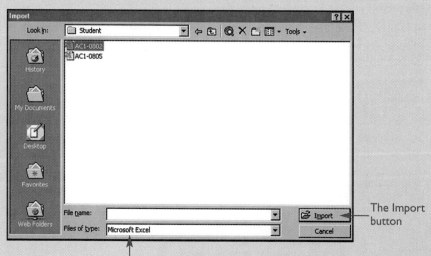

The Import button

The Microsoft Excel file type has been selected

5 Click the Import button.

The Import Spreadsheet Wizard dialog box is displayed. Make sure the Show Worksheets option button is selected and that Sheet1 is highlighted. Notice that the column headings in the first row are displayed as data (see Figure 8.13).

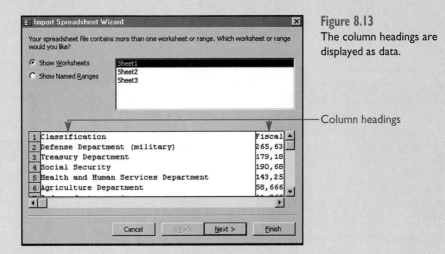

Figure 8.13
The column headings are displayed as data.

Column headings

6 Click Next. Click the check box next to First Row Contains Column Headings, if necessary.

The row that contains the words Classification and Fiscal is converted to headers, which will appear as field names in the database table (see Figure 8.14).

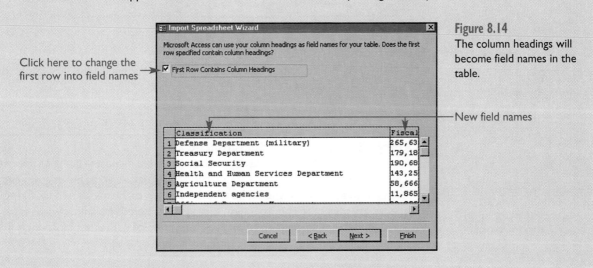

Click here to change the first row into field names

Figure 8.14
The column headings will become field names in the table.

New field names

7 Click Next. Make sure that the In a New Table option button is selected.

8 Click Next.

Do not add indexes to any of the fields.

9 Click Next. Select Let Access add Primary Key, if it is not already selected.

In this case, there are no unique fields, so you can let Access add a field that gives each row a unique number.

continues ▶

To Import a Table from Excel (continued)

10 Click **Next**. Type Government Expenses in the **Import to Table** text box.

11 Click **Finish**. Click **OK** when Access prompts that the import is finished.

The Government Expenses data is added to the database as a new table.

12 Click the **Open** button in the database window.

The Government Expenses table is displayed (see Figure 8.15).

New field names

Figure 8.15
The Excel worksheet has been imported as an Access table.

Primary key field

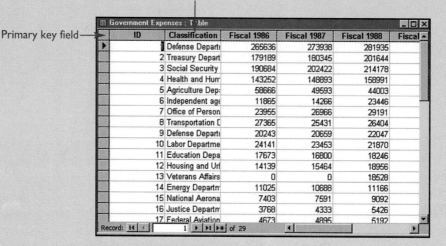

ID	Classification	Fiscal 1986	Fiscal 1987	Fiscal 1988	Fiscal
1	Defense Depart	265636	273938	281935	
2	Treasury Depart	179189	180345	201644	
3	Social Security	190684	202422	214178	
4	Health and Hum	143252	148893	158991	
5	Agriculture Dep:	58666	49593	44003	
6	Independent age	11865	14266	23446	
7	Office of Person	23955	26966	29191	
8	Transportation D	27365	25431	26404	
9	Defense Depart	20243	20659	22047	
10	Labor Departme	24141	23453	21870	
11	Education Depa	17673	16800	18246	
12	Housing and Url	14139	15464	18956	
13	Veterans Affairs	0	0	18528	
14	Energy Departm	11025	10688	11166	
15	National Aerona	7403	7591	9092	
16	Justice Departm	3768	4333	5426	
17	Federal Aviation	4673	4895	5192	

Record: I◄ ◄ 1 ► ►I ►* of 29

13 Click the **Close button**.

This table is now available to use. Leave the Associates database open for the next lesson.

⚠ Preparing to Import a Spreadsheet

A spreadsheet must be set up like a database table if you are going to import it successfully. Check to make sure that the Excel data is arranged in rows and columns. Each column should be a field type, and each row should be a record. If necessary, copy the data to a new spreadsheet. Remove blank rows or rows that contain decorative characters, such as long rows of dashes set up to look like a line.

Lesson 5: Saving a Form as a Data Access Page

Access 2000 is capable of saving forms as interactive Web pages. To save an interactive Web page, save your object as a **data access page**, which is a special type of Web page that has been designed for viewing and working with data from the Internet. You can place a database on a Web server and interact with it using an interactive Web page. To view an interactive Web page, you must have a browser that supports this feature, such as Internet Explorer 5.0.

In this lesson, you create a Web page that would allow your sales people to look up contact information.

To Save a Form as a Data Access Page

1 **In the Associates database window, click the Pages object button and then click <u>N</u>ew.**
The New Data Access Page window is displayed.

2 **Select Page Wizard, choose the Addresses table as the data source, and then click OK.**
The first page of the Page Wizard is displayed.

3 **Use the Add button to select the following fields: FirstName, LastName, Address, City, EmailAddress, HomePhone, WorkPhone, WorkExtension, and FaxNumber.**
Your dialog box should look like Figure 8.16.

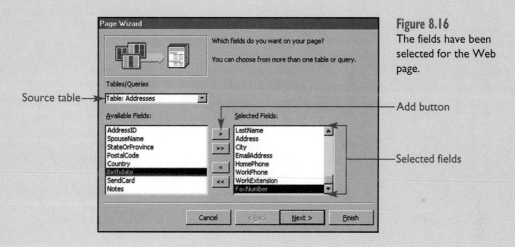

Figure 8.16
The fields have been selected for the Web page.

Source table
Add button
Selected fields

4 **Click <u>N</u>ext.**
The second Page Wizard dialog box is displayed. Do not use the grouping option at this time.

5 **Click <u>N</u>ext.**
The third Page Wizard dialog box is displayed (see Figure 8.17). This page is used to sort the records.

continues ▶

To Save a Form as a Data Access Page   (continued)

Figure 8.17
The third Page Wizard
dialog box enables you
to sort the records.

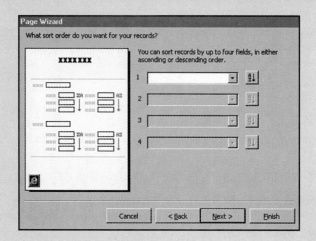

6 **Click the list arrow next to the first sorting box, and select LastName. Click Next.**
The fourth Page Wizard dialog box is displayed, asking you for a title for the page.

7 **Type the title** Contact Information **and click Finish.**
The wizard creates the Contact Information data access page. It is opened in Design view.

8 **Click in the Click here and type title text area, and type** Business Contacts.
You could also type introductory text above the data area (see Figure 8.18).

Figure 8.18
The Design view of
the Page window enables
you to add titles and
supplementary text
to the page.   Supplemental
text area

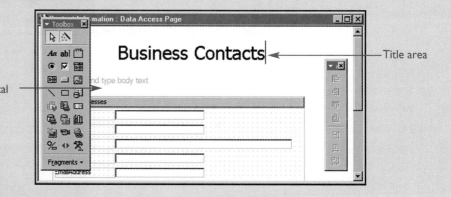

9 **Click the View button to switch to Page view. Maximize the window.**
The title is displayed at the top of the page and the first record is shown. A set of navigation buttons is displayed below the data (see Figure 8.19).

Figure 8.19
The Web page is previewed in Page view.

— Title

First record

Navigation buttons

⑩ **Use the navigation buttons at the bottom of the page to scroll through the records.**
The mouse pointer may be in the shape of an I-beam rather than a pointer when you point at the navigation buttons. You can, however, still click on the navigation arrows to scroll through the records.

⑪ **Close the page and choose Yes to save the changes.**
The Save As Data Access Page dialog box opens.

⑫ **Type Contact Access Page in the File name text box. Click Save to save the data access page.**
Make sure the Save in box displays the location of your database. In addition to saving this in the database, the page is also saved separately with an .htm extension in the same location as your database. In this case, the filename is Contact Access Page.htm.

⑬ **Close the Associates database, and close Access.**
In the next lesson you will view the data access page as you would on the Internet.

 File Structure of Data Access Pages
When you create a data access page, it is saved as a separate file that you can view as you would a Web page on the Internet. Microsoft Access automatically creates a shortcut to the file, which is what you see in the Database window. The process of creating a data access page is similar to creating forms or reports; however, there can be several different ways a page can be used. The design of the page is influenced by its ultimate purpose. For more information about designing a data access page, open Help and review the topic "Data access pages: What they are and how they work."

Lesson 6: Using a Browser to Interact with the Database

If the database table and a related interactive Web page are placed on a Web server (or in a shared folder on a local area network), then others can use the database with a Web browser. A **browser**, such as Internet Explorer or Netscape Navigator, is a program that enables you to view Web pages on the Internet. When you interact with the table on the Web, you can browse through the data. You can also sort and filter the data using any field. You can even change the data.

In this lesson, you use Internet Explorer to interact with the database on your disk as if it were placed on a Web server.

To Use a Browser to Interact with the Database

1 Launch Internet Explorer.
You must have Internet Explorer 5.0 or greater to run the Web page you created in Lesson 5. You do not need to connect to the Web, so click Cancel to work offline.

2 Click in the Address box, and type the disk location and name of your Web page (for example, `A:\Contact Access Page.htm`), then press `←Enter`.
As you type, the program will automatically start to search for the file. A list of files that have been accessed previously by your computer may be displayed. The arrow at the end of the address box opens and closes this list.

The browser displays the page and a toolbar (see Figure 8.20).

Figure 8.20
The Web page is previewed in Internet Explorer.

Type the location and filename here

First Record button

Next Record button

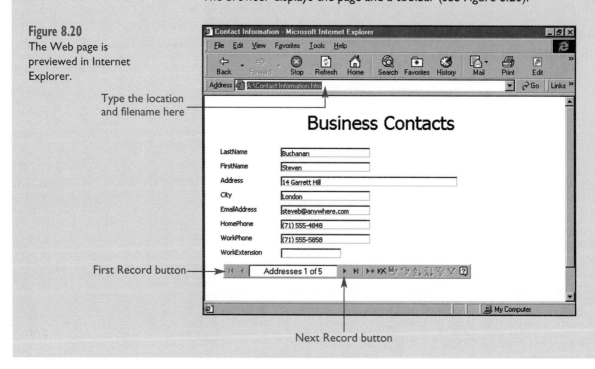

X If you have saved your file to a folder, the folder may be opened and icons for the various files will be displayed. Click the file with the explorer icon and the name Contacts Access Page.htm. to view your data access page.

3 Click the Next Record navigation button to scroll through the records.

4 Click the navigation button at the far left of the navigation bar to return to the first record.
Notice that the area codes for the two phone numbers are incorrect.

5 Edit these two phone numbers to change the area code to (717).

6 Click in the LastName field, then click the Sort Descending button.
Scroll through the records using the navigation buttons. Notice that the records are displayed in reverse alphabetical order by last name.

7 Close the browser.
Notice that the Access program was not running during this lesson.

8 Launch Access, and open the Associates database.

9 Open the Addresses table, and scroll to the right until you can see both telephone numbers.
Both area codes that you changed in the Web page are changed in the database table (see Figure 8.21).

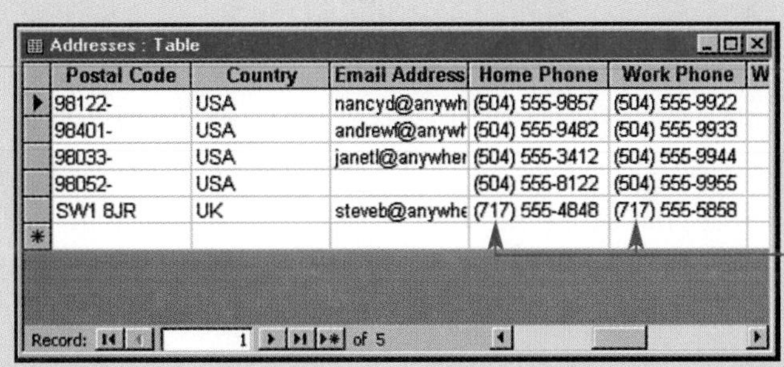

Postal Code	Country	Email Address	Home Phone	Work Phone	W
98122-	USA	nancyd@anywh	(504) 555-9857	(504) 555-9922	
98401-	USA	andrewf@anywł	(504) 555-9482	(504) 555-9933	
98033-	USA	janetl@anywher	(504) 555-3412	(504) 555-9944	
98052-	USA		(504) 555-8122	(504) 555-9955	
SW1 8JR	UK	steveb@anywhe	(717) 555-4848	(717) 555-5858	

Record: 1 of 5

Figure 8.21
The area codes that were changed on the Web page are also changed in the table.

The area codes have been changed

10 Close the table, and close the database.

i **Entering Addresses in Internet Explorer**
When you are typing the address in Internet Explorer, once it has determined that you are typing a drive name, it will offer you a drop-down menu. For example, after you type A: (if your page was saved on drive A:), a drop-down menu is displayed, showing all the files available on that drive.

If you have completed your session on the computer, exit Access and Windows before you turn off the computer. Otherwise, continue with the "Checking Concepts and Terms" section of this project.

Summary

In this project, you were introduced to some of the tools and techniques that enable you to work with information from other sources and to publish Access files for use as Web pages. Specifically, you learned to convert an existing Access database to the current version, Access 2000. You also imported data from an Excel spreadsheet into Access. You then created a data access page and viewed it using a Web browser.

To learn more about the capability of Access to import data from other sources, go to Help and look at the topic "Data sources Microsoft Access can import or link." Also, examine the links on the "Data access pages: What are they and how do they work" page. This will expand your knowledge about the design consideration when you want to make your database accessible using a Web browser.

Checking Concepts and Terms

True/False

For each of the following, check *T* or *F* to indicate whether the statement is true or false.

__T __F   **1.** To merge an Access database with a Word document, you must first create the document, and then open the database and merge it with the document. [L3]

__T __F   **2.** One reason to view your merged document before printing is to ensure that the document looks the way you intended. [L3]

__T __F   **3.** When you print a merged Word/Access document, you must print all the records, rather than just a few records. [L3]

__T __F   **4.** The Merge function in Access adjusts for multiple address lines and empty fields when it prints a merged document. [L3]

__T __F   **5.** Excel files cannot be imported into an Access database. [L4]

__T __F   **6.** When importing a spreadsheet file into Access, it is important that the first row of the spreadsheet is set up with field names, and each subsequent row is a record. [L4]

__T __F   **7.** If you want to use an Access 2000 database on a computer that has Access 97, you can use the Save As option on the File menu. [L1]

__T __F   **8.** Saving a form as a Web page produces a file that can be viewed by an Internet Browser such as Internet Explorer 5.0. [L5]

__T __F   **9.** It is possible to change the data in the database by using a browser and a Web page. [L6]

__T __F   **10.** You can sort the data in a data access page in Ascending or Descending order. [L6]

Multiple Choice

Circle the letter of the correct answer for each of the following questions.

1. What can you do with a database created using an older version of Access? [L1]

  a. Enter data with Access 2000, but do not change any objects.

  b. Convert it to Access 2000.

  c. Share the database with people using different versions of Access.

  d. All of the above.

2. How do you set up a Microsoft Word mail merge document while you are using Access? [L2]

a. Click the MailMerge button in the toolbar.

b. Select the appropriate table, click the OfficeLinks button, and choose Merge It with MS Word.

c. Select the appropriate table, open MS Word, and choose Link to Access from the Tools menu.

d. Open the appropriate table, click the OfficeLinks button, and choose Merge It with MS Word.

3. By what method can you send a mail merge document? [L3]

a. a fax machine

b. a printer

c. email

d. All of the above.

4. When you create a Web page using the Page Wizard, how is the Web page saved? [L5]

a. as a separate file only

b. in the database as a shortcut and as a separate file

c. only in the database

d. on a file server only

5. What can you do when you open an Access table on the Web? [L6]

a. Edit the data.

b. Sort the records using any field.

c. Filter the data.

d. All of the above.

6. Your company has just changed to Access 2000. What must you do to be able to add a field to a table in an Access database created in an earlier version? [L1]

a. You must use the earlier version to change the database.

b. Open the database in the earlier version, and choose the save as command to save it to the newer version.

c. Convert the database to Access 2000 and use Access 2000.

d. Open the database in Access 2000 but do not convert it.

7. When you import data from Excel into Access, how does Access interpret the data? [L4]

a. Rows of data are interpreted as records, and columns are interpreted as fields.

b. Columns of data are interpreted as records, and rows are interpreted as fields.

c. Access does not make any assumptions, and asks you to identify the records.

d. You enter the names of the fields in the Import Wizard.

8. Which of the following is not true about merging data from Access into a Word document? [L2]

a. You can begin the merge process by first opening Word and using the Word merge procedures.

b. You can base the merge on a query or a table.

c. You can use each field in the table only one time in the Word document.

d. You can include calculated fields in a merged document.

9. What is the command used to import data? [L4]

a. Choose File, Get External Data, Import from the menu.

b. Click the Import button.

c. Choose Insert, Data, Import from the menu.

d. none of the above

10. How do you begin the process to create a page from your database that can be viewed on the Web? [L5]

a. Click the Create Web page button on the toolbar.

b. Click the Pages object button and select New.

c. Select the object you want to use and choose File, Save as, Web page from the menu.

d. Select the object you want to use and click Officelinks, Publish as Web page from the menu.

Screen ID

Label each element of the Access screens shown in Figure 8.22 and 8.23.

Figure 8.22

A. Merge field

B. Returns to first record on a Web page

C. Sort descending button

D. Displays next record on a Web page.

E. Places an Access field in a Word document

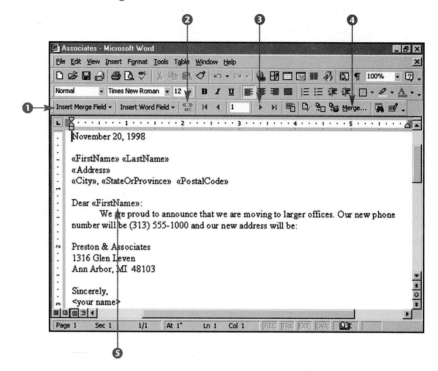

Figure 8.23

F. Press to start mail merge

G. Displays next merged record

H. Location of Web page on your disk

I. View merged data button

J. Data access page title

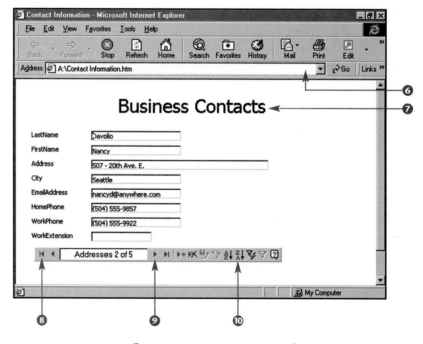

1. _____	5. _____	8. _____
2. _____	6. _____	9. _____
3. _____	7. _____	10. _____
4. _____		

Discussion Questions

1. What methods have been commonly used in the past for sharing files and information between co-workers? What was done before people used personal computers? What was done before people used networks and the Internet?

2. How has the communication technology used today impacted businesses? How does it affect the way we work? How can it make businesses more successful?

3. Of the various forms of communications technology that are used today, which do you think has had the greatest impact? Why?

4. For databases that you commonly use, how would the capability to share the data with coworkers affect your work? What are some of the issues involved in sharing databases?

Skill Drill

Skill Drill exercises reinforce project skills. Each skill reinforced is the same, or nearly the same, as a skill presented in the project. Each exercise includes a brief narrative introduction, followed by detailed instructions in a step-by-step format.

1. Open a Database Created in an Older Version of Access

To practice converting databases from older versions of Access, convert this database of Michigan Tornadoes and give it a new name.

To open a database created in an older version of Access, follow these steps:

1. Launch Access.
2. Find and select the file AC1-0803 on your CD-ROM.
3. Click the Convert Database option button.
4. Give the file a new filename of `Michigan Tornadoes`.
5. Choose to save the file on drive A:.
6. Open the Michigan Tornadoes—Last Decade table to make sure the file translated properly.
7. Close the table and close the database.

2. Creating a Memo Using Mail Merge

Your company is going to have a summer picnic. You have already invited all of your employees, but you decide it would also be a nice gesture to invite your contacts. You will use a new version of the Associates database you worked with throughout this project to create a quick memo to send to the people in the Addresses table.

To create a memo using mail merge, do the following:

1. Find the AC1-0804 database file on your CD-ROM, send it to drive A:, and name it `Associates2`. Select the Addresses table.
2. Edit the Addresses table and enter `a guest` in the empty spouse field.
3. Click the OfficeLinks button (select the database window to activate the Database toolbar), and select Merge It with MS Word. Create a new document in Word, and click Open.
4. Create a mail merge memo announcing a company picnic. Invite each person by name. Also invite their spouse by name. Use Figure 8.24 as a guide.

Figure 8.24
Your document should include fields for your name, your contact's first and last name, and his or her spouse's name.

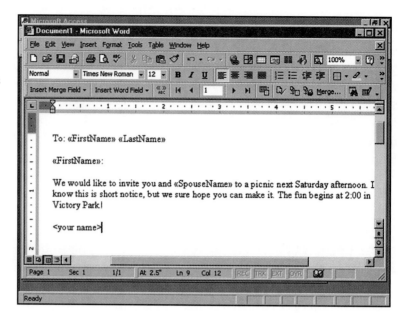

5. Use your name at the bottom of each letter where it says <your name>.

6. Save the document as `Picnic Invitation`. Leave it open for the next exercise. Leave the Associates2 database open.

3. Merging and Printing a Mail Merge Document

Now that you have created the mail merge document to invite your contacts to the company picnic, it is time to make sure it works properly, and then print the memos.

To merge and print a mail merge document, here are the steps:

1. In Word, click the View Merged Data button to test your mail merge document.

2. Scroll through the records to make sure the record you edited flows smoothly.

3. Choose File, Print from the menu. Print the letters for records 1 and 5. To do this in one step, type `1,5` in the Pages box; then click OK.

4. Close the Picnic Invitation document, but leave the Associates2 database open.

4. Importing a Table from Excel

Your company's sales are based on population growth, so you would like to have some population forecasts available to make long-range sales projections. One of the marketing people has put the information into an Excel worksheet. You want to move it into your Associates database.

To import a table from Excel, follow these steps:

1. Choose File, Get External Data, and Import from the menu.

2. Specify Microsoft Excel in the Files of type box.

3. Find the AC1-0805 Excel file, and Import the first sheet.

4. Specify that the first row contains column headings.

5. Select the Choose my own primary key option button, and select the Year column as the primary key.

6. Name the table `Population Projection`.

7. Open the table, and review it to make sure it translated properly.

8. Print the table; then close it.

9. Leave the database open to use in the next exercise.

5. Creating a Data Page to Use on the Web

You want to put the government budget information on a Web page. The first step is to create the data page and decide what information you want to include.

To create a data page to use on the Web, do the following:

1. In the Associates2 database window, click the Pages object button, and click New.

2. Select Page Wizard, and choose the Government Expenses table.

3. Select the Classification, Fiscal 1987, Fiscal 1988, and Fiscal 1989 fields. You will not be using the ID and Fiscal 1986 fields.

4. Sort by Classification.

5. Call the data page Government Budget.

6. Add a title called U.S. Government Budget.

7. Close the Data Access Page design window. When prompted, save the page with the name Government Expenses, then close the Associates2 database.

6. Opening a Data Page Using a Web Browser

Now that you have created a data access page, you need to open it using an Internet browser to make sure it is working properly.

To open a data page using a Web browser, do the following:

1. Launch Internet Explorer or another browser, and enter the location and name of the Government Expenses.htm file you just created. (If you have trouble locating the file, use File, Open, Browse and locate the file in the Microsoft Internet Explorer window.)

2. Double-click the Government Expenses file to open it.

3. Use the navigation buttons to scroll through the records. What could you do to improve the quality of this page?

4. Close the Internet Explorer.

Challenge

Challenge exercises expand on or are somewhat related to skills presented in the lessons. Each exercise provides a brief narrative introduction followed by instructions in a numbered step or bullet list format that are not as detailed as those in the Skill Drill section.

1. Opening and Adding Data to an Older Version of Access

You and your sister have been collecting CDs for years, and entering the information into a database. She has a computer that uses Access 97, whereas you have upgraded to Access 2000. You still want to keep up the database, so you have to open the old version without converting it. You would also like to add another field to help keep track of who owns which CD.

To open and add data to an older version of Access, do the following:

1. Copy the AC1-0806 file to your drive A: and change the name to CD Collection.

2. Open the CD Collection database. Choose the Open Database option, not the Convert Database option.

3. Open the CD Collection table, and add the following record

   Rollins, Sonny

   Saxophone Colossus

   1956

```
Prestige
OJCCD-291-2
Jazz/Big Band
```

4. Go to Design view, and scroll to the first empty field.

5. Add a text field called `Whose?`.

6. Click the View button to switch back to the datasheet. What happens? Why?

7. Close the table without saving the changes. Close the CD Collection database.

2. Importing a Table from an Old dBASE III Database

A common database for personal computers in the 1980s was dBASE III. Many database records from that decade are stored in that format, as are many data sources on the Web. In this exercise, you import data from a 1987 database that shows statistics about retail establishments and their employees in Michigan by postal code. (Sales and Payroll figures are in 1000s.)

To import a table from an old dBASEIII plus database, here are the steps:

1. Create a new database, and call it `Michigan Retail Statistics`.

2. Choose File, Get External Data, and Import from the menu.

3. Specify that you are looking for dBASEIII file types and select the file, ACI-0807.dbf.

4. Close the Import dialog box. Rename the new table `Retail Statistics`. If you do not remember how to do this, use Help.

5. Open the Retail Statistics table. Click the record selector to the left of the first record. Press (⬆Shift) and click the record selector for the tenth record (ZIP Code is 48009) to select the first ten records.

6. Choose File, Print, Selected Records(s), and print the first ten records.

7. Close the table, and close the database.

[?] 3. Importing a Text File

Data is frequently found in text files where the fields are separated by tabs, commas, spaces, or some other character. These data separators are known as **delimiters**. If fields are separated by tabs, for example, the file is referred to as tab-delimited. Access can import such files using the Import wizard.

To import a text file, follow these steps:

1. Find the ACI-0808.txt file on your student disk. Open it in Microsoft Word to find out what kind of delimiter is used. Click the Show/Hide button, if necessary. Close the file.

2. Create a new database called `Hardware Supplies`.

3. Check the available Microsoft help to figure out how to import a text file into a table. Let Access add a primary key field.

4. Name the new table `Plumbing`. Print the table.

5. Close the table, and close the database.

4. Creating a Data Access Page Based on a Query

You can base a data access page on a query as well as a table. This gives you the ability to use query features, such as criteria, to restrict the information you place on the Web. In the following three challenges, you use the CD collection information that you worked with in the first exercise in the Challenge section.

To create a data access page based on a query, do this:

1. Copy the AC1-0809 database onto drive A:, and rename it `New CD Collection`.
2. Create a new query based on the CD Collection table. Include all of the fields. Call the query `The Last 10 Years`.
3. Set the criteria so that the query only shows CDs from after 1988.
4. Create a new data access page based on The Last 10 Years query. Do not group or sort.
5. Add a title that says `CDs Since 1988`.
6. Save it with the name `New CD Collection`.
7. Close the database, and preview your Web page on your browser.

[?] 5. Editing an Existing Data Access Page

You will often look at your new Web page and decide that there should be some changes made. You can always go back to Access and edit your work.

To edit an existing data Access page, do the following:

1. Open the New CD Collection database, and click the Pages object button, if necessary.
2. Select the New CD Collection page, and open it in Design view.
3. Add `From the Collection of <your name>` as body text (type in your name for <your name>).
4. Use the available help to figure out how to add a clip art image to the page. Find an appropriate image, and resize it to about 1" high. Place it to the right of the title.
5. Close the page, and save your changes.
6. Go to the Windows Explorer or My Computer and look at the file you just saved. There should be a new folder that contains a copy of the image you placed in the page. This folder needs to be kept with the page file.
7. Close the database, and close Access.

6. Sorting and Filtering Information on a Data Page

When you open a data access page on the Web, Access gives you some control over the data. You can sort on any field, and you can filter the data by category. This restricts the records in the list to the ones that match the filter you have applied. Applying a filter is like using criteria in a query to limit the records to the ones that match the criteria.

To sort and filter information on a data page, do this:

1. Open the New CD Collection.htm page in the browser. Click in the Artist/Group field.
2. Click on the Sort Ascending button on the toolbar at the bottom of the screen. The records are sorted in ascending order by the Artist/Group field.

3. Scroll to the first record listed as Classical; then click in the Classical field.

4. Click the Filter by Selection button that is near the right end of the toolbar at the bottom of the screen. To the right of the title in the scrollbar, it should display 1 of 92. This indicates that there are 92 classical selections in this list of CDs. Scroll through a few records to make sure that the filter worked.

5. Click the Remove Filter button to turn the filter off. All 198 records should be listed in the navigation bar as shown in Figure 8.25.

6. Close your browser.

Figure 8.25
You can sort and filter records on a data access page viewed with a browser.

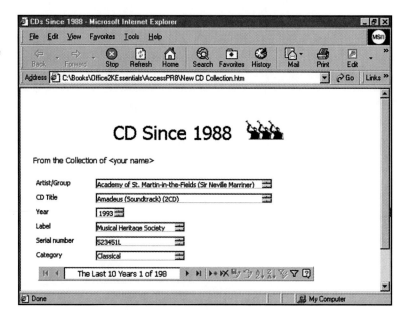

Discovery Zone

Discovery Zone exercises help you gain advanced knowledge of project topics and application of skills. These exercises focus on enhancing your problem-solving skills. Numbered steps are not provided, but you are given hints, reminders, screen shots, and references to help you reach your goal for each exercise.

1. Copying Part of a Table to a Word Document

A convenient way to transfer data from a database table to a document is a simple copy and paste. This results in creating a table in Word that can be formatted in a variety of styles. Try this procedure with the data from the Addresses table in the Associates database that you worked with earlier in this project.

Goal: Copy columns of data from an Access table to a table in Word.

An associate has requested a list of names and addresses from you. Launch Word; then write a short note to your coworker that tells him or her that this is the list of names that was requested. Make sure you include your name at the end of your brief note.

Open the AC1-0804 database as **Associates3** on drive A:, and use the Addresses table. In your memo, you should include first and last name, and home and work phone numbers.

To copy these fields to Word, they need to be next to each other so they can be copied as a group. (Hint: Do not make this a permanent change to the structure of the table; move the fields in Datasheet view.)

Select and copy the First Name, Last Name, Home Phone, and Work Phone fields, then switch to Word and paste it. Format the table by choosing T<u>a</u>ble, Table <u>A</u>utoFormat from the menu. Choose a format that you like. (Hint: Be sure to select the column headings when you are selecting the information to copy.)

Print the document and save it as **Associates3**. Close the Word document, but leave the database open to use in the next exercise.

2. Updating a Table by Pasting Cells from a Spreadsheet

You may want to send a table of data for someone to work on who does not have the Access program, but who does have Excel. To do this, you can export the data to Excel.

Goal: Export a table to Excel, make changes to it in Excel, then paste the new cells back into the Access table.

To ensure that you keep the original data intact, you want to make a copy of the table and export the copy to Excel. Make a copy of the Addresses table and name the copy **Address Updates**. (Hint: right-click on the table and use the shortcut menus.)

Export the table to Excel. Name it **Address Updates**. (Hint: The <u>E</u>xport command is on the <u>F</u>ile menu. When you name it, be sure to change the Save as <u>t</u>ype box to Excel97/2000.)

Launch Excel and open the Addresses Updates file. Scroll to the right and add comments to the Notes field in the Excel sheet. Don't be concerned about the width of the columns.

Now you want to transfer this new information back to the original Access table. Copy the updated cells in the Excel sheet but do not include the heading. Open the Addresses table in Access. Click the Notes column selector and paste the entries from the Excel sheet. The information that was entered in Excel now is entered in the original Access table. Close the database, and then close Excel.

All key terms appearing in this book (in bold italic) are listed alphabetically in this Glossary for easy reference. If you want to learn more about a feature or concept, turn to the page reference shown after its definition. You can also use the Index to find the term's other significant occurrences.

AutoForm   a form created automatically by Access that includes all the fields in a table. [pg. 106]

AutoReport   a tool for creating an automatically formatted report from a database table or query. [pg. 134]

Browser   a program that enables you to view Web pages on the Internet. Examples are Internet Explorer or Netscape Navigator. [pg. 206]

Clipboard   a temporary storage location for whatever you have copied or cut from your document. [pg. 63]

Column selector   the thin gray line above the field name in the query Design view. When you click the column selector, the whole column is selected. [pg. 88]

Control   any object selected from the toolbox or field list, such as a text box, check box, or option button that you add to a form or report. [pg. 112]

Criteria   a test or set of conditions that limits the records included in a query. A single condition is a called a criterion. [pg. 91]

Current record indicator   an arrow in the record selector that points to the record that is currently active. [pg. 57]

Data access page   a special type of Web page that has been designed for viewing and working with data on the Internet. [pg. 202]

Data type   a definition of the kind of data that can be entered into a field. [pg. 29]

Database window   A page that displays a list of the table, query, form, report, macro, and module objects that comprise a database. [pg. 5]

Database   a program that allows you to store, retrieve, analyze, and print large amounts of information. [pg. 2]

Datasheet view   the row-and-column view you use when you enter or edit records in a table. [pg. 32]

Delimiter   a character that separates fields in a text file. Common delimiters are tabs, commas, semicolons, and spaces. [pg. 214]

Design grid   the area used to define the conditions of a query. You can specify fields, sort order, and criteria to be used to search your database. [pg. 83]

Design view   the view of the table you use when you are creating or changing fields. You see columns for the field name, data type, and description of each field. [pg. 31]

Dynaset   a subset of records created as a result of a query. [pg. 80]

Enforce Referential Integrity   ensures that each record in the related table is connected to a record in the primary table. This helps prevent orphan records, and it prevents you from adding records that are not connected to an existing record in the primary table. [pg. 177]

Expression   a predefined or user-defined formula that performs calculations, displays built-in functions, or sets limits. You can include expressions in reports and other Access objects, such as macros. [pg. 143]

Field   a single category of data or information; the column headings in a database table. [pg. 2]

Field label   the field name attached to a field text box in a form or report. [pg. 114]

Field text box   a placeholder for the contents of a field in the database. Field text boxes show the actual data that has been entered into a table. [pg. 114]

Form   a type of object you can use to enter, edit, and view records. Think of a form as a fill-in-the-blanks screen. [pg. 106]

Form Detail   the main part of a form, in which the records are displayed. [pg. 112]

Form Footer   the area at the bottom of the form, containing controls such as labels, dates, or page numbers. This appears at the bottom of each form page. [pg. 112]

Form Header   the area at the top of the form, containing controls such as labels, dates, or graphics. This appears at the top of each form page. [pg. 112]

Import   to include data from a source outside of the existing database. [pg. 199]

Index   a location guide built by Access for all primary key fields that helps speed up searching and sorting for a particular field. Indexes can also be created for other fields, as long as they are not OLE or Memo fields. [pg. 33]

Join   the manner in which the common fields between two tables are associated. [pg. 178]

Label   text on a form or report that is not bound to the table. [pg. 113]

Landscape orientation   the horizontal orientation of a printed page. [pg. 136]

Launch   to run a Microsoft Office program. [pg. 3]

Mail merge   a word processing feature that allows you to customize documents using information from a database table. [pg. 195]

Normalize   to apply a set of design rules to the tables in a database. [pg. 26]

Object Linking and Embedding (OLE)   a set of standards that enables you to insert objects, such as pictures or charts, from one document created with one application into documents created with another application. [pg. 30]

Objects   a general term for the components of an Access database, including tables, queries, forms, reports, pages, macros, and modules. [pg. 5]

Office Assistant   the Help feature that answers questions. [pg. 11]

One-to-many   a relationship in which a record in one table may be related to more than one record in a second table. [pg. 162]

Pencil icon   an icon that looks like a pencil. It is displayed in the record selector when you are editing a record in Datasheet view, and it indicates that the current changes have not yet been saved. [pg. 60]

Portrait orientation   the vertical orientation of a printed page. This is the most common page orientation. [pg. 136]

Primary key   a field that contains a unique value for each record and is used to identify the record. [pg. 26]

Properties   the characteristics of a screen element. For example, a number has such properties as number of decimal places, format, font size, and others. [pg. 23]

Query   a question posed to the database that determines what information is retrieved. A query can be used to restrict which fields are shown and what conditions the displayed data must meet. It can also be defined as one of the objects in a database. [pg. 80]

Read-only   a database file that has been opened but cannot be changed. This occurs when you open a database file copied from a CD-ROM. [pg. 3]

Record   a group of data pertaining to one event, transaction, or person. The categories of information in a record are called fields. [pg. 2]

Record selector   the gray area to the left of a record. It indicates whether the record is selected or being edited. Clicking on it selects the whole record. [pg. 55]

Relational database   a database that has two or more tables that are linked together. [pg. 27]

Relationship   the connection between two tables. [pg. 33]

Report   a database object that is designed to print and summarize selected fields. [pg. 134]

Row selector   the gray area to the left of a field in the table Design view. Clicking a box in this area selects the entire row. [pg. 35]

Section   a division of a report, such as the Detail, Page Header, or Page Footer, that can contain controls, labels, formulas, and images. [pg. 134]

Select query   lists data that meets conditions set by the user. [pg. 83]

Selection handles   small squares that appear at the corners and on the edges of boxes that are used to change the size of the box. [pg. 116]

Tab Order   the order in which the insertion point jumps from field to field on a form. [pg. 118]

Table   one of the objects in an Access database. Tables store data in row-and-column format and are the foundation of the database. [pg. 2]

What's This?   the Help feature that describes the functions of different parts of the screen. [pg. 11]

Task Guide

A book in the *Essentials* series is designed to be kept as a handy reference beside your computer even after you have completed all the projects and exercises. Any time you have difficulty recalling the sequence of steps or a shortcut needed to achieve a result, look up the general category in the following alphabetized listing, and then quickly home in on your task at hand. For your convenience, some tasks have been duplicated under more than one category. If you have difficulty performing a task, turn to the page number listed in the third column to locate the step-by-step exercise or other detailed description. If a task does not include a page reference, it is a bonus task from the author that was not within the scope of the book. To use this Task Guide with the greatest efficiency, take a few minutes to familiarize yourself with the main categories and keywords before you begin your search.

To Do This	Perform These Steps	Page Number
Application and File Management		
Close database	Click the Close button in the database window.	[pg. 8]
Convert database	Launch Access. To convert from a previous version, select and open the file. Choose to Convert or Open the database. When prompted, give the database a new name, and specify the location to save it.	[pg. 194]
Create new database	Launch Access, and click Blank Database; then click OK. Type a filename and select the drive or folder location for the file. Click the Create button.	[pg. 28]
Exit Access	Click the Close boxes for the object, the database, and the Access program.	[pg. 15]
Exit Windows	Click the Start button on the taskbar and choose the Shut Down option.	[pg. 15]
Launch Access	Turn on your computer, and click Start in the Windows taskbar. Choose Programs, Microsoft Access.	[pg. 3]
Open database	Launch Access, select Open an existing file, and click OK. From the Open dialog box, find the file you need using the Look in text box. Select the file, and click Open.	[pg. 5]

continues ▶

To Do This	Perform These Steps	Page Number
Field		
Add to form	In form Design view, drag fields from the selected field list box and place them on the grid until you have included all the fields you need. Use the rulers to help align the fields.	[pg. 113]
Add to query	In query Design view, click and drag the field from the field list box to the design grid; or, in the design grid, click the drop-down arrow, and choose the field you want; or double-click the field in the field list box.	[pg. 83]
Add to report	In report Design view, click and drag the field you want from the field list box to the desired position. Click the Print Preview button to view the report.	[pg. 145]
Add to table	In table Design view, go to the first blank row and insert the new field name, data type, and description for each field to be added.	[pg. 36]
Default value: enter	In table Design view, click the field selector of the field you want to change. In the Field Properties area, click the Default Value box. Type a default value on this line. Quotation marks may be required for certain words that are used by Access in formulas.	[pg. 166]
Delete	In table Design view, use the row selector to select the row you want to delete. Click the Delete Rows button.	[pgs. 43, 165]
Edit	In table Design view, go to the field name, data type, or description you want to edit. Select the information you want to change, and type the new information. Use the drop-down box in the Data Type column to change the type of data allowed for that field.	[pg. 37]
Format: select	In table Design view, click the Format property box in the Field Properties area; then click the down arrow. Select the type of format you want.	[pg. 169]
Insert	In table Design view, click in the row below the position where you want to insert a new field. Click the Insert Rows button. Enter the name of the field, type of data, and description in each column.	[pg. 164]
Move, in form	In form Design view, click in the field you want to move. When the pointer becomes a hand, you can click and drag the field to a new location.	[pg. 116]
Move, in table	In table Design view, use the row selector to select the row you want to move. Click once to select the field, then click and drag the row to a new location and release the mouse button.	[pg. 41]
Resize, in form	In form Design view, select a field text box or label. Click and drag the handles of the text box or field label until it is the desired size.	[pg. 116]

To Do This	Perform These Steps	Page Number
Field		
Size: change	In table Design view, click in the column of the field you want to change. Click in the Field Size property box of the Field Properties area. Drag across the number and type the size you want.	[pg. 171]
Type: change	In table Design view, click in the Data Type column of the field you want to change. Click the down arrow, and select the type of data you want.	[pg. 169]
Form		
AutoForm: create	Click the Forms object button. Click the New button. Choose a table or a query to get the data from, and choose an AutoForm style.	[pg. 107]
Close	Click the Close button.	[pg. 111]
Create from scratch	Click the Forms object button, Click the New button, and select the table or query you want to use. Choose the Design View option from the list, and click OK.	[pg. 112]
Create, use AutoForm	Click the Forms object button, click the New button, choose a table or a query to get the data from, and choose an AutoForm style.	[pg. 107]
Edit data	Use the navigation buttons to move around the form. Click the field you want to edit and enter new data.	[pg. 109]
Enter data	Open the form in Datasheet view. Click the New Record button to add a new record.	[pg. 109]
Field: add	Drag fields from the selected field list box, and place them on the grid until you have included all the fields you need. Use the rulers to help align the fields.	[pg. 114]
Field: move	In form Design view, click in the field you want to move. When the pointer becomes a hand, you can click and drag the field to a new location.	[pg. 116]
Field: resize	In form Design view, select a field text box or label. Click and drag the handles of the text box or field label.	[pg. 117]
Header/footer: add	In Design view, choose View, Form Header/Footer. Adjust the size of the header area by dragging the edge. Use the Label tool to drag a label box within the header. Type the label text inside the label box. Click outside the label box to deselect it. Click the box to select it again; then change the font, font size, or other characteristics.	[pg. 118]
Open	From the database window, click the Forms object button, and double-click the form you want to open.	[pg. 111]
Save	Click the Save button. The first time you save a form, type a descriptive name in the Save As dialog box, and click OK.	[pg. 111]

To Do This	Perform These Steps	Page Number
Help		
Help Contents: use	Click the Show button in the Office Assistant Help window. Click the Contents tab. Scroll down until you find a topic of interest, then click the topic to see the subtopics.	[pg. 12]
Help Index: use	Click the Show button in the Office Assistant Help window. Click the Index tab, and type the word you would like to look up.	[pg. 12]
Office Assistant: use	Choose Help from the menu bar. Select Microsoft Access Help. Type a question, and click the Search button.	[pg. 11]
What's This?: use	Choose Help from the menu bar. Select What's This?; then, point and click on any area of the screen that you would like to know about.	[pg. 14]
Integration		
Browse Data Access Page	Open Internet Explorer 5.0 or a later version. Type the location of the page in the Address box. Scroll through the records.	[pg. 206]
Import an Excel table	Choose File, Get External Data, Import from the Access menu. Select Microsoft Excel as the file type. Select the file you want. Use the Import Spreadsheet Wizard to refine the table.	[pg. 200]
Link table to a Word form letter	Select the table; then click Merge It with MS Word from the OfficeLinks button. Click Create a new document. When Word is launched, type in text and place fields by selecting them from the Insert Merge Field button on the Mail Merge toolbar. Save the Word document.	[pg. 195]
Merge table with a Word form letter	Click the View Merged Data button in the Word Mail Merge toolbar to check for errors. Click the Merge button, and choose a source. Send the document to the printer, email, or fax.	[pg. 198]
Save form as a Data Access Page	Click the Pages object button. Click New and select a table or query. Choose your fields, grouping and sorting options, and page name in the Page wizard. Make changes in Design view, and move to Page view.	[pg. 203]
Query		
Create	Open the database, and click the Queries object button. Click the New button, Design View, and then OK. Select the table(s) you want to use, and click Add. Close the Show Table dialog box.	[pg. 81]
Create, multiple-table	Click the Queries object button in the Database window. Click New, New Query, and then click OK. Select the tables to be included and click Add after each selection. Close the dialog box. From the field list box, drag the fields to be included in the query to the design grid. Place the fields in the order they are to appear in the query. Click the Table View button to view the results. Save your work.	[pg. 179]

To Do This	Perform These Steps	Page Number
Query		
Criteria: match	In query Design view, click in the Criteria row of the field you want to match. Type the criterion you want to match. Add a second criterion by going to the or: row in the design grid. Use quotation marks if punctuation is included in the criterion.	[pg. 91]
Edit	In query Design view, click and drag fields, or double-click a field to add it to the query.	[pg. 88]
Field: choose	Click and drag the field from the field list box to the design grid; or, in the design grid, click the drop-down arrow, and choose the field you want; or double-click the field in the field list box.	[pg. 83]
Field: delete	Select column, choose Edit, Delete.	[pg. 89]
Field: insert	In Query Design view, insert a field between existing fields in the design grid by clicking and dragging the field.	[pg. 88]
Field: move	Click on the column selector and drag left or right to rearrange columns.	[pg. 89]
Open	Open the database, click the Queries object button, select the table, and click the Open button; or, double-click on the query name.	[pg. 94]
Open, multiple	From the Database window, select and open one query first, then use the Database Window button to select another. Open the Window menu, and choose Cascade to view title bars for all queries.	[pg. 95]
Save	Click the Save button. If it is the first time you have saved the query, the Save As dialog box opens and asks for a query name.	[pg. 86]
Save with a new name	Open the File menu, and choose the Save As command. Type a new name in the dialog box, and click OK.	[pg. 94]
Sort	In Query Design view, click in the Sort row of the design grid of the field to be sorted. Select Ascending or Descending order.	[pg. 90]
Report		
Create, use Report Wizard	Go to the Reports object tab. Click New, select the wizard you want, and click OK. Select the fields you want to include in the report and click the Add button (>). Click Next. The Wizard leads you through several more screens. Make your selections, click Next until you reach the final screen, name the report, and click Finish.	[pg. 138]
Field: add	Work in Design view. In the field box, click and drag the field you want to add to the desired position. Click the Print Preview button to view the report. Adjust the size and location of the fields until you are satisfied with the report design.	[pg. 145]
Label, add to report	Click the Label button in the Toolbox. Click and drag where you want to create a text box. Type the text for the new label; then format the text and move it to the desired location.	[pg. 148]

To Do This	Perform These Steps	Page Number
Report		
Modify report design	Work in report Design view. The same techniques used when designing a form apply here. Click and drag the fields you want to move, add, or delete. Use the tools in the toolbox or the Format menu to help align fields, add labels, modify fonts, or change headers and footers.	[pg. 143]
Preview	Open the database, click the Reports object button, select the report, and click the Preview button. From report Design view, click the Print Preview button.	[pg. 145]
Print	In Report Wizard, when you click the Finish button, you see a Print Preview of the report. If you are satisfied with the report, click the Print button.	[pg. 142]
Rename	Select the Reports object button in the database window. Right-click the report title you want to change. The box around the title will change, and you can edit the report title by typing over the existing name.	[pg. 142]
Save with a new name	Open the File menu, and choose the Save As command. Type a new name in the dialog box and click OK.	[pg. 147]
Table		
Close	Click the Close button in the Table window.	[pg. 8]
Column: hide or unhide	In Datasheet view, click in the field selector. Open the Format menu, and choose the Hide Columns command. In the Format menu, use Unhide Columns to display the column again.	[pg. 65]
Column: move (reorder fields)	Select the column, click on the field selector, and drag it to its new position.	
Column: resize width	In Datasheet view, place the mouse pointer between columns in the field selector area until it changes to a thick vertical bar with arrows on either side. Click and drag the line between the columns to the right or left to adjust the column width. Select several columns at once, and double-click one of the bars between the selected columns for automatic adjustment of all selected columns.	[pg. 64]
Create	In the database window, select the Tables object button. Click the New button, choose Design View, and click OK. Enter the field name, choose the data type, and enter a description for each field.	[pg. 30]
Field: add	In table Design view, go to the first blank row and insert the new field name, data type, and description for each field to be added.	[pg. 36]
Field: delete	In table Design view, use the row selector to select the row you want to delete. Click the Delete Rows button.	[pg. 43]

To Do This	Perform These Steps	Page Number
Table		
Field: edit	In table Design view, go to the field name, data type, or description you want to edit. Select the information you want to change, and type the new information. Use the drop-down box in the Data Type column to change the type of data allowed for that field.	[pg. 38]
Field: move	In table Design view, use the row selector to select the row you want to move. Click once to select the field, click and drag the row to a new location, and release the mouse button.	[pg. 41]
Modify table design	Open the database, click the Tables object button, select a table, and click Design.	[pg. 163]
Open	Open the database, click the Tables object button, select the table, and click the Open button.	[pg. 7]
Primary key, create	Use the counter field by clicking Yes when prompted by the save sequence; or in table Design view, use the row selector to select a field; then click the Primary Key button.	[pg. 34]
Print table data	Open the table. Click the Print Preview button. Alter the layout by using the Page Setup command in the File menu, if necessary. When you are satisfied with the page's appearance, open the File menu and choose Print.	[pg. 136]
Record: add	Open the table in Datasheet view. Click the New Record button. Type the appropriate information in each field. Move from field to field with ↵Enter or Tab↹. At the end of the last field, press ↵Enter. This moves you to the next row and saves the record just entered.	[pg. 55]
Record: delete	Click the record selector of the row to be deleted. Click the Delete Record button; then click Yes to confirm.	[pg. 63]
Record: edit	Move to the record and field you want to edit. Click in the field and add, delete, or change the entry as needed. Press ↵Enter to save your changes.	[pg. 59]
Record: find	In Datasheet view, click the Find button. In the dialog box, type what you want to find. You can search in the current field or all fields. You can also search in Any Part of Field. Click the Find Next button to begin the search.	[pg. 67]
Record: go to first	Click the First Record button.	[pg. 59]
Record: go to last	Click the Last Record button.	[pg. 58]
Record: go to next	Click the Next Record button.	[pg. 58]
Record: go to previous	Click the Previous Record button.	[pg. 58]
Record: insert	Click the New Record button.	[pg. 59]

To Do This	Perform These Steps	Page Number
Table		
Record: sort	In Datasheet view, click anywhere in the field on which you want to sort. Click either the Sort Ascending or Sort Descending button.	[pg. 69]
Relationships: create	Click the Relationships button. Click the Show Tables button if the Show Tables dialog box is not displayed. Select the tables you want to include and click the Add button after each selection. Click the Close button. Resize the field lists as needed. Click the field name from one table and drag it to the field name in the second table where you want to join a relationship. In the dialog box that appears, click Create. Close the Relationships window.	[pg. 176]
Save	Click the Save button. Type a name for the table if you are saving the table for the first time. Click OK.	[pg. 34]

Index